Post-Cosmopolitan Cities

Space and Place

Bodily, geographic, and architectural sites are embedded with cultural knowledge and social value. The Anthropology of Space and Place series provides ethnographically rich analyses of the cultural organization and meanings of these sites of space, architecture, landscape, and places of the body. Contributions to this series will examine the symbolic meanings of space and place, the cultural and historical processes involved in their construction and contestation, and how they are in dialogue with wider political, religious, social, and economic ideas, values and institutions.

POST-COSMOPOLITAN CITIES

Explorations of Urban Coexistence

⊰ ◆ ⊱

Edited by
Caroline Humphrey
and
Vera Skvirskaja

Berghahn Books
New York • Oxford

First published in 2012 by

Berghahn Books

www.berghahnbooks.com

© 2012 Caroline Humphrey and Vera Skvirskaja

Library of Congress Cataloging-in-Publication Data

Post-cosmopolitan cities : explorations of urban coexistence / edited by
Caroline Humphrey, Vera Skvirskaja.
    p. cm.
  ISBN 978-0-85745-510-9 (hbk. : alk. paper) -- ISBN 978-0-85745-511-6
(ebook)
  1. Sociology, Urban. 2. Cosmopolitanism. 3. Urbanization--Social aspects.
4. Immigration and emigration--Social aspects. I. Humphrey, Caroline. II.
Skvirskaja, Vera.
  HT151.P626 2012
  307.76--dc23

                                                                    2011052021

British Library Cataloguing in Publication Data

A catalogue record for this book is available from the British Library

Printed in the United States on acid-free paper.

ISBN 978-0-85745-510-9 (hardback)
ISBN 978-0-85745-511-6 (ebook)

⤳ CONTENTS ⤳

ᗋ LIST OF ILLUSTRATIONS ᕽ

❧ ACKNOWLEDGEMENTS ☙

The project that introduced the idea of the post-cosmopolitan city and that led to this book was generously supported by an AHRC grant for speculative research (2005–2006) and the Centre for History and Economics at King's College, Cambridge. Our subsequent long-term ethnographic research in Odessa, Ukraine was made possible by the AHRC programme 'Migration, Diaspora and Identity' designed by Professor Kim Knott. Various conferences organised within the framework of the programme enabled us to discuss our ideas on post-cosmopolitanism at interdisciplinary fora and to meet some of the contributors to this volume. We are grateful to Katie Roche for facilitating our participation in these events.

ᦣ Introduction ᦣ

CAROLINE HUMPHREY AND VERA SKVIRSKAJA

This book is about the kind of cosmopolitanism found – or not found – in cities. It arose from a perception that many great cities, from Bukhara in Central Asia to Venice in Europe, once famous for being cosmopolitan places, are no longer so in the twenty-first century, or at least not in the same way as before. Discussing this, we arrived at the tentative notion of the 'post-cosmopolitan' city that is explored in this volume. Our book first of all draws attention to the fact that the inhabitants of many contemporary cities, diverse as they are, share at least one thing: a sense that something precious has been lost, or sidelined, and that other less generous relations have taken their place. We do not carry out a sustained investigation of the worldwide causes of recent transformations in great cities in general, which would involve an inevitably complex analysis of different concatenations of political and economic forces such as new forms of capitalism, globalisation, the emergence of nation states from former federations, migration, changes in work patterns, and so forth, and has been the subject of a large literature. Rather, we concentrate on particular cities with a history of vibrant combination of many cultures; we describe the way in which cosmopolitanism was practised and sustained in them, the hostility it nevertheless often had to contend with, and the fragility of cosmopolitanism in recent years. The main part of the book then focuses on an anthropological study of the new kinds of relations that are being formed today in more nationalistic contexts. We hope thus to draw attention to an important trend in present-day urban life in many parts of the world, but also to illuminate precisely what the changes are in the quality of relations in these places.

To begin we explain what we mean by the cosmopolitan city. In contrast to some sociological approaches that equate cosmopolitanism with globalisation in the form of cultural commodities, languages, (im)migrants, diaspora networks and dual citizenships, etc. (e.g. Beck 2002, 2008), we avoid such a straightforward conflation. Historically, the presence of social multiplicity in a given place, although a necessary precondition, does not by itself imply or lead to cosmopolitanism. We agree with Vertovec and Cohen that there are many varieties of cosmopolitanism, or, as they put it, several 'windows' through which relations between 'us' and the 'other' are articulated in urban settings (2002: 2). Nevertheless, the term must always imply a capacity for openness, an appreciation of others and an ability to stand outside the givens of one's own community. The research undertaken for this book suggests that this does not simply arise from particular cultural dispositions or the pragmatic requirements of trade regimes (for example), but crucially can also be encouraged, imposed and enforced by particular political practices and ideologies.[1] All the cities that are discussed in this volume share the situation of having been incorporated into political regimes (imperial, colonial, socialist, authoritarian) that in one way or another imposed their own kind of cosmopolitanism.

Cities offer a privileged vantage point from which to investigate people's coexistence with difference – they are places for face-to-face contact of great diversity and intensity that produce friction and conflict as well as accommodation. Imperial expansions, conquests, movement of populations and long-distance trade shaped cities in Europe and Asia as meeting points of different cultures, religions and tongues. Empires, such as the Russian, Ottoman, British, and Hapsburg, and subsequent multinational regimes (notably the USSR), facilitated the emergence of cosmopolitanism not only by re-locating populations to cities and designing divisions of labour there for imperial purposes, but also by providing ideas of unity along with laws and protected spaces regulating inter-communal coexistence. Historically, we observe that the enforced character of such urban coexistence, setting down and regulating lives cheek-by-jowl with others, was not a barrier to benign inter-relations, although such an observation goes against the classical Kantian version of cosmopolitanism, according to which the 'cosmopolite' is a citizen of the world by virtue of transcending state structures (Kant 1991). Even if citizens did not buy into imperial unifying ideologies, they often created everyday cosmopolitanisms *faute de mieux*, which have to be accounted for by different theories. It is telling that with the end of empires and authoritarian regimes, when people were free to leave these cities – which they did in great numbers, notably in the 1990s – they jettisoned the previous unheralded cosmopolitan relations often without much thought, only to look back on them years later with nostalgia. For in the nation-states that succeeded the 'empires', or to which these people emigrated, be they post-colonial, Western or post-socialist, narratives emphasising the city's experience as a crossroads of cultures, peoples and religions are not a matter of prime concern. Both policies and 'memories' of the past are construed first and foremost around nations. The old, practical rationales ('we just had to get along with them') have less and less purchase as cities are bleached of their former diversity. Indeed, as the places of the emigrating 'minorities' were often taken up by mass in-movement of rural people from the national 'majority', earlier cosmopolitan links to a great extent evaporated or were swamped by a central indifference, or even hostility, to people seen as others.

That said, the broad picture thus outlined, of cosmopolitan cities in multinational states succeeded by largely mono-ethnic cities in nation-states, is a radical oversimplification. The nation-state rhetoric may claim hegemony in countries like Ukraine or Greece (see chapters 2, 3 and 7), but in our era of ever-greater interconnectedness the cosmopolitan pasts of 'world cities' and smaller towns have been brought back to fantasy life and enhanced as contemporary cultural commodities. They appear in the local literary market for nostalgia, in tourist hype and travel writings, often trying to give an impression of urban continuity and working in contradistinction both to national mythologies and to the complex, harsh (often not cosmopolitan) reality of history and present-day life in the city. This singling out and objectification of 'our traditional cosmopolitanism' as a thing of value finds its place among the complex processes of globalisation that affect the mid-size cities studied here.

Transnational activities and 'global assemblages' such as international banking, microchip technology, trade and its regulation, cultural borrowing, science, international standards of tourism, or accountancy regimes are spreading to previously separated regions (Ong and Collier 2005), and it is not just world cities like London, New York or Tokyo that can claim the status of global city (Mayaram 2009: 6–7). Perhaps the 'cosmopolitanism' upheld today as a common and desirable urban brand is an epiphenomenon of the desire to participate in global practices that are often seen as inevitable and necessary. Thus even if nation-states and cities attempt to put the brakes on globalising processes such as migration and informal trade (Appadurai 1990; Humphrey and Skvirskaja 2009), it is widely argued that the city's position as a bounded territory within a nation-state has become blurred (Donald et al. 2008). Instead, the city is increasingly seen as a hub or a node in global networks and processes that effectively remove it from its national context and undermine its national loyalties. Nowadays we often read that urban solidarities and engagement with outsiders and global actors tend to supersede national allegiance (see, for example, Appadurai 2003; Sassen 1999, 2000), and that the homogeneity and idea of exclusive oppositions endorsed by national ideologies are destabilised by the internal diversity of de-territorialised places and by the 'place-polygamy' of their inhabitants (Beck 2002: 19–27).

Our studies, however, only partially bear out these generalisations. The point can be made by comparing the material in the chapters to follow with the observations made by Richard Sennett (2008), who argues that, with changes to capitalism, urbanists' understanding of cosmopolitanism has changed radically from the early twentieth century to the present. In the past, migrants to a city such as Berlin, as studied by Simmel in 1908, were seen as unknown and strange; these people had a provoking quality, a 'force of alterity', and thus cosmopolitanism for urbanists of the time was about the notion of being engaged by the puzzling attraction of the unknown. The tension here was with the ever-greater solidity and rigidification of capitalist enterprise. Sennett argues that this dialectic between alterity and rigidity is unravelling itself in the present-day city. Globalisation in terms of labour and capital flows is insufficient to account for the radical change in capitalism itself and its new subjectivities: because of risk taking in which one does not know the outcomes, and groups of workers happy to take on short-term single tasks, previously rigid structures have been replaced by a new flexibility. In this situation, the presidents of the top corporations in New York, for example, have little civic or political engagement with the city and the groups of specialist employees have scant interest in temporary co-workers or neighbourhoods. The dialectic has become one of flexibility and indifference (2008: 42–47). In the cities we studied, however, the kind of high-end globalised capitalism described by Sennett is merely a thin upper layer, in some places vanishingly small, and in any case the revolution in consciousness does not seem to have taken place. Many people who are forced to be flexible, such as Ukrainian merchant seamen who have to work on contracts for international companies, nevertheless have a life ashore 'at home' in Odessa, while highly mobile Afghan businessmen who have experience of serial migration are still constrained by the decision-making power of their family patriarch in Afghanistan (see chapter 3). As others have pointed out, globalisation can be anchored in places, encouraging the fusion of cultural forms, hence 'glocalisation' (Robertson 1995). 'Rooted cosmopolitanism' (Appiah 1998), in which self-declared cosmopolitans state their allegiance and sense of belonging to their home(s), is not compatible with Sennett's idea of flexible workers nor with Zygmunt Bauman's uncommitted subjects of 'liquid modernity' – an incompatibility that reflects real differences in the world.

In Sennett's diagnosis, cosmopolitanism drops away when the 'churning instability of capitalism produces a standardized environment' and non-interaction becomes a guarantor of public order (2008: 47). He is right that there has to be some intensity to local social interaction for cosmopolitanism to be possible. But what ideas can be brought to bear when we are faced with another, more complex reality than Sennett's futuristic vision, when the 'indifference' or (mere) 'tolerance' that is indeed prevalent in many post-cosmopolitan cities cannot be seen as an epiphenomenon of hyper-modern flexibility? It may indeed be difficult to discern cosmopolitan interactions in these cases, but interestingly perhaps they can be traced

– morphed into different forms than before, located in unexpected parts of the city, or etiolated into vulnerable skeins, as the chapters by Skvirskaja and Marsden show. At this point let us think again about how cosmopolitanism actually works in cities.

Derrida (2001) conceived of the cosmopolitan city as a place of hospitality where a non-indifference to the 'other', a positive welcome rather than mere tolerance, operates as a norm of sociality. But the ethics of actual hospitality, as Derrida continues, does not presuppose that the cosmopolitan city is a melting pot where difference/foreignness poses no limitations on inter-cultural interactions. A boundless universal hospitality, an empathetic identification with humanity as a whole (see also Nussbaum 1996), must always be incompatible with the limits embedded in human institutions (e.g. the law, the state) in which any given example of cosmopolitanism is always embedded. Historians and sociologists have shown that, as an actually existing phenomenon, cosmopolitanism is conditioned by various political, social and cultural limitations (Pollock et al. 2000, Cheah and Robbins 1998).

For example, in his discussion of a provincial multiethnic town in Galicia, the historian Redlich describes the specific dynamics of cohabitation among different ethnic communities (Jews, Poles and Ukrainians) as living 'together and apart at the same time' (2002: 164). Although each group tended to keep to itself, during the periods of relative stability (in this case in the early twentieth century and again in the interwar period) there were also joint celebrations of distinctly ethnic events, sharing of public spaces and common participation in urban institutions. Proficiency in other groups' languages was also taken for granted. Many elements of this urban 'togetherness' – the cosmopolitan modality of living in one place – were annihilated by interethnic hostility and/or indifference during the periods when the town experienced the disintegration of previous political frameworks. Others elements, like the practical skill of speaking many tongues, gradually became obsolete when the old ethnic communities were either exterminated during, or moved away after, the Second World War.

It is the delicate balance of 'living together and apart' that this book seeks to elucidate. Once the balance is destroyed, the cosmopolitan relations within a city can cease to exist, giving way not merely to the ethics of 'tolerance'/indifference but sometimes to rabid xenophobia and violence. Appadurai (2000) has called such a process 'decosmopolitanisation' in his study of the global city Bombay. In this 'cosmopolis of commerce', the growing contradiction posed by global wealth and local poverty, together with the national encouragement of religious exclusivity in urban spaces, resulted in violent riots in the early 1990s. The city's diversity, its status as a centre of trade, finance and tourism remained in place, but the riots marked the end of a cosmopolitan city, Bombay, and the emergence of a more intolerant, xenophobic city, Mumbai, in its place. Caroline Humphrey's study of a comparable port city, Odessa, in this volume also charts the descent of a cosmopolitan environment into violence. But taking a longer historical view than Appadurai, she is also able to show how violence may recur repeatedly in the same city, to describe its social character in crowds, and to investigate how surges of hostility broke into the periods and spaces created by a number of different kinds of cosmopolitan moralities present during the nineteenth and early twentieth centuries. It is because this chapter attempts to theorise the co-presence of cosmopolitanism and its opposite, ethnic violence, in the same city over time that we have given it extra space in this volume.

Whereas 'decosmopolitanisation' in Appadurai's analysis refers to the process whereby nationalism brings about the complete disintegration of the urban social fabric into mutually hostile groups, the idea of the post-cosmopolitan city that we advance here implies a certain incompleteness embedded even in radical shifts and designates a wider range of processes and experiences that challenge the concept of multiethnic 'togetherness'. It allows us to reach beyond habitual analytical oppositions between cosmopolitanism and nationalism that run the risk of oversimplifying the complex ways in which urban reality is construed in everyday life and intertwined with ideologies. It indicates that, as with any 'post' phenomenon, including those marked by critical ruptures in social and political structures (e.g. post-socialism or post-colonialism), some cosmopolitan sensibilities, dispositions and affiliations can linger on. In other words, we take into account both the legacy of past cosmopolitanisms and the manifestations of ethnic tensions and nationalisms; cosmopolitanism can survive in 'the post' although it may take new forms, come to occupy different social spaces, be pushed to the margins and be overshadowed by indifferent tolerance. We argue that these new forms have a special quality of relating to the past in cities like those studied here, which everyone acknowledges to have been historically cosmopolitan in character. Hence these forms differ from the ad hoc 'multiculturalism' encouraged in many western countries after mass immigration, and it is also poorly described by the 'new cosmopolitanism' (Hollinger 2008: 230–33), a generalising attempt to reconcile the primal need for belonging with a blanket engagement with human diversity. In the post-cosmopolitan city earlier links and boundaries are not forgotten; cosmopolitanism can shrink and attenuate, it can also mutate and transform into nostalgia for a city that is no more.

Coexisting and successive dynamics in the life of cities

The practice of non-interaction marked, among other things, by low levels of violence, poses a problem for cosmopolitanism (Sennett 2008), for while it safeguards peaceful cohabitation, it also inhibits a wide range of engagements and attachments. In discussions of urban coexistence, however, it is not the mutual turning of backs but intercommunal and interconfessional violence that has commonly been seen as the antithesis of cosmopolitanism par excellence. Many accounts focus on 'crowd mentalities', while psychoanalytical approaches have been widely used to explain conflicting underlying human dispositions, such as an inclination towards racist violence, people's difficulty in living with diversity – be it diversity of ideas or peoples (see, for example, Kristeva 1991) – or the need for inclusivity, even when it entails great personal risk.[2] Contributors to this volume have not engaged with such psychological arguments; instead they have focused on how diverse processes in the city – migration, national and religious revivals, globalised tourism, the dispositions of marginalised minorities and rural incomers – impact on urban sociality and aesthetics.

The volume opens with a chapter by Humphrey that, while acknowledging the antithetical character of generous interactions with others (cosmopolitanism) and violence against them, notes that both phenomena are urban assemblages whose recruitment, social content and dynamics can be studied together, and which have variously advanced and retreated in relation to one another over time in the same city. While these theoretical concerns establish a broader analytical background for other discussions in this volume, Humphrey's case study deals with the city of Odessa during the last few decades of the Russian Empire. At the time, the city was famed for its vibrant diversity, multinational mercantile elite, lively café society and cosmopolitan milieux. Yet, it was also a site of recurrent pogroms throughout its imperial history and 1905 saw the most violent attack against Jews in the whole of Russia. Drawing on Tarde's idea of imitation-cum-repetition and his analysis of 'crowds' and 'publics', as well as Deleuze's discussion of 'molecular multiplicities', Humphrey shows how both pogrom mobs and cosmopolitan networks (e.g. Freemasons, socialist revolutionary movements, trading networks) were dynamic, temporary assemblages that moved across social boundaries. The two were to some extent reactions to one another and kept reappearing at different historical junctures.

This historical example of repetitive violence and amicable sociality across ethnic, religious and class divisions, which were sometimes co-present and sometimes mutually displacing, suggests that pogroms and cosmopolitanism should be understood as temporary patterns of relations. In retrospect, Humphrey argues, it is possible to see Odessa as a 'post-cosmopolitan' city after its very first pogrom in the early nineteenth century – and it was repeatedly so, as various cosmopolitan networks were successively shattered by pogroms over the decades. But if pogroms were repetitive, recursive and stasis inducing, the cosmopolitan networks that formed again and again were different. They moved with the times, linked to new trading opportunities, fashions, changing moral sensibilities, or the effect(s) that swept through the city via music and cinema in the period before the Russian revolution. This perspective, which draws attention to the place- and time-specific character of urban assemblages, is relevant also to the new kinds of cosmopolitan sensibilities and attachments that have emerged (and vanished) since then, during the Soviet period and after. The sharpest blow occurred during the late 1940s when Stalin's 'anticosmopolitan' campaign directly assaulted the day-to-day multiethnic life in work places and institutions (Humphrey 2004). Although Odessa today is a world away from pogroms or public attacks on cosmopolitanism, many people there have nevertheless found new ways of privatising their living spaces or of withdrawing from engagements with those who are seen as 'foreign' in some unaccustomed way (see chapter 4 and 6 for similar phenomena in Tbilisi and Venice).

The history of Thessalonica (Salonika) is, interestingly, comparable with that of Odessa, for both were port cities with large Jewish populations and were distinctive enclaves within huge and sprawling empires. Hatziprokopiou, in his chapter on Thessalonica, traces temporary and shifting patterns of urban relations from the late nineteenth century until the present. He explores a series of contradictions and dynamics related to the city's cosmopolitan history and those that have structured urban diversity more recently. During the late Ottoman rule, which was associated with the flourishing of commerce and cosmopolitanism in Mediterranean port cities, relations with difference were nonetheless regulated by socio-spatial segregation based on religious affiliation; meanwhile, the formally recognised religious 'communities' (Muslim, Christian and Jews) were heterogeneous groups in terms of mother tongues, origins, occupations and class. The Ottoman style cosmopolitanism was first challenged, albeit unsuccessfully, by the class-based solidarity propagated by the early labour movement, and was later ousted by competing nationalisms in the city and beyond.

A succession of dramatic events (the great fire of 1917, the exchange of populations and emigration of Muslim inhabitants, the Second World War and the annihilation of the city's Jews in camps) delivered devastating blows to the remnants of Thessalonica's cosmopolitanism. Its memory has been evoked only recently to deal with the increasing flows of foreign migrants to the city and to endorse calls for European 'multiculturalism' currently in vogue. These evocations of 'traditional' cosmopolitanism have not, however, made the nationalist, Hellenic agenda in the city less dominant politically. The point is that these uneasy 'partners' are themselves in contradiction with processes of homogenising urban development and competition in a globalising economy. It is precisely these active aspirations and rhetoric, Hatziprokopiou suggests, that have turned Thessalonica into a post-cosmopolitan city, a city once more acutely aware of its heterogeneity, past and present, and still somehow 'stuck' in parochial nationalism.

Yet, in the post-cosmopolitan city, cosmopolitanism does not have to be reduced only to the awareness and reconstructions (e.g. in media, literature, art and architecture) of the past or to the political intentions of some limited social circles. In her chapter, Skvirskaja looks at the ways in which cosmopolitanism is sustained at the margins of mainstream, Slav, post-Soviet Odessa. Here, as in present-day Thessalonica, a city divested of its former diversity (both that of the Tsarist era described by Humphrey and the Soviet implantations of workers from all over the USSR) indulges in public and nostalgic commemorations of its 'unique' cosmopolitan outlook, including the mixed Odessan language and vibrant street life. Focusing on recent, mainly post-Soviet, Afghan immigrants and local old-timers, Ukrainian Gypsies, as representing different modalities of exclusion from the city's wider circles of sociality, she investigates what kinds of coexistence strategies proliferate among these minority groups.

Negative racial stereotypes of the Gypsies inherited from the Soviet epoch have merged in the contemporary city with negative attitudes towards 'dark-skinned', and especially Muslim, newcomers. Although these xenophobic impulses are, more often than not, kept in check by public and official appeals to Odessa's historical tolerance, they play an important role in the minorities' view of themselves in the city. While wider society can resort to frigid tolerance as a mode of engagement with difference and can 'afford' to be simply ignorant about the ways of its different members, groups on the social margins do not have such a choice. Instead, Afghan and Gypsy communities practice what Skvirskaja calls 'endogamous' and 'selective' kinds of cosmopolitanism, both of which constitute a stock of integral and highly valued cultural skills. In this way, the minorities' cultural skills contribute to Odessa's post-cosmopolitan repertoire of practices.

In many post-Soviet cities there is a widespread nostalgic identification of the socialist era with a certain rough and ready ethnic equality, companionship in hardship, and the sociability of illicit practices, and the demise of all this – conducive to an everyday cosmopolitanism, along with the officially sanctioned Soviet internationalism – tends to be regretted today. But in his chapter on Warsaw Murawski picks up a different chronology of cosmopolitan imagination. He argues in chapter 5 that the cosmopolitan era is identified with the pre-war Polish national state, with its free inter-relations with France and Western Europe. Meanwhile the Soviet-dominated period is seen as oppressively homogenising, to be resisted and then gladly jettisoned and replaced by a 'renewed', and yet in fact more global, cosmopolitanism today. Two points can be drawn from this case: first, that what counts as 'cosmopolitan' varies in different loci with distinctive perspectives on what otherwise might seem like a shared socialist history. Secondly, as the chapter is largely concerned with architecture and architects, we see the relevance of the idea of the 'assemblage' (Humphrey, in this volume; Ong and Collier 2005) as a network of techniques, abilities and values that exists within a city but cannot possibly comprise all of it. Murawski documents how '(Polish) cosmopolitan' architectural styles, i.e. those inspired by pre-War international modernism, were used to contest the officially approved, heavy pseudo-Baroque of Stalinist architecture (which, if one put on a different pair of glasses, could itself be seen as 'cosmopolitan' within a certain Soviet paradigm). As the chapter then shows in its discussion of the recent buildings by international design stars, globalisation is not accepted with open arms, and architecture continues to be a battleground associated with cherished visions of what it means to be both Polish and cosmopolitan.

Migration and minorities

This raises a more general question about the place of minorities and migration in the configuration of the post-cosmopolitan city. Our initial inspiration for this study arose from our earlier ethnographic research on coexistence in the post-Soviet cities of Bukhara and Odessa. Today these cities have very different cultural and economic profiles and are located within different political regimes. But they also have many things in common: both were important commercial centres in the pre-Soviet period; and different ethnic-religious communities comprised the building blocks of the urban economy. At present, both have inherited the (vanishing) legacy of Soviet internationalism and are situated in new nation-states that promote cultural homogenisation, both have experienced mass emigration of the city's core ethnic groups (Jews, Russians and Tatars in Bukhara; Jews, Germans, Greeks in Odessa) to their 'countries of origin' or the USA.

At the same time, both cities have experienced significant inflows of migrants from the surrounding impoverished countryside, together with a trickle from abroad. Even though the cities can boast the presence of a diverse population (and statistics are often used to claim that a multiethnic plural society is an ongoing key feature of the city in question), the new diversity constitutes only a thin layer around a largely homogenous majority. The complex interplay of ideological and demographic changes (especially top-down nationalism, new religious loyalties and continuing out-migration) could not but modify the dynamics of urban relations and sharpen perceptions of difference. Some long-standing urbanites have developed 'diasporic' sensibilities at home, suddenly perceiving themselves as a 'minority' surrounded by a homogenous mass of new urban dwellers. According to this vision, it is the authentic city, its language and modus operandi that have been 'moved' abroad (Skvirskaja 2010). Newcomers from the rural hinterlands are seen as alien to the urban habitus with its open, cosmopolitan spirit (Skvirskaja and Humphrey 2007), and neither newcomers nor native urbanites have

Figure 0.1. 'Hey! We know all these faces.' Poster of an exhibition illustrating an idealised image of cosmopolitan Odessa. Odessa 2006. Photo by Vera Skvirskaja.

been enthusiastic about the flows of foreign traders, transnational migrants and refugees.[3] These processes of immigration and emigration are not, of course, independent of the ideological changes in the new nation-states and beyond, and taken together they undermine the old cosmopolitan ways.

Several contributors to this volume focus specifically on the social effects of international and internal migration in post-Soviet cities. Sapritsky (chapter 2) discusses the largely simultaneous processes of mass Jewish emigration from Odessa and the entry of Jewish international organisations and emissaries whose efforts and economic means are aimed at helping the remaining Jewish inhabitants as well as the growing trend of return migration. The story of Odessa's distinctiveness owes a great deal to its Jewry, and, especially during the Soviet period, being Jewish in Odessa was nothing like being 'the Other' – the alien face of modernity (see Chaudhuri 2009). Jewish visibility – in language, faces, jokes, etc. – was integral to the character of the city. Sapritsky analyses how this 'ordinariness' has been undermined by the new religious and political formations created by various connections to overseas diasporas. Old local models of Jewish identification, informed by the cosmopolitan orientation and idealised internationalist practices of the Soviet regime, have been confronted with foreign models of Jewishness. Although many remaining Odessan Jews perceive the foreign models as isolating and narrowing, these more exclusive forms of Jewishness have taken root in the city. The paradox of the situation is that although the majority of Odessan Jews left the city, the small present-day Jewish community appears to be far more visible and distinct than its Soviet counterpart, and this very visibility and distinction tends to contribute to new forms of social exclusion.

Chapters by Marsden and Frederiksen that deal respectively with Dushanbe, the capital of Tajikistan, and Tbilisi, the capital of Georgia, focus on the ways in which conflicts, negotiations and transformations in the urban forms of diversity are not only processes that take place between social groups, but also within individual selves. In Dushanbe, people talk about the ongoing effects of Tajikistan's civil war on their society, something that shapes the multivalent and complex strategies through which they seek to negotiate city life. In the 1990s many Russians and others fled Tajikistan fearing employment discrimination on political, linguistic and religious grounds. The situation, however, was more complex that this implies, and different takes on what it meant to be a Muslim became important markers of internal diversity. Marsden explores the perspectives of rural-urban migrants who might easily be assumed to be the key agents behind the degeneration of the previously more open and versatile kinds of urban subjectivities. He argues that 'rural migrants' have diverse origins and orientations: while some reflect critically on state-derived discourses of national culture and hardened forms of identity, others endorse them.

Tbilisi is yet another city that is represented officially as traditionally cosmopolitan. Yet the city's historical situation as a trading route between Europe and the Central Asia inflected inter-ethnic relations in different ways at different times. Today, what might look from the outside like cosmopolitan influences – Chinese traders, international NGOs, oil consultants – are often viewed as unwelcome intrusions. Frederiksen contrasts these contestations with the image of pre-Soviet Tbilisi as the thriving 'gate' between East and West. And the new hostility to incomers also contrasts with the sentiments of belonging to the supra-national geopolitical realm of the Soviet period. While the authorities highlight the old cosmopolitan atmosphere in Tbilisi, urban dwellers are more inclined to recall the Soviet heritage and they therefore tend to accept various peoples from the former USSR (as distinct from 'foreigners') as the natural parts of the city. Frederiksen suggests that in a city that has lost much of its ethnic diversity, all that remains is at best a type of 'encapsulated' cosmopolitanism – i.e. pertaining in this case only to post-Soviet compatriots. The long-standing inhabitants of Tbilisi seem to privilege links with Russians in particular, despite the ongoing military clashes and ideological wars with Russia.

Rapid changes in urban population due to the mass emigration of native minority residents are a common feature of many post-Soviet cities, but similar processes also take place elsewhere. Kostylo, in chapter 6, discusses the case of Venice, which has been experiencing an exodus of the native population in the last few decades. Just like 'native' Odessans, the Venetians were never an autochthonous population but emerged as an urban population with a strong identity and its own dialect as a result of cultural mixing. Motivated by economic considerations native Venetians have recently moved en masse to the mainland. Kostylo argues that mass tourism and flows of transnational capital – the key sources of the city's prosperity – are at the same time what have brought about the demise of Venetian culture and its cosmopolitan orientation. From the point of view of the remaining Venetians, foreigners are taking over the city: they are taking over local trade and they are the ones who can afford to live in the city. The cosmopolitan façade of the city, famous not only for its splendid architecture but also for high profile international events such as the contemporary arts Biennale and film festivals, barely disguises the polarisation of a city split between a small inward-looking community of Venetians, tourists and wealthy transnational elites. Kostylo describes how the ghetto that had been in itself a quasi-cosmopolitan enclave, as it was inhabited by Jews from different places with diverse traditions, is today transformed into a tourist attraction. With distant echoes of the situation in Odessa, the ghetto is now run by foreign orthodox Jews.

Conclusion

Of all the cities studied in this volume, Odessa is the only one that resembled for a brief period Derrida's cosmopolitan ideal. Built on the site of a fort abandoned by the Ottomans, it was founded as the hospitable City of Refuge that welcomed all incomers – runaway serfs, Greek and Italian merchants, German homesteaders, French aristocrats, religious dissidents and diverse refugees of revolutionary bent. The openness and harmony that prevailed under the first governorships could not, and did not, last. This book shows how in other Eurasian cities too, cosmopolitan formations were sustained for a period, only to shrivel up or collapse altogether at times when they were shouldered aside by other, harsh and exclusivist social forces or abandoned by the people who had kept them alive. The present time seems to be such an epoch. The 1990s–2000s have seen mass movements of people abandoning cosmopolitan cities in search for national identities and economic advancement, or running away from their old homes in fear – a dread or premonition, not unrelated to historical experience – that these places would no longer be cosmopolitan and they would be the ones to suffer. The cascading effect of out-migration has left huge gaps in cities from Venice to Dushanbe, for although the apartments were rapidly filled it was not by the same kind of people. Villagers, tourists, new hoteliers and businesspeople, NGO representatives, traders from all corners of the world may not be quite like the Sennett/Bauman 'flexible capitalist subjects', but all the same none of them know or care about the niceties of the former cosmopolitan interactions. Just as a mere settler in London does not make a Londoner, let alone a Cockney, similarly an inhabitant of Odessa does not make an Odessit. Yet this sense that cities have their native denizens, and that their way of life encodes a relaxed openness that should be treasured, has not vanished; and at the same time at least some of the old timers and newcomers are creating their own – even if 'selective', 'encapsulated' or 'endogamous' – types of cosmopolitanism. This book aims to describe the kinds of diverse assemblages that have arisen in post-cosmopolitan cities and that are symptomatic of the state of the city at a particular historical juncture.

NOTES

1. See for example Isin's (2009) discussion on the Ottoman Empire and Humphrey (2004) on the Soviet case. That is not to say that ideology and political will alone can secure a cosmopolitan society; see also Lefebvre (1996) for an analysis of this situation.

2. For a concise outline of this argument and an elaboration on 'visceral cosmo-politanism' see Nava (2007).
3. Humphrey, Marsden and Skvirskaja (2009) and Skvirskaja (2010).

REFERENCES

Appadurai, Arjun. 1990. 'Disjuncture and Difference in the Global Cultural Economy', in M. Featherstone (ed.), *Global Culture*. London, pp. 295–310.
———. 2000. 'Spectral Housing and Urban Cleansing: Notes on Millennial Mumbai', *Public Culture* 12(3): 627–51.
———. 2003. 'Sovereignty without Territoriality: Notes for a Postnational Geography', in S.M. Low and D. Lawrence-Zuniga (eds), *The Anthropology of Place and Space*. Oxford, pp. 337–50.
Appiah, Kwame A. 1998. 'Cosmopolitan Patriots', in P, Cheah and B. Robbins (eds), *Cosmopolitics: Thinking and Feeling Beyond the Nation*. Minneapolis and London, pp. 91–114.
Beck, U. 2002. 'The Cosmopolitan Society and Its Enemies', *Theory, Culture and Society* 19(1–2): 17–44.
———. 2008. 'The Cosmopolitan Perspective: Sociology in the Second Age of Modernity', in S. Vertovec and R. Cohen (eds), *Conceiving Cosmopolitanism. Theory, Context, and Practice*. Oxford, pp. 61–85.
Chaudhuri, A. 2009. 'Cosmopolitanism's Alien Face', *New Left Review* 55, Jan/Feb: 89–108.
Cheah, Pheng and Bruce Robbins (eds). 1998. *Cosmopolitics: Thinking and Feeling Beyond the Nation*. Minneapolis and London.
Derrida, J. 2001. *On Cosmopolitanism and Forgiveness*. New York and London.
Donald, Stephanie, Eleonore Kofman and Catherine Kevin. 2008. 'Introduction: Processes of Cosmopolitanism and Parochialism', in S. Donald, E. Kofman and C. Kevin (eds), *Branding Cities: Cosmopolitanism, Parochialism, and Social Change*. New York and London, pp. 1–13.
Hollinger, David A. 2008. 'Not Universalists, not Pluralists: the New Cosmopolitans find their own way', in S. Vertovec and R. Cohen (eds), *Conceiving Cosmopolitanism. Theory, Context, and Practice*. Oxford, pp. 227–35.
Humphrey, C. 2004. 'Cosmopolitanism and *Kosmopolitizm* in the Political Life of Soviet Citizens', *Focaal: European Journal of Anthropology* 44: 138–54.
Humphrey, C., Magnus Marsden and Vera Skvirskaja. 2009. 'Cosmopolitanism and the City: Interaction and co-existence in Bukhara, Uzbekistan', in Sh. Mayaram (ed.), *The Other Global City*. New York and London, pp. 202–32.
Humphrey, C. and V. Skvirskaja. 2009. 'Trading Places: Post-Socialist Container Markets and the City', *Focaal* 55: 61–73.
Isin, Engin F. 2009. 'Beneficence and Difference Ottoman *Awqaf* and "Other" Subjects', in Sh. Mayaram (ed.), *The Other Global City*. New York and London, pp. 35–53.
Kant, Immanuel. 1991. 'Perpetual Peace: A Philosophical Sketch', in H. Reiss (ed.), *Kant: Political Writings*. Cambridge, pp. 93–130.

Kristeva, J. 1991. *Strangers to Ourselves*, trans. Leon S. Roudiez. New York.

Lefebvre, H. 1996. *Writings on Cities*, selected, translated and introduced by Eleonore Kofman and Elizabeth Lebas. Oxford.

Mayaram, Shail. 2009. 'Introduction: Rereading Global Cities: Topographies of an Alternative Cosmopolitanism in Asia', in Sh. Mayaram (ed.), *The Other Global City*. New York and London, pp. 1–34.

Nava, M. 2007. *Visceral Cosmopolitanism. Gender, Culture and the Normalisation of Difference*. Oxford.

Nussbaum, M.C. 1996. *For Love of Country*, ed. J. Cohen. Boston.

Ong, Aihwa and Stephen J. Collier (eds). 2005. *Global Assemblages: Technology, Politics and Ethics as Anthropological Problems*. New York and London.

Pollock, Sh., H. Bhabha, C. Breckenridge and D. Chakrabarty. 2000. 'Cosmopolitanisms', *Public Culture* 12(3): 577–89.

Redlich, Sh. 2002. *Together and Apart in Brzezany. Poles, Jews, and Ukrainians, 1919-1945*. Bloomington and Indianapolis.

Robertson, Roland. 1995. 'Glocalization: Time-Space and Homogeneity-Heterogeneity', in M. Featherstone, S. Lash and R. Robertson (eds), *Global Maternities*. London, pp. 25–44.

Sassen, Sakia. 1999. 'Globalisation and the Formation of Claims', in J. Copjec and M. Sorkin (eds), *Giving Grounds. The Politics of Propinquity*. London and New York, pp. 86–105.

———. 2000. 'New Frontiers Facing Urban Sociology at the Millennium', *British Journal of Sociology* 51(1): 143–60.

Sennett, Richard. 2008. 'Cosmopolitanism and the Social Experience of Cities', in S. Vertovec and R. Cohen (eds), *Conceiving Cosmopolitanism. Theory, Context, and Practice*. Oxford, pp. 42–47.

Skvirskaja, V. 2010. 'New Diaspora in a Post-Soviet City: Transformation in Experiences of Belonging in Odessa, Ukraine', *Studies of Ethnicity and Nationalism* 10(1): 76–91.

Skvirskaja, V. and C. Humphrey. 2007. 'Odessa: skol'zskii gorod i uskol'zaiushchii kosmopolitizm', *Acta Eurasica* 1(35): 87–116.

Vertovec, S. and R. Cohen. 2002. 'Introduction', in *Conceiving Cosmopolitanism. Theory, Context, and Practice*. Oxford, pp. 1–24.

৭ Chapter 1 ৬

Odessa: Pogroms in a Cosmopolitan City

CAROLINE HUMPHREY

How can we explain the case of a city famed for its cosmopolitanism, where nevertheless pogroms have taken place? In the early twentieth century, when Odessa was renowned for its enlightened multinational mercantile elite, its magnificent opera house, its irreverence and street humour, it was also the city where Russia's most violent pogroms against the Jews took place. It cannot be convincingly argued that they were only a matter of externally-incited passions unleashed in the city, for attacks on Jews had taken place in Odessa many times in previous decades (notably in 1821, 1849, 1859, 1871, 1881 and 1900, as well as countless minor raids). So although the most devastating pogroms were related to great political events in Russia, specifically to the assassination of the Tsar in 1881 and the revolution of 1905, there is still something to be explained about the city itself that so regularly produced these spurts of hatred. This chapter does not aim to provide a causal account of the pogroms, on which there is already a distinguished literature;[1] nor is it a study of the suffering inflicted and the subjectivities of those involved. Rather, focusing on the late nineteenth and early twentieth century, it is an attempt to explain how the pogroms happened and to characterise the complex – disjointed yet mutually aware – make-up of a city undergoing radical change in which such events could take place.

The destructive energies of violent mobs vented against people seen as alien (pogroms) were the reverse of cosmopolitanism, if by this we mean generous and appreciative interactions between those who recognise one another as different. This incompatibility, the difficulty of thinking them adjacently, is reflected in the literature on Odessa, which tends to focus either on its complex cosmopolitan culture or on pogroms, but not on their co-presence (see, however, Gerasimov 2003). But perhaps there is a way of conceptualising such a situation when it is seen that in some respects these undoubted opposites – pogroms and cosmopolitan interactions – were not dissimilar kinds of phenomenon. Both were changeable heterogeneous assemblages, for which an analysis in terms of epistemological pluralism – rather than individualism or holism – is appropriate. Both were unstructured, leaderless, relational and contagious, and for these reasons best understood, it will be suggested, through Tardean notions of 'imitation' and 'opposition'.[2] The historical conditions of cosmopolitanism and pogroms changed during the nineteenth and early twentieth centuries, but on any given occasion they consisted of the spontaneous enactment, in slightly altered form, of specific sets of things that were said and done, including ritualised and symbolic elements (Löwe 1998: 457–59). I shall argue, however, that there were several distinctive kinds of cosmopolitanism and that they tended to be mutable and creative, whereas the pogroms were recursive and backward looking. This dire repetition of pogroms has been interpreted as standardisation, giving rise to the notion of the 'pogrom paradigm' (Klier 1992: 13–18). However, that interpretative-explanatory theory cannot account for the absence of pogroms in Odessa after the culminating orgy of ethnic violence in 1905. A more convincing perspective, and one that chimes with the Tardean approach taken here, is Il'ya Gerasimov's idea (2003: 251) of 'immunity' to pogroms that developed in Odessa after 1905.

Cosmopolitan networks and pogrom crowds created their own separate, patterns of relations, which can be seen as topographies, defined by the overall connectivity of their different elements as assemblages. They had characteristically different ways of changing over time, seeping, coagulating, or leaping like wildfire across the boundaries of civil estates, ethnic groups, religions, classes, neighbourhoods and professions. Furthermore, they interacted in different ways with the same physical features of the city. The central avenue, the fashionable Deribasovskaya Street, for example, was a key attractant for destructive rampage but it was also, more constantly, one of the most prominent venues for displaying courteous interactions. What complicates this picture is that because the two opposite activities were played out in public, they were to a degree rhetorical, and thus their actors were aware of one another's potential emergence and long histories in the town. Some people at the time, as well as historians, have seen them as reactions to one another (Sekundant 2005) or as 'counterbalancing mechanisms' in the turbulence of economic modernisation (Gerasimov 2003: 252). However, in a longer history we should consider the idea of balance carefully, for these were inimical movements that had different dynamics. Pogroms in the pre-Soviet period, I shall suggest, were a recurrent part of an archaic politics of the autocratic state, and the 'immune reactions' were a refusal of this politics; whereas cosmopolitanisms were inventive in their own right, were more than just a rejection of ethnic violence, and should always be thought of in the plural: the forms of cosmopolitanism were very different at the beginning of the nineteenth century from those at the end.

Still, whatever form cosmopolitanism took at various times, the violence of pogroms dealt their fragile relations a brutal blow. If the term 'post-cosmopolitan' refers to the sense of there having been a former benign state of social harmony, now evaporated, then Odessa was repeatedly prey to this awareness throughout its history.

Some ideas used in this chapter

Pogroms against Jews could be analysed in the light of the anthropology of ethnic violence, with its characteristic themes of social suffering, resistance, cultural rights, legitimacy, the moral economy of the mob, blame and healing (Das 1995; Kleinman, Das and Lock 1997) or the relation between collective violence and everyday practice (Kapferer 1988; Spencer 1990). This chapter, however, attempts a different, both material and communicative, approach. The pluralistic epistemology just mentioned is inspired by the work of Gabriel Tarde and Gilles Deleuze, in particular Tarde's notion of 'imitation', which he endowed with an everyday quality, describing it as the repetition, always in an infinitesimally different way, of 'a word or phrase spoken, a job executed, or a legal procedure enacted' (Tarde 1969: 143) and Deleuze's idea of the 'molecular', a wave-like assemblage (or multiplicity) of tiny immanent differences that do not submit themselves to any totalisation (Deleuze and Guatari 1987: 34 and 248–50). This chapter will not deal with these theories as philosophical explanations of phenomena in general, but will focus instead on certain ideas relevant to the subject at hand.

Because it is founded on the notion of incremental additions, in Tardean theory the spatial and the temporal dynamics of the social occupy a single conceptual gesture (Born 2010: 237). This chapter will show how seasonality and timing was crucial to the formation of pogrom raids. Externally given times, such as religious holidays, or dramatic political events, brought crowds together – crowds that, if they formed pogrom mobs, 'cascaded' through time in characteristic patterns. Separately, there were times of cosmopolitan interactions. Just as important were the engagements with material places. I therefore pay attention to the physical layout of Odessa: its districts, market squares, port, and places of social display. These places had names (Greek Street, Polish Street, Jewish Street, Cathedral Square, etc.) which reflect their associations with different kinds of people; but an engagement in a theoretical sense with the materiality of place also means taking seriously changeable emergent qualities, rescuing, as Matei Candea has put it, 'a more dynamic version of place from the premature foreclosure of approaches in which the relevant (political) actors and the relevant (political) issues are known in advance' (Candea 2009: 1).

What might this mean? In the case of pogroms, it was not just that the crowds of people were active, creating places of ruin from city edifices, but that the mobs themselves were enticed, frustrated, divided, blocked off, or channelled by the emergent qualities of the sites they encountered. Looking at what actually happened, however, it is difficult to assign predominant agency to one side or the other, to assemblages of people or to architectural ensembles, since they transformed one another. In a way we know this well. Before the great sale on 'Black Friday' (the day after Thanksgiving) at Walmart on Long Island in 2008, the glass doors held back a heaving queue, but when the doors shattered, instead of opening in an orderly way, the 'customers' were suddenly transformed into 'a dangerous stampede' that resulted in death and injury. The glass doors, which had earlier welcomed customers and offered an enticing look at the goods inside, turned into sharp instruments of blood-letting (Brockes 2009: 21–25).

Let me take the example of Odessa port. The transformative possibility of the port was suddenly made evident in the dramatic stand-off in June 1905 when the rebel battleship Potemkin steamed into the harbour and trained its guns on the merchants' palaces. The spatial setting, which presented the range of the elegant Primorskii (Seashore) Boulevard to the purview of the armed ship, became an essential and powerful agent in the emergence of a new landscape. This was the arc in which it was possible to be a target from the sea, behind which extended a similarly emergent zone, that of the 'safe areas', to which the frightened merchants could retreat. In pogroms, the running patterns taken by crowds were to a great extent formed by the disposition of objects that became their quarry, from rows of trading stalls to imposing banks.

It might seem that the undramatic and small-scale activities of cosmopolitanism would be less apt for such an analysis, but as I hope to show, they too formed, and were formed by, the affordances of specific places, from market squares to basement taverns to elegant clubs: places that had indeed often been built to enable certain kinds of cosmopolitan sociality. All this implies that we should pay attention to what Lisa Blackman (2007: 574) calls the 'suggestive realm', i.e. where embodied experience and material encounters engage with fantasies that are both affective and ideational.

If Blackman outlines a largely unspecified 'intersubjective zone' of relations between human subjects, Bruno Karsenti (2010), also inspired by Tarde, takes us directly to what passes between individuals. This content – crucially beliefs and desires – is in effect the 'social'; or to put it another way, the items that are learned (imposed, copied, rejected, etc.) from someone else are the 'vectors of sociality'. Focusing on such vectors raises the question not of the origin of the relation, but simply of what it consists in, what it is made of, what it is, precisely, that makes it a relation. These are psychic phenomena that are beyond the individual and yet are not subsumed into collective representations. As Karsenti continues, 'In a strict sense, beliefs and desires imitate each other, not individuals' (2010: 45), and they constitute 'an impersonal milieu in which imitative flows are built up and clash with one another' (2010: 49).

One does not have to go the whole hog with Tarde's social theory – that is, to accept his three analytical categories of imitation, opposition and creation as the key to understanding all (social, political, economic, biological, psychological) phenomena – in order to see that the focus on impersonal content proposed by Karsenti is particularly apt for understanding the unstructured change-making activities of the kind discussed in this chapter. For in fact, as can be seen from eyewitness accounts, specific kinds of breakages, blows, shouted slogans, etc. constituted pogroms, but it could not be known in advance who would participate, nor even who would be a victim. In other words, pre-existing social categories, such as 'the Russians', 'the Greeks' or 'the Jews', did not determine who were the acting subjects. Rather, during pogroms such named categories, together with representations and symbols of them, were some of the key vectors (i.e. 'content') that temporarily linked people – people who otherwise had quite variegated and multifarious identities.

We should pay attention, therefore, to crowds by examining the synthesis of the properties of such emergent assemblages (DeLanda 2006: 4) rather than assuming them to be organic totalities pervaded through and through by culturally-given ideologies. If crowds are seen as temporal processes of gathering and dispersal of diverse components, it is then possible to examine the micro-histories of particular crowds, the way they become attached together by specific contents, encounter internal and external resistance as well as further agglutination, and thus form changing topologies over the time of their existence.

Such an approach may seem to fly in the face of our intuitions. Surely, it might be protested, everyone in Odessa knew who was a Jew and who was not, and at the very least, the Jews themselves knew who they were, and that their pre-existing ancestral status was why they were victimised. But with the idea of assemblages things would never be so clear, since the relations envisaged by Deleuze imply that a component part of one assemblage can be subtracted from it and plugged into a different one (DeLanda 2006: 10). And in fact, ethnography bears out this idea: not only were ambiguous/multiple social identities widespread during the turbulent period of suppressed modernisation that was late Imperial Russia (Haimson 1988), but more specifically there were Jews who converted to Christianity, there were Slav Christians who joined Jewish defence militias, and sometimes, as in 1871, people identified as Jews even joined the mobs of pogromists (Morgulis 2001: 31). Rather than defining particular subjects, such as 'the cosmopolitan' or 'the pogromist', I prefer to describe inimical ways of communicating, acting and imagining that passed among people, sweeping them temporarily into groups.

Still, this brings up what one might call the sticking point – or inconsistency – of the Tarde-inspired presentist theory: the delineation of the actors. The vocabulary of imitation and suggestion seems to imply a blank subject, on whom impressions are made. If individual people have consistency over time, it is relevant that the sets of vectors passing between people in crowds could act as reminders of stored-up prior experience, or act as touch papers for earlier emotions. Indeed, Tarde's own idea of opposition implies an actor whose previous ideas and experiences jar against the new inputs and make her reject them. Some of the most telling vectors in the events I shall describe were memories. Occasionally they consisted of a combination of memories and promises, such as the threat made at the start of the 1871 pogrom that unless a Jewish cabstand was removed from near the Greek cathedral, 'the events of 1829' (i.e. the pogrom of that year) would be unleashed again (Morgulis 2001: 42–43). The Blackman-Karsenti portrayal of the subject as merely a processing zone, stacking up inputs, sorting them out, and opting amongst among them – the theory according to which a memory is merely a passing acquisition – runs counter to the alternative 'humanist' vision in which memories and the capacity to make promises are central to what the subject is.

The present chapter does not attempt to resolve this issue of the subject (see Humphrey 2008) but I conclude the section with an insight, again derived from Tarde, which sheds some light on the dispositions of people in social multiplicities. Tarde distinguishes between a 'crowd' and a 'public'. Tarde's use of the terms crowd and public is non-judgemental, unlike that of other social theorists of his time and later, in whose works 'crowds' are anxiously invoked as unruly phenomena, whereas 'the public' and more recently 'multitudes' appear as positive phenomena of vitality and autonomy (see Mazzarella 2010). For Tarde, a crowd, a physical assemblage in which communications are passed by direct contact, is different from a current of opinion, a diffuse 'inorganic transformation', in which ideas are transmitted at a distance, a public: 'The transportation of force over distance is nothing compared to this transportation of thought across distance. Is not thought the social force par excellence?' (Tarde 1969: 279)

The people transfigured by ideas in a public, Tarde writes, do not meet or hear one another, but there is a social bond between them, 'their simultaneous conviction or passion, their awareness of sharing at the same time an idea or a wish with a great number of other men' (1969: 278–79). In pre-modern times, Tarde writes, publics were the small and occasional audiences produced by oratory, but they were succeeded in later centuries by more intense, persistent and widespread publics enabled by printing, newspapers, radio, political parties, etc. Society has become entirely pervaded by the 'mobile atmosphere' of countless publics ('there is not one sect that does not wish to have its own newspaper in order to surround itself with a public extending far beyond it', 1969: 284). The most salient point for this chapter is that a person can be physically present in only one crowd, but 'one can belong – and in fact one always does belong – simultaneously to several publics' (1969: 281).

Thinking about Odessa enables one to see that cosmopolitanism and pogroms bore different relations to publics as defined above. By the end of the nineteenth century the city was host to countless newspapers, journals, public reading-rooms, libraries, professional newsletters, legal publications, political leaflets, etc. and there could hardly have been any educated person who did not regularly read many of these. But in 1897 around forty-two per cent of the population of Odessa was illiterate (Herlihy 1986: 242–43) and the publics they belonged to, if any, were the old audiences of oratory in churches, synagogues and political meetings. The evidence is that pogrom incitements were overwhelmingly transmitted person-to-person orally and material-symbolically, among workers, indigents, local peasants and similarly non-literate migrants from central Russia looking for work, as I will describe later. There were undoubtedly anti-Jewish publics in Odessa at the end of the nineteenth century. One was the middle-class readership of the newspaper *Novorossiiskii Telegraf*, which, although its editorials condemned the use of violence against Jews, also published anti-Semitic articles inciting hatred, accusing Jews of exploitation of peasants and workers, of disloyalty to the state, and of masterminding the assassination of Tsar Alexander II in March 1981 (Aronson 1990: 68–75). Irresponsible journalists publicised rumours predicting pogroms. Nevertheless, the anti-Semitic campaign run by the paper in spring 1881 did not result in a pogrom at the time (1990: 79). The mass of pogromists was not this literate public sprung to life, but consisted rather of a heterogeneous gathering of people threaded together by various signs, rumours and slogans, sometimes focused, but often confused. Sometimes it was wealth, or privilege, or perceived economic advantage that was attacked, rather than 'Jews' as such. Working-class antagonism towards Jews was not universal and where it existed, its main stream could perhaps be seen as a pre-modern 'sub-public', conveyed intimately, by ancient calumnies, grandmothers' fables, resentment at a bad deal, or a neighbour's invective. The coming together of these various flows was crucially energised by malignant rumours, as I shall describe later. The pogroms could not have come about without these various – oral and literate – kinds of public. But pogroms were not publics: in Tarde's terms they were 'crowds', having their own crowd-like characteristics of spontaneity, physical ferocity, excitement, attraction of bystanders, and brute imitative actions.

Cosmopolitan engagements were unlike this in one crucial way. The people co-present on these occasions were consciously different from one another and were often members of divergent publics. Whatever form it took, cosmopolitanism meant the tacit, and sometimes explicit, understanding that any mutually hostile identities or publics the individuals may have belonged to in other settings would be set aside. In this sense, cosmopolitanism implied creating spaces/times of detachment from exclusivist ethnic, political and religious forms of belonging. 'Detachment' in this case should not be construed, as it often is in recent anthropology, in negative terms as a 'debilitating alienation from organic forms of life ... a sickly privileging of rationality over creativity' (Anderson 2001: 20) but as a practical interrogation of irredentist social norms, a piercing of boundaries, in the interest of a broader courtesy and sometimes of social justice. In this sense, cosmopolitan actions implied certain kinds of re-attachment and were indeed creative.

Odessa city and its inhabitants

Odessa was founded from scratch by Europeans in the late eighteenth century and rapidly became a thriving mercantile city. Its history is made up of disjunctive yet co-existing processes and temporalities: the growth of industry alongside trade, repeated attempts by the Tsarist state to suppress the 'foreignness' of the city, out-migration of old mercantile groups and in-migration of others, abject impoverishment alongside great wealth, the modernising of infrastructure and transport, the sharpening of anti-Semitism, and the emergence of different forms of cosmopolitanism.

After Russian armies defeated the Turks in the 1780s, Catherine the Great determined to populate the more or less deserted region called New Russia (*Novorossiia*). The authorities invited colonists, merchants, political refugees and artisans from all over Europe to settle, notably Italians, Greeks, Jews and Poles. Odessa prospered till 1857 as a *porto franco*, subject to lesser customs tariffs than the rest of Russia, and was visited annually by thousands of ships from trading countries around the world. Its 'foreign' and 'southern' character was loved by poets, but feared and disliked by Russian nationalists who regularly criticised Odessa during the nineteenth century for its potential disloyalty (Atlas 1992: 109–19). Gover-

nors appointed from St Petersburg by the autocratic Tsarist state made repeated attempts to Russianise the city. Still, a powerful image (often known
as 'the Odessan myth') was born: that of cosmopolitan, witty, sunny, free
and beautiful Odessa, the city that welcomed all strangers.

Odessa was built on a high plateau overlooking the sea. Its grandest boulevards reach right to the edge of the cliff, where a palatial crescent faces
out to sea. Here stands the statue, erected by a grateful citizenry, of the
duc de Richelieu, who gazes down the magnificent stairway that descends
to the harbour – steps made famous in Eisenstein's film *Battleship Potemkin*. In the narrow strip of land below the cliff known as the 'port' clus-
tered warehouses, customs and quarantine buildings, dormitories, sailors'
clubs, engine shops, grain transporters, railways and docks. Above was the
baroque order of aristocrats' palaces, gardens, department stores, grand
hotels and restaurants, the Opera House, cathedrals and synagogues, the
university and conservatory. Below was a disordered hash of dusty streets
teeming with dockers, prostitutes, and sundry incomers (sailors, drunks
and people looking for work). The early twentieth-century journalist Isaev
drew a picture of the port's otherness: its inhabitants were 'barbarians' (*di-
kari*) or 'ghosts' who had never been to the city above; its 'repulsive' flop-
houses, taverns and eateries were 'dark, smelly and sepulchral' (quoted in
Sylvester 2005: 33–34).

All through the nineteenth century, the port had been seen in contradictory terms. On the one hand, it was busy and industrious, the gateway
of wealth. It was part of what Emma Rothschild calls 'the seaside world'
cultivated across the globe by primarily commercial empires like the British, the world of commissions and consignments, of exotic goods, strange
languages, and fortunes to be made (Rothschild 2005: 226). However, Russia was not centrally a maritime polity. Almost all of its rulers upheld the
contrasting Ciceronian view, in which a virtuous inland Rome was opposed
to the morally suspect seaboard cites of Carthage and Corinth. Seen from
this perspective, ports were sources of dangerous foreign ideas, debilitating dreams of far lands, ignoble scrambles for wealth, and, most practically
of all, invisible 'germs' bringing epidemic diseases. In the late nineteenth
century, plague was still understood by Russia's medical establishment as
always having a foreign origin and Odessa was seen as one of its main por-
tals (Mikhel' 2008: 143–44).

Beneath the city centre was a warren of catacombs. These were often
used for storing contraband and guns and other nefarious activities, contributing to Odessa's fame as a criminal capital (Sylvester 2005: 24). This is
relevant because destructive disorder, including pogroms, was thought to
originate 'from below', spatially as well as socially. After the 1871 pogrom,
one of the first actions of Antonov, the chief of police drafted in to restore

order, was to block the entrances to the catacombs and study their topography (Gubar' 2004: 48).

Central Odessa was built in a grid, with wide, straight avenues. All of the prominent citizens lived here, as well as countless people in poverty, squeezed into basements and crannies. Many of the large houses, consisting of numerous apartments as well as servant quarters and stables, had a fairly transient population. They were 'income houses' (*dokhodnye doma*), whose various parts were rented out by the owner on shorter or longer contracts. In such a house people of different nationalities often lived as neighbours – central Odessa had no ethnic quarters and there was no ghetto. Beyond the centre were manufacturing areas and working-class housing, such as the mainly Jewish neighbourhood of Moldavanka, and the low-lying, huddled streets of Peresyp and Slobodka-Romanovka, mostly inhabited by Slavic workers.

Patricia Herlihy calls the cosmopolitan image of Odessa a myth not just because it formed the chimerical fear-object of Tsarist loyalists, but because it was far from evident that relations between the various ethnic groups and religions were so strikingly benign. A major reason for strained relations was the trajectory of the economy. The boom that attracted the incomers, which lasted approximately to the 1860s, was the result primarily of the massive grain export trade. This faded for various reasons, including the inadequacies of the Odessa docks (Herlihy 1986: 222–27), and the city lost out to other Black Sea ports. Competition sharpened for the remaining trade as well as for manufacturing opportunities. As was commonly the case throughout Russia, ethnic groups lived largely separate lives. Mazis, a Greek scholar, writes about the late nineteenth century: 'Although Odessa was cosmopolitan, it was not a melting-pot; the various ethnic groups interacted in the market place but outside it there was little contact' (2004: 25). Close friendships and even common social occasions between Jews and non-Jews remained unusual at all levels of society (Zipperstein 1985: 65, 189), and while business partnerships were frequent, they were increasingly strained due to the difficult economic conditions. Meanwhile, the proportions of the various groups shifted greatly. Italian merchants, architects and engineers had been a strong presence in the founding years and indeed from an Italian point of view Odessa was regarded as 'the last Italian Black Sea colony' (Makolkin 2004). But their influence waned; they lost out in the struggles to obtain real estate in the city centre and were overtaken by Russians and also by the Greeks, who of all the inhabitants had the oldest presence around the Black Sea coast and who regarded Odessa as in some sense 'their city' (it was named after Odessos, an early Greek settlement, Mazis 2004: 17)). The Jews were not initially among the great trading communities, but they increased in number and influence by leaps and bounds during the nineteenth century. By 1897 they represented over a third of the population (138,900 according to the census) and came to dominate banking and many merchant spheres, including the still crucial grain trade. Until the 1917 Bolshevik Revolution Russian society was officially organised according to its own archaic politico-legal system of estates. This was an imperial vision, which ignored nationalities and religions in favour of 'layers' (estates, *soslovie*) of subjects categorised according to their occupations and hence their duties to the Empire. By the beginning of the twentieth century people were coming to think of themselves more in terms of 'classes' and the surging political loyalties of the time. Yet Haimson argues that estates continued to provide 'significant clues to the collective mentalities of certain social groups', especially the landed aristocrats and the hereditary nobles who dominated the bureaucracy and all those who depended on, or admired them (Haimson 1988: 3). Freeze (1986) and Löwe (2004) go further, arguing that the operating dynamic of the estate order was not just imperial will but also collaboration by particular groups.

> Much of society continued to think in terms of the prereform *soslovie* system. The strong hereditary patterns, the persisting legal distinctions, the segregation of groups in administration and law, the deeply-rooted cultural differences among various groups, and the conscious effort of the state to preserve the *soslovie* separation – all acted to maintain the old social structure even in the face of far-reaching social and economic change. (Freeze 1986: 36)

This relates to my argument, because although the estate system was increasingly irrelevant to practical life, it stood symbolically for the entire social order of the Old Regime, loyalty to the Tsar and Russian Orthodoxy. Thus, when patriotic processions made their way through the streets – some of which morphed into crowds intent on pogrom – there should be no surprise at the form they took. As late as 1912, during the great celebration in Kishinev of the inclusion of Bessarabia into the Russian Empire, the procession marched according to the estates: the nobles and officials, the merchants, the clergy, the *meshchanstvo* (lower middle-class townspeople), and the 'peasants' (mostly factory workers), each walked in their own groups (Löwe 1998: 445–46). Bringing together loyalists who were otherwise sharply divided by wealth and power, this system was, of course, the hated target of revolutionaries.

If the Tsarist order evoked fealty, emulation, even passionate devotion – and conversely contempt and revolt – other kinds of clusters, such as adherents to a religion, ethnic group or language, were non-systemic and particularistic. It can be seen therefore that ethnic identity and membership of an estate were different kinds of category. Unambiguous legal designations assigned people to estates, but in the case of ethnicity, although the populace in general was sure that some people really were Jews, just as others were Greeks or Russians, the criteria for this kind of belonging were varied and ambiguous in many individual cases. Yet it was the essentialised ethnic categories, offering a simplified way of imagining the city, which became the currency of pogrom crowds.

Economic 'vertical integration' linked the craftsmen, industrialists, wholesalers, traders, etc. of the larger ethnic groups, and there were other ethnic institutions too. The Greeks were perhaps the first to introduce, in 1814, a Greek Friendly society, then a Commercial School (to which every Greek sea captain docking at Odessa had to pay a tithe each visit), a Philanthropic Society, the Brotherhood of the Holy Trinity, and the Greek Benevolent Society of Odessa, a Greek students' union, etc., as well as three Greek newspapers published in Odessa. (Mazis 2004: 52–57; Sifneos 2005: 101). The Russians, Jews and Germans came to have even more elaborate arrays of their own organisations – churches and synagogues, schools, hospitals, friendly societies, clubs, music societies, newspapers, women's groups, orphanages, reading-rooms, and old people's homes (Plesskaya-Zebol'd 1999; Brodovskii 2001: 39, 43, 49; Zagoruiko 1960: 99–105). Even the 800 or so Tatars had their own economic niche and social life based on their mosque, cemetery, school and club (Kalmykov 2008: 27–30). However, the image of the city thus conjured up – of a series of separate, ethnically integrated, vertical columns – is seriously deficient.

A chasm separated bourgeois German-speaking Jewish magnates and intellectuals from the swarms of poverty-stricken Jews streaming into the city from the *shtetls*. The collapse in the second half of the nineteenth century of the Jewish economic niche as middlemen in provincial towns and villages had caused hardship and mass migration to cities. In 1899–1900, a commission was set up to distribute bread and coal to the most needy households. In order to discover how many of these there were, a street-by-street, house-by-house investigation was carried out. Brodovskii wrote about the university students who carried out the investigative survey and had not known about the 'filthy Jewish basements and hovels, where destitution and disease were woven together into durable nests':

> For many of these young people their first survey of the area allocated to them opened up a whole new world of the most appalling poverty. Right nearby tens of thousands of well-supplied people were living calmly in full ignorance. Many of the students were simply struck dumb by what they saw, and they collapsed in spirit. We will never forget the humiliated voice and bitter smile with which one student told us about his impressions. (Brodovskii 2001: 17–18)

Such shock occurred because people supposed the ethnic groups to be integrated and homogenous, and as a result of this bias their diversity was difficult to perceive. Occasionally glimpses are given, when it becomes evident that mobile and varied activities gave rise to multiple cross-ethnic identities rather than a single one. Among Greeks, even the most prominent representative, the grain baron John Ralli, saw himself as a man with a multinational identity: 'I am a Russian subject, was born on the island of Chio in the Archipelago and am by birth of Greek origin' (Sifneos 2005: 101). Grigorios Marazlis, who became Mayor of Odessa between 1878 and 1895, kept a house in Paris where he spent time every year and he seems to have envisaged himself not so much as upholding Greek traditions as becoming a conduit for the openness of Odessa to Western European culture. Greek and Jewish entrepreneurs invested in substantial building projects, inviting foreign architects to construct European styles, such as Renaissance, Baroque and Anglo-Gothic. As members of the municipal council, they promoted innovative economic methods and civic institutions that had already been implemented successfully in European metropolitan centres – all of which was resented by more conservative Greeks (Sifneos 2005: 105).

A similar opening to, and absorption of, European culture by the Jews included the strong development of the Haskalah ('Enlightenment') movement, which maintained that Judaism was entirely reconcilable with the modern world. Many rejected orthodox ritual, wearing Jewish clothing, or giving their children Jewish names, such that in some orthodox eyes they had ceased to be Jews (Zipperstein 1985: 105–106). Meanwhile Jewish professors mastered the Russian national canons of literature and music. The well-known Zionist Vladimir Jabotinsky observes that they were 'just too good at it … assimilated Jews found themselves in the role of the public bearers and propagandists of Russian culture'. Another Jewish nationalist wrote, 'We Jews administer the spiritual possessions of a people that denies us the capability of doing so' (both quotations in Slezkine 2004: 71). Some Jews converted to Christianity. Far more, among the younger generation, became revolutionaries and ardent opponents of ethnic exclusivity. Such breaches of cultural boundaries – inside-out or outside-in – aroused deep anxieties and resentments among both Jews and Russians and contributed to the atmosphere in which pogroms became possible.

In nineteenth-century pogroms, 'the Jews' were often attacked ostensibly on the religious grounds of Judaism's hostility to Christianity – a bitter irony when one realises that many Jews came to Odessa precisely to escape the restrictions of religious orthodoxy in small towns and villages. For decades, the city had been renowned for its lack of seriousness about religion, characterised by a merchant's remark: 'I have so much to do with the present world that I have no time to think about a future one' (Zipperstein 1985: 64). In Jewish folklore Odessa was rarely associated with high-minded pursuits. Rather, the word Odessa became 'synonymous with disbelief, sinfulness and frivolity' (Dawidowicz 1967: 26).

The 'ethnic communities' were virtual signs hanging over associations whose edges were hazy and whose make-up was internally fragmented and changing. Apparently solid cogs joining people together – even something as seemingly unquestionably Jewish as the Odessa Mutual Aid Society of Jewish Salesclerks (OMASJS)[3] – could metamorphose into something completely different. In a brilliant article, Robert Weinberg (1990: 427–45) has described how the OMASJS began as a *hevrah* (Hebrew for 'association') of male salesclerks attached to Poele Emuna prayer house. In the 1860s a group of young members, frustrated at the religious orientation of the *hevrah* and its unwillingness to provide material assistance, established a mutual aid society for all (male) Jewish salesclerks, not just those attached to the prayer house. It began operation in 1863 and furnished loans, medical aid, and death benefits. So far, it did not engage in bargaining with the employers about work conditions. By the 1880s, professionals – grain brokers, doctors, lawyers, etc. – began to take control of the society, sidelining the salesclerks. The same happened in a mutual aid society catering to Christian shop assistants, resulting in complaints in both cases. By the early 1900s Socialist Revolutionary agitators began to pay attention to salesclerks throughout the city and proposed an illegal union among the rank and file, without regard to sex or nationality. Young members of both mutual aid societies forced their organisations to fund a new legal entity, a common Trade Union. There soon followed a split over whether the Union should engage only in narrow professional activity (wage rates, work conditions, etc.) or campaign for political goals, basic civil rights and a constituent assembly – the latter prevailed.

This example shows not only that the institutions forming the glue of the ethnic edifice called 'the Jews' could shift and change their character (from 'religious' to 'economic' to 'political'), but also that new, non-ethnic, social categories were increasingly important in the city. The occupational category 'salesclerks' (*prikazchiki*, of whom there were 26,000 in Odessa in 1902; Weinberg 1990: 429) was of course just one of these. By now the language of class ('proletariat', 'intelligentsia', etc.) was everywhere. People had to choose how to describe themselves in diverse political circumstances. Industrialists, for example, oscillated between representing themselves as *kuptsy* ('merchants', a category of the ossified system of estates) and *krupnaia burzhuaziia* ('big bourgeoisie', a class and increasingly a political designation).

Most encompassing of all was the concept of *publika*, not to be confused with the Tardean 'public' mentioned earlier. *Publika* in a literal translation meant all of 'society' (*obshchestvo*), i.e. excluding the unlettered common people; but it implied a zone of debate.[4] By the late nineteenth century *pub-*

lika referred to the public both as spectators and as judges of personal and civic behaviour (Sylvester 2000: 803). The Odessan public sphere was the sea-like milieu in which currents of opinion (Tarde's publics) surged. In the lively, varied press, popular songs, satires, or journalistic coups, national concerns were debated together with the city's moral and social problems such as taverns as dens of alcohol-fuelled iniquity, wild street children, overly greedy match-making and dowries, thriving thievery and prostitution in Odessa, or the deceptively 'well-dressed man' who was a cunning seducer (Sylvester 2005: 94–95 et. seq.). It was in the *publika* that we find one important kind of urban cosmopolitanism, as will be described later.

In brief, by the beginning of the twentieth century it was possible to describe Odessa in largely non-ethnic terms. The university, markets, cafés and theatres were places where people of any nationality could meet, where lowly origins and straightened incomes could be disguised for an evening out, and where the characteristic Odessan speech was bandied about and local jokes were made.[5] Yet class and ethnic divisions were still acutely felt. Preoccupations with common social justice came to dominate in revolutionary political parties and the serious press. In fact, from the beginning of the century, the city was seething with economic and political anger, riots, labour demonstrations and strikes.

This bursting out of presumed social categories – ever more frequent and uncontrollable over the years – are central to my theme, for, paradoxically, pogroms were instituted by the poor against a category ('Jew') they themselves considered as 'out of order'. Odessa experienced a confused multiple anticipation of mob volatility: the authorities were afraid that workers' pogroms against Jews would blaze into general revolutionary uprising (Judge 1992: 28), while this was precisely what many revolutionaries hoped for. Meanwhile, the socialists feared that their own political demonstrations would degenerate into anti-Semitic violence. In 1903 the proposed May Day (labour) procession was cancelled because the potential participants, both Jews and non-Jews, feared that a march through Odessa would unleash a pogrom against Jews as prime representatives of the 'exploitative bourgeoisie' and/or 'traitorous revolutionaries'. With the cancellation of the march, worker solidarity prevailed on this occasion (Weinberg 1987: 57).

'Worker solidarity' was newly forged through emergent socialist political action at the end of the century and it can be seen in Tardean terms as 'invention', i.e. as a practice introducing a 'difference that makes a difference', i.e. departing from the usual temporal curve of imitation, repetition that inevitably involves minute changes (Born 2010: 242). Worker solidarity created a new kind of social assemblage. In contrast, the pogrom, whatever the misplaced fears/hopes of transformation into revolution, seems to have been a recursive, non-creative kind of practice.[6]

A regional geography of pogroms

In 1881, in the agitated atmosphere that followed the assassination of the Tsar and the anxieties that his successor would redistribute land or even re-impose serfdom, Jews were accused of being behind the treasonous plot and several surges of pogroms hit southern Russia (Ukraine). Historians have recorded 259 attacks, of which 219 happened in villages and only 36 in towns. Yet it is clear that pogroms started in towns. Before they had run their course there, they had already spread out to villages. By the time they reached more distant villages, they had been 'put out' in the originating city. This suggests a wildfire or wave-like pattern.

The readiness to form aggressive crowds can be understood in relation to the ethnic separateness, industrial conflict, political revolt and general violence in Ukraine at the end of the nineteenth century. Russians and Ukrainians lived in separate villages and regularly attacked one another in knife fights. Jews were not the only non-Slav victims of attacks. Muslim Tatar migrant workers also suffered in the industrial Donbas (Kuromiya 1998: 41–42) and in 1905 there was a pogrom against Greeks in Kiev (Mazis 2004: 36), though by far the most numerous and serious attacks were carried out by Christians (Russians, Ukrainians, Greeks, Moldovans, etc.) on Jews. Political and religious accusations, economic desperation and class antagonism curdled with ethnic hatred in these pogroms. What this chapter draws attention to, however, is not the continuity of pogroms with everyday aggression (Spencer 1990), but the particular dynamics of pogrom crowds.

This is where we see the contagion, copying and molecular spreading highlighted by Tarde. Careful study by I. Michael Aronson (1980; 1990) has cast doubt on earlier theories that nineteenth-century pogroms in Ukraine were conspiracies, i.e. planned and initiated by officials within the Tsarist government or by the Holy Brotherhood, a secret counter-revolutionary organisation of loyal aristocrats serving in government positions. He shows how pogroms moved from towns to villages along the routes used by ordinary villagers and workers, spreading via highways, railway lines, and rivers. For example, the pogrom in Kiev on 26 April 1881 was repeated in nine nearby villages the next day; it spread by the river connection to Kanev on 27 April, to Cherkasy on 29 April, and to Smela on 3 May (1980: 19), and via rail to two stations also on 27 April (1990: 51). Such a rapid radiation is entirely understandable if we imagine people returning from the city with a practice to be copied. One witness described how 'a person in a white cap' got off the train from Kiev and went straight to nearby workshops and shouted, 'Now we'll work in the Kiev way!' and a new pogrom started (1990: 116). Railway employees, and machine-shop workers who had free passes to travel on the lines for which they worked, seem to have been most active in spreading news and creating pogroms (Aronson 1980: 23). The movement was continuous in some cases, sporadic in others, stopping for days or even weeks, only to break out again, generally at quite a distance from the previous area of action. The patterns, Aronson suggests, strongly suggest spontaneous imitation rather than a master plan.

In the 1881 wave, to which Aronson's analysis refers, incitements to violence found particularly ready acceptance among people who themselves were dislocated. Together with Russians who normally sought seasonal jobs in the rich agricultural lands of Ukraine, there also arrived throngs of people who had lost their jobs in St Petersburg and Moscow due to the industrial crisis of 1880–1881. However, Ukraine was in the grip of local crop failures and near famine. People wandered from place to place looking for work: 'Many must have lost hope ... a pogrom had the advantage that it promised, as a bare minimum, a bellyful of vodka' (Aronson 1980: 21).

Odessa concentrated these patterns. As well as local peasants who had settled there seeking 'to inscribe themselves in the *meshchanstvo* estate and forget about their hard rural past' (Atlas 1992: 175), thousands of poor, overwhelmingly male, Russian migrants arrived from the north (Herlihy 1986: 243–51). By the 1890s there were 20,000 homeless dockworkers, hordes of street children, widespread theft and street muggings (Skinner 1986: 228). Every year seasonal hands from a wide network of towns and villages gathered at hiring places, waiting huddled in the dust along fences, willing to work for a pittance and some '*borshch* (beetroot soup) with a layer of fat on top', or even for *borshch* with no fatty layer (Zagoruiko 1960: 77). These people travelled back to their villages in winter. Pogroms occurred more rarely in regions that experienced less social upheaval, migration, and economic deprivation than Odessa (Löwe 2004: 22). From Odessa pogroms would spread quickly outwards to the region. For example, the pogrom that started there on 16 July 1900 'as always, exerted a malign influence' in nearby Russian and Bulgarian villages; within days there were attacks on the few poor Jewish shopkeepers in those places (Karakina 2005: 9).

Within Odessa, pogroms were highly mobile, dispersed and difficult to pin down; no one ever saw the whole picture. Contemporary accounts often avoid the word 'pogrom' and describe 'the disorders' (*bezporiadki*), which conflated pogroms with other riots, strikes, uprisings, and Jewish self-defence actions. This practice could indicate a deliberate blindness to the character of events, but it is also true that many onlookers did not know what they were seeing. 'Should we be afraid of the Russians, or the Jews?' wrote one bewildered merchant in his diary of the years 1903–1905 in Odessa (Kotliarevskii 2005: 136). Eyewitnesses describe a mob disappearing down a street, or streaming past like an elemental force or a fire-ball. 'They sent out for Cossacks [to quell the riots]', writes one observer. 'But it was difficult for the soldiers to run after the fast moving crowd, which now dissipated in clumps down the streets and side passages, and now gathered together in one place in a compact mass to destroy (*razgromit'*) a particular building' (quoted in Karakina 2005: 9).

Rumours

What is interesting about rumours is how they may escalate from things said by one person to another, often as 'secrets', into widely shared knowledge, whether true or false, in which case they become indistinguishable from public news. Like street oratory, rumour-news is seen here as the active preparatory content of the sociality of publics and crowds. Some pogroms started with trivial fights in taverns, whereupon shouts would bring others running (Karakina 2005: 10). But it is the shouts – the minimal elicitations of oratory – more than the brawl that matter. Often the significance of rumours is obscured because explanations focus on a causative incident and neglect the relay of communications that spread so mysteriously, like electric transmission. In pogroms eyewitness observations of the alleged initial event were often absent or confused, and the effect of this was to confound incidents and rumours. An invisible or distant provoking incident was said to have happened, was objectified in the form of a rumour, and passed from person to person as a suggestion until someone used it actively to initiate an attack.

As Homi Bhabha has observed concerning the slaughter in Rwanda, we need to understand the figural nature of language as an agent – not a reflection – of violence. In contrast to slow-moving corrosive socio-economic 'causes' such as poverty or political injustice, the rhetorical elements of propaganda constitute fast time-lines of imminence and emergency which convert such 'causes' into rapid-fire, affective responses that often lead to violence (Bhabha n.d.).

The first pogrom in Odessa in 1821 began in the wake of an event that happened in Turkey: the Ottomans had beheaded Gregory V, the Greek patriarch of Constantinople, and displayed the head to an enthusiastic crowd. The body was brought to Odessa for burial, the city being a major centre of Greek anti-Ottoman revolutionary activity. Greek sailors travelling with the body carried the story that the corpse had been dragged through the streets by a furious Jewish mob. This rumour spread like wildfire in the crowd gathered in Odessa for the funeral and attacks on Jews in Odessa began immediately afterwards. Many rumours had an archetypal quality, being resuscitated through the centuries, such as the one that arose the following year (1822) through reports by Greek sailors of a ritual murder of a Christian child by Jews in Moldavia; this initiated a further pogrom (Zipperstein 1985: 119–20). In short, each of these initiatory event-rumours is both what I called earlier 'fantasy', a vivid image of something some people wanted to believe, and the content of a social relation. This was not inward fantasy, like a daydream; it elicited affects, memories, and incited to action.

Rumours had their own life and durability in publics already created by previous rumours, invective and rhetoric. In this recursive arena, the question one has to ask is: what did people have to believe (before) to believe that? An unending genealogy of previous 'grounds' opens; rumours cascaded into other rumours. The rumour of the Tsar's order (*ukaz*) to attack Jews, which flared recurrently across southern Russia, sheds light on how this worked, as well as indicating the problematic workings of autocracy in conditions of orality. With the accession of the hyper-conservative Tsar Alexander III in March 1881, officials realised belatedly that the unfounded rumour of his order would result in pogroms, but they were unable to dispel it, as it was linked in people's minds to the suspicion that Jews had been behind the assassination of his father, the previous Tsar. The rumour of the order then became the productive grounds for even more unlikely speculations. According to one version, the Tsar was going around the villages disguised as a high-ranking official (in order to hide from landlords opposed to the rumoured land redistribution) and was giving the peasants money to beat the Jews and the landlords for murdering his father (Aronson 1990: 84). Peasants had a ready explanation for why the Tsar's order had not been announced publicly – the Jews had bribed the state officials to suppress it. The same rationale was reiterated in order to explain why police and troops acted to dispel riots against Jews in Odessa in 1905 (Kotliarevskii 2005: 136).

Aronson observes that one does not have to ascribe deep belief to an acceptance of the rumours, since they could serve various purposes and in any case could form part of the peasant repertoire of false naivety presented to officials (1990: 89). Indeed, these anarchic, mistrustful currents ran counter not only to official proclamations but also to the everyday neighbourliness that was also present, as if injected as a specific layer of hate-filled consciousness identified with 'obeying' (some higher power). Peasants would sometimes provide their own carts to help Jewish neighbours remove their property that would otherwise 'have to be destroyed' on the morrow. In one town, when ordered by local officials to desist from a pogrom, rioters refused and demanded a written guarantee that they would not be punished for failing to comply with the Tsar's *ukaz*. The official gave the guarantee, but the mob remained unconvinced and destroyed six Jewish homes 'as insurance'.[7]

Written communications from the government, including the reading out of manifestos, etc. in churches and public squares, had little impact, as Aronson shows. This was a long-standing problem in Russia. In 1858, a commission on local government observed:

> Manifestos and decrees are read unintelligibly by deacons or police officials; most of the people cannot hear; barely five per cent are present; and finally, even the most attentive and informed listeners are seldom able to get a true understanding of the substance of the decree from a single reading... Priests and police officials not only do not care about the correct meaning of the law but, unfortunately, are sometimes prepared to confuse the people intentionally in hopes of serving their own interest. (quoted in Aronson 1990: 93)

So rumours flourished. They were often publicised in the anti-Semitic press (Judge 1992: 40), whose articles were handed as scraps of paper from person to person, from policeman to clerk to factory worker to peasant (Aronson 1990: 80), but they travelled faster and further by word of mouth. Traders and shopkeepers sometimes deliberately augmented the rumours, calculating that people anticipating trouble would buy up supplies and that prices could therefore be raised (Kotliarevskii 2005: 132).

Tarde highlighted the importance of belief and desire in publics, emotions that, however, could always be tempered by other sources of ideas. In crowds, on the other hand, passions become heightened through mutual contact (1969: 288–89). Descriptions of the Odessa riots show how in the body of a crowd verbal information was reduced, perhaps just to the archetypal shout 'Beat the Yids!' Other kinds of vectors of sociality came to the fore: the noises of breaking, whistling, and yelling; the press of bodies in a certain direction; the craning forward to see what is going on; eye-contact and facial gestures; the excitement, fear and loss of self through being part of a throng: in short, that complex combination of affects that make up the 'suggestive realm' mentioned earlier.

1871: case study of a pogrom

The pogrom of 1871 in Odessa was less bound up with class warfare and political revolt than later pogroms, yet it illustrates many of the points made earlier: the role of rumours and timing, the transformation and spatial splitting up of crowds, and the impact of materiality/architecture. The case study also enables me to illustrate some further points, notably to show how the specific actions 'imitated' in pogroms produced not just one but several thresholds, and it brings to the fore two important actors hitherto barely mentioned: the authorities and bystanders.

By 1871 economic competition had sharpened and Greek traders were rapidly losing out to Jews. Every year on the eve of Easter Sunday, Greeks, including many sailors and dockworkers from the port, would gather at their church. This was situated right beside an area thickly populated by Jews, on Ekaterinskaia and Evreiskaia Streets. In the large church compound Greek crowds would carouse, shout, whoop and whistle, and let off rounds of revolver fire. Sometimes wilder youths would dash out of the compound and break a few windows in Jewish houses nearby. The Odessan Jews dreaded the Easter holidays and those living further away sympathised with the unfortunates whose apartments were close to the Greek church (Morgulis 2001 [1910]: 21–22). In 1871 the celebrations were more aggressive than usual: people sensed that something was about to happen. A rumour spread among the Greeks: a cross on the compound railing was bent and it was said to have been 'the Jews' who had caused this damage to the holy object. There was little reaction to this rumour. But soon the cross disappeared and now 'the Jews' were said to have stolen it. On Easter Sunday, an angry Greek posse ran to the courtyard of Kornfel'd's, a rival Jewish trader, attempting to grab the tables standing there. Repelled by the guard, they went back to the church compound. Gathering a larger crowd, they stormed back to Kornfel'd's, beat the guard, carried the tables back into the church compound and made a celebratory bonfire of them. Dashing out again, they did the same to Shukhman's shop. All this was more or less usual for Easter. But the following morning, more determined efforts were made to destroy nearby Jewish businesses. The fire brigade was called in, and jets of water directed into the compound dispersed the crowd. Once the rioters had been forced out of their church precinct something resembling a pogrom began. The men set out on raids in the surrounding streets, armed with axes, clubs and staves (Morgulis 2001: 23).

The iron fence around the Greek compound enabled it to become a 'citadel', transforming the church from religious edifice to fortress. This was recognised by the city authorities after the pogrom. They ordered the fence to be demolished and moved close to the church. Now aggressive crowds could no longer gather inside and rely on the railings for protection.

The recursive character of rumour-actants is shown by information given by the Odessa historian Gubar'. The Greek Patriarch Gregory V, whose funeral initiated the 1821 pogrom, had been buried at this same Greek church. In spring 1871, his remains were to be repatriated to Athens for reburial; a few days after the pogrom, a mass procession accompanied them to the Russian orthodox cathedral, and thence to the port, where they were embarked on a ship meaningfully called 'Byzantium'. Around the time of the pogrom lithographs of Gregory V were circulated in the town, and along with the old story of the Jewish mob in Constantinople, a new evil rumour spread that 'people of a different faith' were planning to steal his sacred remains and prevent the repatriation. Gubar' argues that it was not just economic competition between Greeks and Jews but indeed these rumour-memories that enraged the pogromists (Gubar' 2004: 50–51).

Descriptions of the 1871 pogrom (Morgulis 2001; Gubar' 2004; Zipperstein 1985: 114–28), together with those of other pogroms, indicate that there were 'stages' of pogroms, consisting of distinctive actions. First was destruction of Jewish property, like the grabbing of the tables and shop fittings just mentioned, along with the breaching of material boundaries (breaking windows, smashing doors and window-frames, chopping at external staircases, setting fire to shops). Accounts describe acts of imitation which seem to be almost without thought. A band of very young boys took two hours to break the glass of every window of the main Jewish synagogue (Morgulis 2001: 26). According to one Russian eyewitness, 'I walked round the streets where the crowd was raging, trying to catch any conscious motive for the rampage, like anger about "Jewish exploitation" and so forth, but I could not pick up anything at all'. As this witness was walking by a row of poor market stalls at the New Market he saw a woman, 'absolutely not ferocious in appearance', who was holding a lighted taper to a stall. He asked her why she was setting fire to the stall of someone as poor as herself. In great confusion, she groped for an answer and in the end replied, 'Do you think we could destroy and beat Jews for three whole days if that had not been the will of the authorities?' (Gubar' 2004: 40–41).

Morgulis notes the use of certain tactics, such as the deliberate breaking of windows in the house opposite the police station on the first day. When this test received no effective response and the one policeman who dared to intervene was beaten up, the crowds sensed that further boundaries could be breached and they went on the rampage. What they did is described as 'wild', 'insane', beyond any likeness to another kind of activity and absolutely impermissible in everyday life. Noise was integral to pogroms: hordes 'rolled through' the streets (Gubar' 2004: 39) yelling, whistling and greeting breakages with shouts of 'Hurrah'. Squads of soldiers marched to the beat of drums. Mobs also attacked Christian businesses, indeed they ransacked randomly to loot particular goods; they even beat policemen and threatened Orthodox priests if the latter requested them to disperse ('Get lost, father, or you'll get a stone in your face!') (Morgulis 2001: 40). At one point the highest official in Odessa, the City Prefect, ventured into the streets to see what was going on. The crowd surrounded him, tearing up a big eiderdown and emptying feathers over his head, so he looked as though he had been in a snowstorm – all this to guffaws of laughter and cries of 'Hurrah!' ((Morgulis 2001: 26).

On all sides there were mimetic acts. They could crystallise into stark phantasmagorical inversions, projecting onto the feared Other the aggression of the crowd itself. After the widespread destruction of Easter Monday 1871, a massive crowd gathered, stretching seven blocks down Richel'evskii Street, forming the masquerade of a cortege. In its centre Morgulis could just see a horse's head bobbing, behind which followed a cart bearing a wounded pogromist. The bier was being born by the 'aggrieved' crowd to the Governor General, to demonstrate to him the aggression of the Jews who had dared to wound a Russian person. In fact, the man had been wounded by one of the soldiers called in to quell the riots (Morgulis 2001: 32). If pogromists mimed the role of victims/mourners, soldiers mimed 'providing protection'. A doctor saw the following scene on the third day: a crowd was stirring, while an army troop stood idly by. Through the throng there slowly moved a carriage bearing an old Jewish woman, probably a trader, with her trunk. The carriage was 'guarded' by eight soldiers with weapons at the ready, four closely walking on each side. The crowd reached through the guards, dragged out the woman and grabbed the trunk. She was beaten; the trunk was broken up. But the carriage moved on at the same pace and the soldiers continued to hold up their weapons, as if there were still something requiring protection (Morgulis 2001: 39).

Another stage began when the mob split up into 'task forces' and tore into Jewish homes across the city. Here the actions were above all demonstrative, consisting of the breaking and scattering of objects. The palatial buildings of banks (which were also the bankers' homes), whose baroque balconies afforded public display, were particular targets. Crockery and furniture was smashed and splintered and thrown out onto the street. Even grand pianos were heaved out to triumphant shouts. A speciality was ripping up cushions and bedding, and tossing them in the air so feathers covered the streets as if it were snowing. It is significant that the word used by eyewitnesses was often not pogrom but *razgrom* – the prefix *raz* added the meaning of 'breaking apart' to *grom*, which means 'thunder, annihilation'. Looting was partly for immediate consumption (groceries, drinks, alcohol, clothes, shoes) but its excesses can also be seen as the destruction of (hated, desired) stores of wealth (jewellery and precious watches were particularly targeted). Morgulis attributes the destruction of account books to more tactical thinking: people heavily in debt deliberately shredded the pages to ribbons. The street outside the palace-bank of Hans Rafalovich was covered with pieces of paper, just as other streets were white with cotton and feathers (Morgulis 2001: 28), and the torn pages of sacred books fluttered outside the synagogues.

Onlookers flocked to these scenes and formed crowds, uneasily poised between looking and doing. Jabotinsky describes such a crowd, not at a pogrom, but gathered on a cliff-top one summer night in 1905 to watch the revolutionary confrontation of the battleship Potemkin and dockworkers against the soldiers. People wondered about using opera glasses – you could see better, but would it not appear too frivolous for such a horrific sight? As flames appeared below and shots rang out, something changed in the mood of the crowd like the 'swinging of a common pendulum'. Jabotinsky writes, 'Now I could scramble down the cliff into that group laughing under gunfire below, who only half an hour before had been just whispering to one another, and the men and women there would accept me as one of themselves and go on pouring out defiance' (2002: 150). This phenomenon of the fascinated mass of onlookers tipping towards joining in was present in both pogrom and revolution. In the 1871 pogrom, the sight of looting attracted poor street boys (*bosiaki*) and 'shady people in torn clothes with haggard angry faces' (Karakina 2005: 13). Some middle-class onlookers shouted encouragement to the rioters from the safety of their carriages. Other bystanders merged into the crowd, notably 'the whole estate of the city's thieves, who did not bother with religious or social grievances, but quite simply set about lifting other people's wealth'. This kind of crowd did not destroy anything. They picked shops bare, leaving them clean and tidy, as if the owners had left with their goods, and then moved on to new premises (Morgulis 2001: 34–35).

It was a different stage of pogrom, condemned by the authorities (Morgulis 2001: 43), to commit mass physical violence on Jewish persons, since that might result in death. The city fathers were complacent, ineffective, even conniving when it came to attacks on property. When a prominent Jew succeeded in getting through to the Governor General to beg for help, the reply was, 'I know, I know, and so what? The Jews are responsible for this; they started it. And don't make a fuss: I have already taken the necessary measures' (Morgulis 2001: 30). As happened in several other pogroms, Cossack troops called in to restore order were uncertain what to do for two days while the City Prefect and military commander exchanged messages about who was in charge. Some soldiers and police took part in looting, though some fought fiercely against the pogrom mobs. When a troop was sent to the Old Bazaar to calm the crowd, the Cossack captain first of all set about dispersing the Jews, who had gathered to protect their property. Then he said to the pogromists, 'Do what you like, just don't kill anyone'. From on high, the orders were to stop and go home, but the inconsistent statements and lack of determined action on the part of the authorities had already established that such 'orders' could be breached with impunity. People, including women, died.[8] It was not until the crowd, appearing with the carriage bearing the 'victim' at the Governor General's house, called him out to the balcony and threw stones at him when he sharply refused to accept their complaint (about Jewish attacks), that he eventually decided the next day to use determined force to put down the pogrom (2001: 32–33).

On the third day, the Wednesday of Easter Week, the pogrom had spread to Slobodka and Moldavanka. Meanwhile, in the town centre, a crowd of peasants had massed near the New Bazaar, having heard the rumour of the Tsar's order to attack Jews, and they had looted two streets by eleven o'clock in the morning. The pogrom did not simply fade away, but ended through a public demonstration of the violent supremacy of the state. Just after eleven o'clock, a troop of soldiers arrived with a cart of birch rod whips. In the midst of the market, they set about thrashing everyone in sight, pogromist or not, amid shrieks and yells. One woman 'from society' was slashed just for raising her voice against this 'barbaric mass punishment'. Hearing the whistle and crack of the rods, people at the back of the crowd shouted, 'Oi, they're shooting!' and immediately eyewitnesses heard the creak of wheels and saw clouds of dust as the peasants set off en masse in their carts. Within a couple of hours, convinced that the authorities were now serious, the villagers were nowhere to be seen and all the pogromists melted away (Morgulis 2001: 41–42). Such scenes became part of urban memories. Crowds did not always disperse before the soldiers' rods; some laughed defiantly, even those being flogged (De-Ribas 2005: 248). It is possible to see the brutality of pogroms, the thrashing of Jews with sticks and cudgels, as a repetition of the archaic, disordered brutality of the sovereignty exercised by the state.

Pogroms as punishment

After the revolutionary uprising of June 1905 – the Potemkin revolt, the burning of the docks, strikes, bombings and shootings – central Odessa pulsated to the sway of fervent, conflicting crowds. Armed, black-shirted, Jewish groups appeared and warned others not to attack;[9] the University doors were opened to mass meetings of workers; and Tsarist loyalists, angry and frightened, their emotions highly wrought by the recent return of heroic sailors from the Japanese defeat, held parades and religious processions. The 'hydra of revolution' spread even to children, who occupied their schools, breaking windows and making threats, and then went through the city waving red flags, 'taking' school after school throughout the city. The police called in to deal with them were accused of beating children (Malakhov and Stepanenko 2004: 104–105). Prices rocketed, and state employees were beaten up if they refused to strike. Faced with chaos across Russia, Tsar Nicholas II issued his Manifesto granting civil liberties. News of the

Manifesto reached Odessa on 17 October and the following morning thousands of people thronged the streets to celebrate. Demonstrators ripped down portraits of the Tsar and a red flag was substituted for the Imperial colours in the city Duma building. Crowds forced passers-by to doff their caps to red flags. Simultaneously, an Orthodox religious service was held to declare loyalty to the Tsar, an action that was to lead straight to the 1905 pogrom. The procession of loyalist dockworkers, proceeding from the port to the cathedral, came under gunfire from newspaper office windows, killing a boy bearing an icon. Meanwhile, Jewish youths belonging to 'black shirt' defence groups attacked two other parades with bomb and gunfire. Fighting broke out across the city. However, loyalists who disapproved of the concessions granted by the Tsar took action, not by attacking Russian workers celebrating in the streets, but by turning on all Jews (Weinberg 1987: 61–62; Malakhov and Stepanenko 2004: 106–107).[10] In the horrific pogrom that took place over the next three to four days, over 300 Jewish people were killed, including women and children, and tens of thousands made homeless. Unprecedented in its brutality, it was the culmination of all the pogroms in the city. The following days saw a spate of pogroms across the Pale of Settlement in hundreds of towns and villages.

Evidently new kinds of political fury were mixed with other emotions in 1905; all sides were more organised and aware than they had been in the 1881 event described earlier. But I would still wish to suggest here that the pogrom – unlike the revolution – was a continuation of an archaic political modality concerned with enforcing imperial supremacy and hierarchical order, and that it was therefore different from the seemingly similar violence that has latterly come under the name of 'ethnic cleansing'. Processes of 'de-cosmopolitanisation' (Appadurai 2000: 627) come in diverse guises. The Odessa mobs were not intent on ridding the city of all Jews or creating a purified religious space, as in the case of Shiva Sena Hindu activists in Bombay-Mumbai in 1992–1993 (Appadurai 2000: 630), but on punishing the Jews, destroying or grabbing their wealth, and enforcing their lowly place in the imperial arena. For in nationalist ideology (and often in practice), were the Jews not ostracised half-citizens who were beyond the common law? The concept of a hierarchical – imperial yet also racist – polity, in which it was possible to imagine a people who had 'risen beyond their station', explains the variable and indeed, contradictory character of the accusation-rumours. 'The Jews' could be attacked both as representatives of the exploitative bourgeoisie and as revolutionary activists.

The urge to enforce hierocratic order is evident in the symbolic acts reiterated by the crowds that preceded the outbursts of violence. By 1905, religious processions with icons and gonfalons had become common in Russian cities; to the accompaniment of church bells, hymns, the national anthem and military bands, they mobilised support for the loyalist cause. They would call on the workers of a railway depot, people at a market place, a government office and so on; a priest orator would then address the crowd, but it did not much matter what he said – any admonishments not to start a pogrom went unheeded (Löwe 1998: 456). What mattered were the material signs, icons, banners, and above all the portrait of the Tsar: the smallest sign of disrespect to these would unleash an attack on revolutionaries, students and Jews alike. The processions enforced a reverential stance on all people in the spaces that surrounded it. Passers-by were made to stand to attention and doff their hats, revolutionary students forced to come out of their buildings and 'ask forgiveness'. At Nezhin (Chernigov) in October 1905, the crowd forced students to bring out the university's portrait of the Tsar, so that it could witness their surrender, the ceremony of repentance, and the oath taken to the sovereign. The idea was that the portrait would thereafter work upon the students to remain loyal subjects – evidence as Löwe notes (1998: 457–58) of the mystical or fetishist power that was attributed to this particular portrait (since the crowd was carrying several other portraits that would not have had this specific long-lasting effect). The university portrait was therefore set up in the main square, to shouts of '*Buntovshchiki* (seditionists), on your knees!' One by one, students and Jews had to step forward, kneel down, kiss the portrait, and take the oath to Nicholas II. A list of supposed democrats in the town was produced; they were rounded up and forced to go through the same ceremony, which went on deep into the night (1998: 458).

Similar events took place in Odessa just before the 1905 pogrom started, and were copied on both sides. On 17 October, Jews had attempted to convince a group of Russian workers to doff their caps to the red flag. The next day, a vast loyalist procession, substituting Imperial colours for the red flag, made Jews kiss icons, etc. (Weinberg 1987: 61–62). All of this was part of a repertoire of well-understood practices that went back to nineteenth-century pogroms. Evidently, external signs such as distinctive clothing, headwear, or perhaps overheard conversations in Yiddish, enabled the mob to distinguish 'Jews', and it was also by external marks that they could escape. As soon as a pogrom mob was sighted, Christian icons appeared in windows, on doors, in shops and stalls, those belonging to Jews as well as Russians (Karakina 2005: 8 for 1900). If someone begged for mercy, they would be let off if they agreed to wear a cross (Morgulis 2001: 26 for 1871). A similar enforcement of 'sameness' or subordination on passers-by was copied in all subsequent pogroms.

All of this tended to deflect anger away from the state as a political target. Yet the state itself was the fount of demonstrative public violence, both physical and symbolic, as we saw in the description of the suppression of the 1871 pogrom.

Counter-acts, opposition, hesitation, shame

There were also Russians who acted bravely to protect the Jews. For example, in 1871 the Avchinnikov brothers, who were landlords, succeeded with the help of an Orthodox priest holding up his cross in stopping the mobs by the 'power of good words' (Gubar' 2004: 43; Morgulis 2001: 36). Many other ordinary people hid known Jews in their homes and cellars. Some prominent citizens of 'cosmopolitan Odessa' organised protection for the businesses of Jewish acquaintances (Gubar' 2004: 44). Morgulis mentions others who, 'although they were full of the Christian feeling of sympathy, were unable to reveal it because of weakness of character' (2001: 36–37).

These observations recall what Tarde writes about 'opposition'. The rejection of an imitable act ('opposition') can occur between different entities or within the same entity. In other words, such rejection can take place between people, or within one person – in the latter case involving the splitting of subjectivity by the contradiction between a person's previous value or habit and the potentially imitable aim or notion of some other person (Tarde 1969: 171). We can see the public standing up for Jews as the first kind of opposition to pogrom violence; however, the internal conflict of an individual might well not be visible and indeed is not recorded in the accounts available to me. Yet the fact that some pogromists evidently regretted their acts afterwards and went to Jews to return stolen property and to ask forgiveness suggests that inner conflict may have been present among some people in the crowd even during the riots.[11] Let us recall Deleuze's remark that Tarde's focus on opposition within a being suggests that 'hesitation [can be] understood as "infinitesimal social opposition"' (quoted in Born 2010: 237). Hesitation, or the inability to express one's inner revulsion, is a micro-process occurring internally that parallels the oppositions taking place overtly between people.

However, after the culminating pogrom of October 1905 – even during it – public revulsion spread immediately: the entire Duma blamed the City Prefect for not taking prompt action, he was forced to resign and called to St Petersburg to face questioning. The Russian Orthodox Archbishop raged to his flock, 'How can stupid, shameful acts serve to protect honour?' (Malakhov and Stepanenko 2004: 109). It is true that counter-signs of pogromic justifications did seep into the public, such as newspapers exclaiming that 'totally innocent people' had suffered in the pogrom – as if there must be other Jews who were not innocent. But overwhelmingly the discourse of shame prevailed and split the Slavic multitude by labelling the perpetrators as 'non-humans overwhelmed by instincts' (2004: 107).

Cosmopolitan topologies

In some writings about Odessa, pogroms are either not mentioned or appear as incidental aberrations, while the real character of the city is assumed to reside in its free-thinking lightness, wit and beauty (De-Ribas 2005). 'Cosmopolitanism' appears as part of this character, a constant. It will be argued here, however, that cosmopolitan relations were sporadic and historically specific, becoming more fragile through the nineteenth century. Such webs were dissimilar to one another, and formed distinctive situated patterns in the city (Werbner 2008: 1). Whatever their form, they were always a 'thread', a skein of relations that co-existed with other, different and mutually exclusive relations.

Jabotinsky's description of the literary club at the beginning of the twentieth century illustrates this last point. The club had premises at the very centre of 'civilised' Odessa, beside the Opera House and the City Duma on the plaza overlooking the sea.

> Looking back on all this thirty years later, I think that most interesting of all was the peaceful brotherhood of peoples amongst us at the time. All the eight or ten tribes of old Odessa met in this club, and really it entered no one's head, even silently to oneself, to notice who was who. Two years later this changed, but at the very dawn of the century we sincerely got on well with one another. It was strange. Because amongst ourselves at home we held others at a distance: the Poles visited and invited other Poles, the Russians other Russians, the Jews other Jews. There were relatively few exceptions. But we didn't yet think about why it was like that, and subconsciously we assumed that this was just a temporary oversight and that the Babylonian diversity of colours of our common forum was the symbol of a wonderful tomorrow. (Jabotinsky 2002: 26)

Jabotinsky goes on to describe the brotherhood of the literary club as a conciliatory surface lying on top of a threatening underground. The horizontal imagery, I suggest, is not an accident, since cosmopolitanism is almost always imagined this way, rather than vertically. Mutually friendly relations between a landlord and his poverty-stricken tenant are not usually called 'cosmopolitan', even though the difference in culture may be greater than that between, for example, a Polish and a Greek merchant; the same is true of the bridges made between members of professions who would otherwise hardly meet, such as navy officers, musicians, or chemists.

In a city like Odessa, however, it could make sense to stretch the topography of the cosmopolitan in all directions. The skeins of mutually benign relations, co-present with other exclusivist networks, can now be seen as temporary – and readily punctured – three-dimensional assemblages, now expanding, now shrinking. This would allow us to consider cross-estate, cross-class and cross-professional linkages in the same cosmopolitan light as those between ethnic groups and religions. What formed the 'contents' of such relations? There were several kinds of trans-boundary interdependencies in Odessa and they each had their own temporal-spatial topographies.

Let us start with the most visible, powerful and vocal cosmopolitanism, that of the city's European and Russian founders, who consciously pursued the ideals of the Enlightenment. These well-travelled aristocrats, generals and admirals upheld in principle the classic, Kantian version of cosmopolitanism, according to which universal human values such as equality, fraternity, justice, education, and civic responsibility should override partial, nation-bound interests. The 'publics' (in the Tardean sense) of this kind were initially tiny, always opposed by Tsarist nationalists, and they fractioned into diverse ideologies. In this top-down cosmopolitanism one can discern the emergence during the nineteenth century of overlapping networks that spread out in different directions, in each case reinforced by communications with like-minded associates in Russia and across Europe. Most notable were the literary-artistic circles, the Freemasons, and the socialist revolutionary movements.

In the leading circles of Odessa cosmopolitan relations, as distinct from the ideas held by a 'public', could fan out or suddenly shrivel away, as can be seen from two incidents recounted in De-Ribas' memoirs. Abram Brodskii was a well-known Jewish magnate, a friend of the City Prefect, and a proponent of Jewish integration with wider society. One day in 1861 he received a letter asking for help from a colleague from Kiev, who wrote that Jewish university students in that city were being expelled because they were unable to pay the fees and that the Kievian Jewish community was too poor to support them. Brodskii replied with a profession of his beliefs: 'It would agree with the demands of the present time if prosperous people helped those in need without regard for their religion. It would be desirable for the Jewish community to make contributions to poor students in general and not only to Jews. This would be a new step towards eliminating the exclusivity that served, and still serves, as a barrier for Russian Jews in closer, more sincere, relations with their Russian co-citizens.' Brodkskii's reply created a furore. His letter was immediately published in the Odessan and Kievian press, and soon many people from various parts of Odessan society – Jews, Russians, and foreigners – sent contributions to Kiev, stipulating that the money must be given 'without regard to religious belief' (De-Ribas 2005: 210).

At around the same time, however, there occurred the following sad incident. Napoleon-Louis de Turnefor, an elderly Polish-French professor, 'lightly atheist, lightly epicurean', used to give public talks and private lessons on the moral questions raised by contemporary French literature. He was the centre of a wide circle and would give flirtatious confidential advice about sentimental matters to his female students. But suddenly he stopped being invited; almost all his lessons were cancelled. Why? Because he had fallen in love with a Jewish woman, first glimpsed on Richel'evskii Street as a stream of gold coins slid from her purse at a money-changing kiosk. He published a poem about this moment. Was she herself a money-changer or had she just gone to the counter to change her own money? It did not matter – she was Jewish. Professor De Turnefor was shunned and died a lonely man (De-Ribas 1990: 153–54).

These two incidents occurred in broadly the same upper social circles, and their co-presence shows the fragile quality of cosmopolitan relations. If we understand these relations to consist in communicative 'content' in Tardean terms – the published letters, declarations, cheques, invitations, lessons, confidential advice, poems, and so forth – it becomes clear how cosmopolitan practice can fail. One can speculate about the individual motives of the professor's clientele, but quite simply, when someone withdrew the 'content', and that withdrawal was copied by everyone else, this particular cosmopolitan circle ceased to exist.

The Freemasons of Odessa are a good illustration of the contradictions of cosmopolitanism in a divided city. I discuss them in some detail partly because they were important in creating the international economy and population of the town and yet are less well-known than the literary-artistic and revolutionary movements (Skinner 1986; Herlihy 1986; Weinberg 1993; Slezkine 2004), but also because the expansion, retraction and transformation of Freemasonry during the nineteenth century can be analysed profitably through Tardean ideas.

Freemasonry declares devotion to the interests of humanity as a whole, but if we recognise the existence of different cosmopolitanisms (such as 'vernacular', 'postcolonial', 'rooted', etc.) (Robbins 1998: 1–2) it should not be seen as the carrier of cosmopolitanism as such – the one universal Kantian ideal of perpetual peace – but as a particular, situated and self-limiting form, always embedded in some specific historical situation. In Russia, the relational impact of Freemasonry's anti-clerical humanism changed: in the late eighteenth century of Catherine the Great it was seen as 'French madness' and revolutionary (Dixon 2009: 106) but a century later, Trotsky, having initially been attracted while he was in prison in Odessa, came to see it as a stale attempt by the petty bourgeoisie to create moral ties in the face of modernity and therefore antithetical to revolution. However, the *modus operandi* of Freemasonry remained the same: small secret groups of like-minded people splitting to create new groups. The self-limiting aspect of

Freemasonry lay precisely in the combination of declared universality with this imitative pattern of reproduction: universality could be claimed by virtue of detachment from ordinary and ignoble affiliations, a detachment that was manifested in the case of Freemasons by secretive self-choosing of special 'morally superior' members.

Almost all of the founders and early governors of Odessa were Freemasons.[12] It is difficult to know the extent to which this influenced their activities until the main Odessan lodge was founded in 1817. Called Pont Evksinskii after the ancient Greek Euxin Sea between Europe and Asia, it became one of the largest and most multinational in Russia,[13] and its grand master, the Count de Langeron, was also the City Prefect and the Governor General of the region. De Langeron followed the same policies as his friend and predecessor as Governor, the energetic and inspiring duc de Richelieu, also a Mason, who had encouraged Jewish settlement and carefully placed Russian former serfs as free farmers among German, Greek, Moldavian and other colonists 'who would teach them modern agriculture and the practice of liberty' (Ascherson 2007: 138). De Langeron negotiated Odessa's Free Port status, built the architectural ensemble facing the sea, created a botanical garden, founded a newspaper, and established the Richelieu Lycée and a school for girls. The Pont Evksinskii lodge illustrates the long-drawn out, vine-like character of Masonic relations: it was similar to the system of the Grand Orient of France, based in Paris, which was itself descended from the Scottish order. Its members were linked to lodges in Constantinople, Toulon, Geneva, Napes, Paris, Lausanne, Nice, Livorno, Genoa, Marseilles, Weimar, and Leipzig (Serkov 2000: 134, 196). The statue of the duc de Richelieu, standing in a Roman toga at the top of the Odessa steps, holds out a welcoming hand to travellers ascending into the city – the opposite image of the relation between port and city to that expressed by later generations.

The Freemasonry of Odessa was distinctly more secular than the 'heretical' ecumenist Christian Rosicrucian trend that dominated in the rest of Russia (Faggionato 2001: 459–87; 2002). The Pont Evksinkii Masons did not bother with mysticism, and the best among them, according to a Russian visitor, spent their time 'working on French and Italian literature, such as Rousseau and Ariosto' (quoted in Serkov 2000: 135). The members held a great variety of views and their work was carried out in French, German, Italian and Russian, all of which resulted in the visit of a leading mason from St Petersburg in 1818, with the aim of 'creating agreement among the local and newly arrived brothers' through lectures in the Russian language (Serkov 2000: 194). However, by 1820 the lodge was taken over by Decembrist members of the secret Union of Prosperity (*Soyuz Blagodenstviia*) – even De Langeron signed up – and it became the centre of a number of organisations intent on overthrowing autocracy and serfdom (Serkov 2000: 195).

Tsar Alexander I had long been suspicious of Freemasonry. Its secrecy and internal loyalty, the inclusion of people of different estates and ranks, religions and nationalities, foreign members and active links with overseas lodges, and its equivocal relation to Orthodoxy, were all anathema to the autocracy (Serkov 2000: 147). With plots brewing, the Tsar banned Freemasonry and all secret societies in Russia in 1822.

After this Freemasonry was largely suppressed – in Odessa, the few remaining Masons met in extreme secrecy in the country homes of members and hid their paraphernalia in the catacombs; but numerous offshoots hived off and continued to operate through the century, partly through links with émigré Russian masons: the Populists were active in Odessa in the 1870s–1880s; the illegal *Kolokol* paper, printed in London, reached Russia via Constantinople and Odessa; and Marxist organisations began to appear in the early 1890s. By this time, the city's Prefect admitted that Odessa was 'the main hotbed of sedition' in Russia (Skinner 1986: 231). Meanwhile in Europe the Masonic movement had crystallised into restricted bourgeois circles. After the 1905 amnesty, when émigré Freemasons returned to Russia, most of the new lodges supported constitutional reform, but definitely not revolution.

Masonic literature created 'publics', but more sinister to outsiders was the imitative and secretive character of the patterns of association. The lodges hardly ever unified together in a mass convention. The fundamental process was one of budding off, in which individual Masons sought like-minded people to found a new group sometimes in distinction from the parent lodge. In negative relational tension with all this other social assemblages emerged, energised by fending off cosmopolitanism, an example of the 'repelling of others' example that Tarde also sees as spreading contagiously (1969: 171). Dynamic reactive complexes of accretion and retrenchment are one way of understanding such contradictions. Even though the original cosmopolitan Masonry had been defunct for decades, the Russian Far Right, active in Odessa from the beginning of the twentieth century in the upper classes, created a (Tardean) 'public' with the bizarre paranoid myth of a Jewish Masonic world conspiracy; in this they were far from alone as similarly lurid scenarios circulated in the British Foreign Office concerning the Masons and Young Turks of Constantinople (Kedourie 1971: 89–104). The Far Right had its own repertoire of assemblages: private evenings (*panskie vecherinki*), business meetings opened by prayer, singing the national anthem and toasts to 'Orthodoxy, Autocracy and Nationality', raising spirits by arias from Glinka's 'immortal' opera *A Life for the Tsar*, or the street processions with banners and icons mentioned earlier (Löwe 1998: 440–60). The Far Right's hatred of the Masons correlated with its terror of revolution, its disapproval of universities, its disdain of democracy, and its suspicion of 'the people', especially the peasants with their 'coarse drunkenness and un-Christian satanic carnivals' (Löwe 1998: 447).

Meanwhile, if Savchenko is right, in 1910 Odessa already had four Masonic lodges, which gathered together influential professionals (advocates, journalists, industrialists, artists, bankers, merchants, army and navy officers). It is notable that the lists of members included some Jews and many converted Jews (Savchenko 2007: 102, 105–107). In this, masonry in Odessa differed from that in most of bourgeois Russia, and here we can perhaps see a sign of the 'immunity' to interethnic hatred that developed after the 1905 pogrom, as will be discussed later.

Performance of civility

Another kind of cosmopolitanism flourished in the expanses of the middle-lower classes. This was the performance of the admirable – or at least enviable - citizen, stepping out in public and following models of fine persona aspired to by people of any nationality or religion. Such desirable images were created by journalists for the *publika* that formed their readership, for the audiences of plays, comics and popular singers. As Sylvester writes:

> Using newspapers as their rostrum, journalists set out for their readers a clear definition of what it meant to be respectable, describing what was dangerous, safe, normal, barbaric, insolent, cultured. They sorted out and named the faces in the crowd, describing a city inhabited by a range of social 'types', each fitted neatly into a schema of respectability. [...] In order to create this urban typology, journalists posited a significant correlation between visible 'correctness' – in dress, manners, and deportment – and correctness of character. (2000: 905–906)

If only for the sake of commercial sales, the positive images had to appeal to as wide a public as possible and could not be ethnically particularistic. I therefore suggest that the authoring, consumption and acting out of urban 'types' were integrated, reinforcing cycles that had to be cosmopolitan, even if that was not their intention.

If actually existing cosmopolitanism implies not an ideal of detachment, but a reality of (re)attachment (Robbins 1998: 3), what was the object of (re)attachment here? The Masons had clung to their particular vision of social improvement. These other actors, I suggest, were (re)attached to the city of Odessa, or, more exactly, to its style. By style, I refer, by analogy to literary style, to all those shared devices by which Odessans recognised and imitated 'wit', 'elegance', 'respectability', and so forth. Just as rhetoric is not additional to, but a property of, a literary work, so these devices were the objective, 'material' content of urban performance.

Gregorii Moskvich, an early twentieth-century travel writer, commented that:

> Odessans are proud of themselves, flaunting their ability to dress as well as any purebred Parisian or Viennese. [...] The passion for fashion, the desire to impress by external appearances, penetrates all of Odessan society, from the counts to the cooks ... the petty bank clerk, cashier, or salesclerk at the haberdashery, the barber, the lackey, everyone in Odessa ... mingles in the variegated street crowd, full of the consciousness that on the street, in the restaurants, on the promenades, everyone is equal. (quoted in Sylvester 2000: 802)

There is evidence that people put a great deal of effort into such cosmopolitan appearances. Sylvester mentions Valentin Kataev's memoirs of his youth in Odessa, recalling his mother's transformation when she went out:

> At home, she was soft, pliable, warm, and usually without a corset – just an ordinary cosy mamma. But in the street she was a severe, even slightly disagreeable lady, with a black-spotted veil over her face, and a dress with a train, which she held up to one side with her hand, on which hung a little moiré bag with spangles... [This woman was] not my mamma at all, but 'madam' as she was addressed in shops or by someone inadvertently brushing against her on a narrow pavement. (Sylvester 2005: 100)

The elegant 'Robinisty', named after the expensive Café Robina, were dandies who luxuriated amid 'winding ivy, wild grapes and tubs of exotic plants', but who might actually be unemployed salesmen or out-of-work artists (Sylvester 2005: 114). The mimetic pattern in such performances, unlike the lateral liens of Freemasonry, was centripetal – a broad, variegated homing-in on key urban images and on the devices by which an image could be signalled.

This kind of cosmopolitanism perched on the shoulders of the actual economy of the city – predominantly income from international trade – which depended on Turkey keeping open the Dardanelles, through which all shipping reached the city. Journalists satirised two 'ladies in white' meeting in the street:

> 'C'est incroyable!'
>
> 'It's terrible ... it's awful.... Today I should have bought myself a new spring hat but Bazel said, "There'll be no hat for you now, my dear!..."

"Mais, pourquoi donc?" I asked. And he said, "They say the Dardanelles are closed...". I laughed. "But Vlasopulo [a boutique] is open!" And then, my dear, he looked at me fiercely and said something that I simply can't repeat ... and wouldn't give me any money!' (Sylvester 2005: 112)

The urban adventures of such women thus hinged upon a different, maritime cosmopolitanism. That was enacted on a far broader stage, involving the contracts of Odessan merchants with the chief deposit ports of the Mediterranean, the negotiations of passages and fees, the changing import taxes in Holland or England, the development of steamships and the telegraph, bad weather, poor harvests, and the wars that closed the Straits and brought commercial life to an abrupt collapse. The ladies' sprinkling of French was like a tiny multivalent sign: it was a recognised rhetorical form inside Odessa, but also linked boulevard performances to this infinitely larger, uncontrollable, perilously navigable world.

Integral to the urban enactments of cosmopolitanism was the danger of a disastrous unmasking, as we see from an entry in the diary of Kotliarevskii, the Russian owner of one of Odessa's great emporiums:

2nd November 1904. In the last few days there has been disorder in our warehouse. Grebnev's brother, a boy of thirteen whom we had only just taken on, stole a pound of tea. Another boy, Meleshkevich, went to the post-office to collect some money, and today he did not return, having gone off with 365 roubles. Depravity is starting, which must be stopped.

3rd November 1904. Meleshkevich, having taken the money, went to the Kavkaz restaurant, where he dined, and then went by carriage to Malana Ivanovna's [brothel] on Bolgarskaia Street. There he chose two women and took them to the Severnyi restaurant. From there this whole fine company proceeded to the Russian theatre, where they were playing *Ekaterina Maslova*. Our men tracked him down to the theatre. When they took him out he wanted to shoot himself, but he only got a slight wound. It was nasty how everything happened. But he seemed a good and likeable boy. (Kotliarevskii 2005: 126)

Two things are notable about this. First, the magnate's cosmopolitan awareness of sharing the same landscape as the poor boys who worked for him: he knew the uncle, the brothel keeper, the restaurants, the play at the theatre. Secondly, he is not surprised that the boy had a gun. In 1904, Odessa was between pogroms and this was the year before the revolution.

Practical cosmopolitanism

Odessa is most famous, however, for yet another kind of cosmopolitanism – that of the dusty lower-class street, the market place, the courtyards of apartment houses, the beaches, wineries, theatres and other places where people gathered. Countless novels and memoirs celebrate the repartee, dialect jokes, flirtations, strolling singers, thieves, and sellers of anything and everything to be found in such places; these places made possible the kind of inclusive cosmopolitanism that encompassed all those present in temporary amity. Unlike the drawn-out fibres of Masonic sociality or the convergent mimesis of appearances, this sociality could be imagined as a mosaic specific to a certain time and place. The grimy bustling Moldavanka quarter, celebrated in Babel's stories, called forth the following nostalgic evocation. Here were the:

> poor tailors, who spent whole lives re-sewing, patching and ironing old clothes which they later sold at the nearby street market to equally poor purchasers; the sickly girls sewing tiny buttons onto cardboard from morn to night so they can be sold more easily in shops; the tired laundresses; the binders rimmed in paper dust; the gang bosses and the people on the very bottom of the criminal world, the petty thieves; the owners of tiny stalls; the cobblers; and the port workers taking the chance to get some extra cash. These were powerful, strong men, standing firm on both legs, a distinct caste with their own attitude to life and moral precepts (*zapovedi*). Don't express your personal feelings. Too much chatter – well, that is just for hairdressers. Don't shove your nose in other people's affairs – especially not their income, god save us. It is categorically forbidden to curse food, even more so drink; to eat together with funeral workers; or eat your meal before watering and feeding your horses. It is not good to brandish your fists impetuously. And someone is not respected who doesn't join in when company has formed and goes away instead of following everyone else to the tavern and dancing the 'seven-forty', yes, dancing till the heavy glass mugs on the tables jump. [...] People did not live well.... But it was friendly. (Aleksandrov 2002: 126)

This was the sociality of diverse people living in close proximity. The courtyard, the street market, theatre, and the pub all had their own denizens, their own shape and scales; they also had their own ways of behaving, which had to be shared ('imitated') if practical affairs were to be carried out. One had to accept the others, whoever they were, whatever their food, their 'caste' or their dances. The surface was all – customs forbade one from probing into the differences that divided all these people. Yet the mosaic was not superficial in the sense of inconsequential. Rather, it seems from the quotation above that the surface content – the common restraint, the precepts of how everyone should act in a given place – were hallowed, a matter of honour, and to be infringed at one's peril. The mere threat of what 'all Odessa' would say was enough to keep the gangsters of Moldavanka in line (Aleksandrov 2002: 208), at least most of the time.

In reality, this thin amity could easily break down. Some anthropologists like to see 'vernacular cosmopolitanism' as a hazy merging of two normatively desirable things: transnational altruism (good) and ordinary working people (good). But practical cosmopolitanism as I outline it here was precise and not especially altruistic. In fact, it rested on a knife-edge in Odessa. The practical purpose could dissolve in a moment's rage. Il'ya Gerasimov writes that differences of religion or ethnicity were the last thing on people's minds on such occasions: economic need was uppermost. In 1908, for example, Stepenko (a Slav) and Nutovich (a Jew) were neighbours on Bol'shoi Fontan. Nutovich refused to buy something at Stepenko's stall; Stepenko lost his temper and beat his neighbour savagely about the head with a stone. Blood flowed. It is possible, Gerasimov writes, that Stepenko was an anti-Semite, but the paradox is that the Christian beat the Jew not to drive him away from the stall but to attract him to it. 'The logic of interethnic relations in Odessa made him vitally (*krovno* – bloodily) interested in his neighbour' (Gerasimov 2003: 244).

Conclusion: pogrom and 'immunity' to pogrom

Pogroms tore into cosmopolitan places, destroying whatever web of amity was reigning there. The mob perforated the sociality of place, as an alien convulsion with its own violent dynamic, even if some individuals in the mob were not outsiders at all. A short story by the writer Alexander Kuprin describing what happened at the Gambrinus in 1905 provides one kind of account. The Gambrinus was a famous beer-hall in the centre of the city, visited by carters from Moldavanka, factory workers from Peresyp, university students, dockers from the port, and sailors from all round the world. Its popularity came from its star entertainer Sender Pevzner, known as Sashka the Fiddler, a 'meek, droll, tipsy, bald-headed fellow', accompanied by his little dog. Sashka mesmerised audiences with his improvised response to the most varied requests, from Russian folk melody to Viennese waltz to an African chant. When the pogromists burst in, a stonemason's chisel was about to pierce Sashka's head, when someone grabbed the hand and said, 'Stop, you devil, – it's Sashka!' The assailant stared and stopped – and dashed the little dog's brains out instead. In the ensuing melee Sashka was arrested. He returned from the police station crippled in one arm. But the message of Kuprin's story is that the pogrom could not entirely destroy the sociality-conveyed-by-music of the Gambrinus. When Sashka returned, patrons sorrowfully asked if that was the end of the music; he drew an ocarina out of his pocket with his good hand, and, swaying to the beat as much as his broken body would let him, began piping the 'deafeningly-mirthful *Chaban*' (a Ukrainian folksong; quotations from Skinner 1986: 227, 237).

However, this is a fictionalised account (somehow everything continued as before) and does not reflect what actually happened. Visible consequences of the 1905 pogrom were economic crisis for the city, the emigration of many Jews, the disgrace of the City Prefect, and the appointment of at least some officials who were determined to prevent further interethnic fighting. There was also an invisible change of mood. Gerasimov (2003) has suggested that Odessa developed something like an immunity to pogrom after the bloodbath of 1905. No significant pogrom was to occur there again (for archival evidence see Milyakova 2007), despite general ongoing violence and in contrast to the re-emergence of terrible pogroms elsewhere in Ukraine during the Civil War in 1918–1922. 'Immunity' describes a state of having sufficient biological defences to avoid infection or other unwanted biological invasion; it can be non-specific – acting as a barrier to a wide range of pathogens – or the immune system can adapt to each new disease encountered and generate pathogen-specific defences and mechanisms of elimination. If we purloin the term for social analysis, it can work as a way of conceptualising (more specifically than Tarde's 'opposition') how the repetition of harmful ideas and actions can be stopped.

The skin is the first immune barrier of animal bodies and its few openings are the chief entry points of infection. Using this imagery for the sake of illustration, we could see Odessa's earlier cosmopolitan skins as limited, scattered and easily perforated. Strangely, it seems that after 1905 it was the expansion of 'crime' and 'anarchy' – much of which could be alternatively called 'resistance' – that led to the extension of a kind of desperate cosmopolitanism into the very deprived classes that had earlier launched pogroms. The 1905 revolution had made evident the interdependency of ethnic groups in confronting a number of functional situations as well as state terror. People now saw that with more or less equal numbers of Jew and Slavs among the dockers in the Port, ethnic conflict would have meant mutual destruction; to avoid this, the workers formed cooperative *artels* (associations) to improve their working conditions. Strikes continued into 1906–1908, as did shootings, bombing, muggings, extortion and street attacks (Malakhov and Stepanenko 2004: 142–45). The *artels* took part in the general violence, but they fought non-unionised labour, not Jews.

Gerasimov shows how similar to one another were the bands of 'anarchist-communists', the mushrooming Jewish self-defence groups,[14] and ordinary criminal gangs, all of which politicised violent extortion by calling it 'expropriation'. Experienced fighters of any nationality were welcome in all of these groups and could be recruited from one to another (2003: 231). Slav and Jewish neighbours would carry out joint raids on shops, Jewish attacks on other Jews were particularly common, and a well-oiled collaborative division of labour between thieves (mostly non-Jewish) and sellers of stolen goods (mostly Jewish) was widespread (2003: 246).

In the face of this 'crime wave', the City Prefect resigned in 1907 with what seems to have been a nervous breakdown; the next man lasted only a few months, and it was only with the appointment of General Major Tolmachev that some order, albeit heavily repressive, was brought to the streets of the unruly city. Now there was a surge of suicides among all classes, men, women and even children. The fashionable Deribasovskaya Street was chosen as the scene for suicides by shooting; most suicides were carried out in public places, making visible an epidemic of despair that grew until at least 1912 (Malakhov and Stepanenko 2004: 146–48). Thus it was that the critical event of 1905, subsiding from revolution and pogrom into dislocated random violence and self-harm, gave rise to new preoccupations and different configurations.

A specific kind of immune response spread within the city, one which was adapted to the particular threat of pogrom. Between 1906 and 1916 there was a boycott of the Far Right press. The latter suffered from a lack of funds and advertisers, and the widespread refusal of agencies, sales kiosks and deliverymen to accept its publications. When anti-Semitic articles were published, none of the Odessan right-wing papers were prepared to represent their own city – as distinct from 'all Russia' or 'the whole world' – as the site of Jewish conspiracy (Gerasimov 2003: 237–38). In official documents, it became 'not done' to refer to Jews in anything other than neutral language. 'White-collar crime' was not painted as 'Jewish' (although it was quite largely so). Unlike in the days before the pogroms, scare-mongering rumours were ignored by the security service as being absurd (2003: 239–42). Gerasimov argues that all of this was part of a general turning away from ethnic-religious antagonism among individual citizens at the personal level. He notes, for example, the frequency with which marriage advertisements stipulated 'nationality and religion irrelevant' (2003: 247–48).

This is at least in part because there were new elements of pleasure, fantasy, affect and imagination flowing into the content of sociality. Most important, these conveyed not the outer characteristics of other people, but rather their life tragedies and their inner feelings. A new cosmopolitanism of empathy may have formed a significant barrier to blind hatred.

One of the most creative vehicles of such shared sensation was the cinema, engagingly known as '*illuzion*', which spread lightning-fast through the city after the first stationary cinemas were opened in 1904. Visiting an *illuzion* was not a passive activity: while a pianist (the *taper*), glancing at the screen, improvised appropriately affecting music, the audience sat or stood, crunching sunflower seeds, commenting loudly ('Looks like Sonechka from Dal'nitskaia, doesn't she') or yelling to the operator, 'Turn it faster!' Meanwhile, there was a constant murmuring as the literate people translated the subtitles for those who could not read. First a short 'view' film about, for example, Spain or Greece was shown, then a comedy or a Pathé newsreel, and lastly a proper drama; these included Russian and foreign films about Jewish life (*The God of Revenge, Sarah's Sorrow, The Tragedy of the Jewish Student*, etc.). The film programme ended with a *divertissement*, a concert with dancers, one-liner comedians, or singers. In the 1910s, Sashka the Fiddler escaped from his fame at the Gambrinus to perform in the dusky *illuzions* of Moldavanka, along with many other *klezmer* musicians from around the city (Aleksandrov 2002: 246–57).

In these years before 1917, Odessa also saw the flourishing of an inspired, multiethnic musical life, in which Jews were the stars. This reached across classes and ethnicities. Babel's 'tiny, frail creatures', the Jewish boys shepherded to violin lessons by their 'flushed and hysterical' mothers (2002: 628–29), would emerge from squalid basements in Moldavanka to become idols of popular and classical music, worshipped across the whole of Russia and indeed the world. The shared content of musical emotion should not be seen simply in terms of its effect as a 'non-specific antidote' to the hatred of others – though it may have acted in this way – but rather as a creative means of detachment from exclusive religious traditions and a (cosmopolitan) re-attachment to music seen as universal, bringing people together temporarily in feeling.

This chapter has sought to show that certain unstructured social forms, such as pogroms and cosmopolitanism, are best understood not as urban states of being, nor as paradigms with their own development, nor as providing the character of a whole city, but as transitory patterns of relations, expanding and subsiding. Such relations are made by the words, thoughts, gestures, memories, images or rumours which pass between people, and, just as 'imitation' accretes elements to the formation, 'opposition', refusal and hesitation serves to halt or shrink it. Arguing that a blanket re-statement of the Tardean categories alone is not illuminating, since it would result for example in any crowd being analysed as just any other crowd, I have sought to highlight the *contents* in the particular ethnography of Odessa in the late nineteenth and early twentieth century, and to point to the specific topologies of these formations, their places, modes of operation, degrees of inclusivity, and in the case of cosmopolitanisms, their innovativeness in forming new kinds of association.

A large part of the chapter has been taken up with the discussion of anti-Jewish pogroms. Here I acknowledge common features with urban ethnic violence elsewhere, such as the agency of rumour (Bhabha n.d.), the objectifications of ethnic others in conditions of economic desperation (Appadurai 2000), or the frantic, cascading effect of crowd behaviour (Spencer 1990). Yet I have also argued that pogroms took the specific form they did – as spontaneous yet largely repetitive, phobic outbursts – because they occurred in particular, increasingly pressurised political environments. By the early twentieth century pogroms were no longer so backward-looking: the participants saw their political future at stake. Now, booming yet unreliable economic growth, global links, mobile populations, modern technologies, and revolutionary ideas burst against the cage bars of an archaic autocratic state. The account given here therefore does not disagree with accounts of pogroms as one of the reactions to over-rapid modernisation in a restless colonist enclave of the Tsarist empire (Skinner 1986: 237–39; Gerasimov 2003: 260). My discussion of the way in which pogrom beatings echoed the public beatings and subordinations carried out by the police and army also has some similarities with Taussig's (1993) analysis of 'mimesis' and dissimulation in colonial situations.

Such accounts tend to focus on crowd mentalities, or the psychic inventiveness of dualistic confrontations, but we can also conceive of a broader canvas, where pogroms can be seen as one among many diverse, dynamic multiplicities of people and places. Here ideas of crowd, public (in the Tardean sense) and *publika* have been used to try to understand various kinds of assemblage and their trajectories over time. In the city, it was the public character – in the sense of visible, audible, available to others – of all this activity that threw into sharp relief not only the leaching of elements of relational content (slogans, gestures) across boundaries – such as the borrowing in pogroms from right-wing oratory, folk anti-Semitism, Christian imagery, patriotic processions, police operations, or peasant devotion to the realm – but also the refusal of such elements. From the early nineteenth century, revolutionary groupings had concentrated, contracted, and then flourished in Odessa, the antithetical disorderly 'hydra' that emerged not in isolation but through 'solidarity and connection within and among social movements and individuals' (Linebaugh and Rediker 2000: 352). It has not been possible to do justice in this chapter to the cosmopolitan character of revolutionary crowds, but suffice it at this point to recall how the content of their sociality too often consisted of direct, public, counter-acts against the repertoire of loyalty (doffing hats to the red flag instead of to the Tsar's portrait, for example) as well as appeals made in the international vocabulary of fraternity and liberation.

To a great extent the built city itself created the conditions for this public openness: its centre faced right on to the sea and the mercantile world of the port, its grandiose staircase linked the two, its wide boulevards and parks invited the evening strollers – and these very same features could become the arenas of rampage or despairing self-destruction. The balconies built for prosperous families to take the air on stifling nights were the same ones used by pogromists in destructive mockery, or by sharp-shooters to fire on processions. Places thus transformed in events and formed part of the networks of forces and intensities, the flows of psychic energies that created crowds out of merely co-present individuals. This public character of Odessan life was a central feature of its volatility, its ungoverned swings from one direction to another, its fast expanding ripples of intersubjectivity.

Odessa can be seen to have been a post-cosmopolitan city ever since the eclipse of the first city-building Freemasons and the pogrom of 1821. Thereafter it experienced regular surges of hatred. But new kinds of cosmopolitan amity also arose time and time again. Such movements did not consist simply of negation, such as the repudiation of violence and malignant rumours. We have to see them more precisely as signs of positive detachment from exclusivist ties and opinions in favour of a re-attachment to more generous practices and values, citywide and beyond.

Notes

I am particularly grateful to Matei Candea for discussions on Tarde and anthropology, and also to Susan Bayly, Georgina Born, Il'ya Gerasimov, Catriona Kelly, Bruce Grant and Vera Skvirskaja for their comments on earlier versions of this chapter.

1. Examples include: Zipperstein 1985: 114–28; Lambroza 1987; Aronson 1980: 18–31; Aronson 1990; Herlihy 1986: 299–308; Weinberg 1987: 54–75; Klier and Lambroza 1992; Judge 1992; Weinberg 1993: 164–87; Nathans 2002; Löwe 2004: 16–23; Gubar' 2004; Sekundant 2005.

2. Blackman's emphasis on suggestion and suggestibility takes its impetus from Tarde's concepts of invention and imitation, but she takes her argument in a direction that deals with psychological rather than more clearly anthropological questions. She concludes, however, with the interesting argument that investigating suggestion in its various forms enables one to refigure 'the idea of the subject as a node within a network of forces and intensities'. Seeing the subject in this way would involve 'the re-connection and opening up of the relationship between the virtual and the actual through a lived, experiential engagement with fantasy' (2007: 592).

3. *Prikazchiki* ('salesclerks') performed a number of tasks, not only selling in shops but also cleaning the store, taking orders, running errands, delivering goods, stocking the shelves and often manufacturing the goods too (Weinberg 1990: 429).

4. Douglas Smith has shown that the idea can be traced to the late eighteenth century, at least to the time when Catherine the Great published three plays criticising Freemasonry. Merely to stage the plays at the court theatre would have reflected the logic of absolutism (the supreme power conveys its message to a circumscribed audience expected to receive it uncritically), but publication referred to 'a different logic, one in which decisions are reached through the consensus born of critical reasoning. Presupposed in this process were both an expanded sphere of participation and the relative equality of its participants' (Smith 1998: 290).

5. In 1895 a journalist described the language of Odessa as a 'salad', a mixture of Russian, Yiddish, and Ukrainian with some French thrown in and particular uses of cases and pronunciation (Rothstein 2001: 781–801).

6. I disagree therefore with Morgulis's argument that all pogroms had a common kernel with its own phases of evolution (2001: 45). It is true that the events of 1881 and 1905 were more terrible than the pogrom of 1871, but the reasons for this can be sought in the greater meshing with national politics in the later cases, rather than in the internal dynamic of pogroms as such.

7. Maintaining that they were inspired to illegal acts by their devotion to the Tsar had often enabled peasants to escape punishment (Aronson 1990: 89–90).

8. According to Gubar', who corrects the official data, the pogrom resulted in three Jewish dead and tens of wounded; eight pogromists who died from drinking too much alcohol; three wounded by bayonets; and three officers and twenty-four lower ranks wounded in street fights (2004: 42–44).

9. The black shirts signalled membership of the Jewish Bund organisation and self-defence units.

10. Note, however, that after the 1881 pogrom persons who returned stolen goods voluntarily were usually granted immunity from prosecution (Aronson 1990: 152).

11. Jose de Ribas (Iosip Deribas) was an active Freemason, a member of the St Petersburg lodge *Blagotvoritel'nost' k Peliknu* and also of a French lodge and one in the Swedish system (http://soc.world-journal.net/E.Eurmas_3text.html). Other founders of Odessa who were Masons include: the duc de Richelieu (Rjéoutski 2007: 68); General Suvorov (Davies 1996: 634); Prince Volkonskii (Makolkin 2004: 170); the duc de Langeron (Rjéoutski 2007: 40); and his two assistants Meyer and Vegelin (Makolkin 2004: 170). Governor I.A. Inzov was a Mason (Serkov 2000: 194), and Prince Mikhail S. Vorontsov was a follower of the prominent French freemason Saint-Martin.

12. According to Savchenko (2007: 58), who unfortunately gives no sources for his information, the Pont Evksinskii Lodge had over 180 members during de Langeron's time, with a further 100 'brothers' visiting from other lodges.

13. The short-lived Moldavanka Flying Self-Defence Brigade, formed in 1906, engaged in 'expropriation' from the neighbourhood in order to buy arms and set up a print shop. The Brigade did not aim to fight pogromists, however, but saw itself as engaged in a struggle against counter-revolutionaries, despotism and the secret police (Gerasimov 2003: 232–35).

14. The short-lived Moldavanka Flying Self-Defence Brigade, formed in 1906, engaged in 'expropriation' from the neighbourhood in order to buy arms and set up a print shop. The Brigade did not aim to fight pogromists, however, but saw itself as engaged in a struggle against counter-revolutionaries, despotism and the secret police (Gerasimov 2003: 232–35).

References

Aleksandrov, R. 2002. *Istoriia s ran'shego vremeni*. Odessa.

Anderson, A. 2001. *The Powers of Distance: Cosmopolitanism and the Cultivation of Detachment*. Princeton.

Appadurai, A. 2000. 'Spectral Housing and Urban Cleansing: Notes on Millennial Mumbai', *Public Culture* 12(3): 627–51.

Aronson, M.I. 1980. 'Geographical and Socioeconomic Factors in the 1881 Anti-Jewish Pogroms in Russia', *Russian Review* 39(1): 18–31.

———. 1990. *Troubled Waters: The Origins of the 1881 Anti-Jewish Pogroms in Russia*. Pittsburgh.

Ascherson, N. 2007 (1995). *Black Sea: The Birthplace of Civilisation and Barbarism*. London.

Atlas, D. 1992 (1911). *Staraia Odessa. Yeye druz'ia i nedrugi*. Odessa.

Babel, Isaac. 2002. *The Complete Works of Isaac Babel*, ed. Natalie Babel, translated by Peter Constantine. New York.

Bhabha, Homi. June 2009. Speech at University of Cambridge.

Blackman, L. 2007. 'Reinventing Psychological Matters: The Importance of the Suggestive Realm of Tarde's Ontology', *Economy and Society* 36(4): 574–96.

Born, Georgina. 2010. 'On Tardean Relations: Temporality and Ethnography', in M. Candea (ed.), *The Social After Gabriel Tarde: Debates and Assessments*. London, pp. 232–49.

Brockes, Emma. 2009. 'Critical Mass', *Guardian Weekend* (27 June): 19–28.

Brodovskii, I. 2001. 'Yevreiskaia nishcheta v Odesse', [1902] *Yevreiskaia Dusha* 3 (March): 16–63.

Candea, Matei. n.d. 'Don't Go There! A Space for Absence in Anthropological Engagements with Place', paper for conference *Materialising the Subject: Phenomenological and Post-ANT Objects in the Social Sciences*, MS 2009.

Das, V. 1995. *Critical Events: An Anthropological Perspective on Contemporary India*. Delhi.

Davies, N. 1996 *Europe – a History*. Oxford.

Dawidowicz, Lucy S. 1967. 'Introduction: the World of East European Jewry', in L.S. Dawidowicz (ed.), *The Golden Tradition: Jewish Life and Thought in East Europe*. Boston.

DeLanda, M. 2006. *A New Philosophy of Society: Assemblage Theory and Social Complexity*. London.

Deleuze, G. and F. Guattari. 1987. *A Thousand Plateaus: Capitalism and Schizophrenia*, translated by Brian Massumi. Minnesota.

De-Ribas, A. 2005. *Staraia Odessa: istoricheskie ocherki i vospominaniia* [1913]. Moscow.

Dixon, S. 2009. *Catherine the Great.* London.

Faggionato, R. 2001. 'From a Society of the Enlightened to the Enlightenment of Society: The Russian Bible Society and Rosicrucianism in the Age of Alexander I', *The Slavonic and East European Review* 79(3): 459–87.

———. 2002. 'New and Old Works on Russian Freemasonry', *Kritika: Explorations in Russian and Eurasian History* 3(1): 111–28.

Freeze, G. 1986. 'The Soslovie (estate) Paradigm and Russian Social History', *The American Historical Review* 91(1): 11–36.

Gerasimov, I. 2003. '"My ubivaem tol'ko svoikh": prestupnost' kak marker mezhetnicheskikh granits v Odesse nachala XX veka (1907–1916 gg.)', *Ab Imperio* 1: 209–60.

Gubar', O. 2004. 'Skazanie o pogrome', *Moriia* 2: 37–51.

Haimson, L. H. 1988. 'The Problem of Social Identities in Early Twentieth Century Russia'. *Slavic Review* 47 (1): 1-20.

Herlihy, P. 1986. *Odessa: A History (1794–1914).* Cambridge, Mass.

Humphrey, C. 2008. 'Reassembling Individual Subjects: Events and Decisions in Troubled Times', *Anthropological Theory* 8: 357–80.

Jabotinsky [Zhabotinskii], V. 2002 *Pyatero: roman, rasskazy.* Moscow.

Judge, E.H. 1992. *Easter in Kishinev: Anatomy of a Pogrom.* New York and London.

Kalmykov, Z. 2008. 'Odesskie Tatary: proshloe bez budushchego?', *Odesskii Al'manakh Deribasovskaia-Richel'evskaia* 35: 27–32.

Kapferer, B. 1988. *Legends of People, Myths of State.* Washington and London.

Karakina, Y. 2005. 'Pogrom yest' pogrom', *Moriia* 4: 6–16.

Karsenti, Bruno. 2010. 'Imitation: Returning to the Tarde-Durkheim Debate', in M. Candea (ed.), *The Social After Gabriel Tarde: Debates and Assessments.* London, pp. 44–61.

Kedourie, E. 1971. 'Young Turks, Freemasons and Jews', *Middle Eastern Studies* 7(1): 89–104.

Kleinman, Arthur, Veena Das and Margaret Lock (eds). 1997. *Social Suffering.* Berkeley, Los Angeles, London.

Klier, John D. 1992. 'The Pogrom Paradigm in Russian History', in John D. Klier and Shlomo Lambroza (eds), *Pogroms: Anti-Jewish Violence in Modern Russian History.* Cambridge, pp. 13–38.

Kotliarevskii, P.P. 2005. 'Iz dnevnika P. P. Kotliarevskogo (1903–05 gg.)', *Moriia* 4: 121–41.

Kuromiya, H. 1998 *Freedom and Terror in the Donbas: A Ukrainian-Russian Borderland, 1980s-1990s.* Cambridge.

Lambroza, Sh. 1987. 'The Tsarist Government and the Pogroms of 1903–6', *Modern Judaism* 7(3): 287–96.

Linebaugh, P. and M. Rediker. 2000. *The Many-Headed Hydra: The Hidden History of the Revolutionary Atlantic.* London and New York.

Löwe, H.-D. 1998. 'Political Symbols and Rituals of the Russian Radical Right, 1900–1914', *The Slavonic and East European Review* 76(3): 441–66.

———. 2004. 'Pogroms in Russia: Explanations, Comparisons, Suggestions', *Jewish Social Studies* 11(1): 16–23.

Makolkin, A. 2004. *A History of Odessa, the Last Italian Black Sea Colony*. Lewiston, Queenston, Lampeter.

Malakhov, V.P. and B.A. Stepanenko. 2004. *Odessa 1900 – 1920: liudi, sobytiia, fakty*. Odessa.

Mazis, J.A. 2004. *The Greeks of Odessa: Diaspora Leadership in Late Imperial Russia*. Boulder.

Mazzarella, W. 2010. 'The Myth of the Multitude, or Who's afraid of the Crowd?', *Critical Inquiry* 36: 697–727.

Mikhel', D. 2008. 'Chuma i epidemiologicheskaia revoliutsiia v Rossii: 1897–1914', *Vestnik Yevrazii* 3(41): 142–64.

Milyakova, L.B. 2007. *Kniga pogromov: pogromy na Ukraine, v Belorussii i yevropeiskoi chasti Rossii v period grazhdanskoi voiny 1918–1922 gg., sbornik dokumentov*. Moscow.

Morgulis, M.G. 2001. 'Bezporiadki 1871 goda v Odesse (po dokumentam i lichnym vospominaniiam)', [1910] *Yevreiskaia Dusha* 1: 19–45.

Nathans, B. 2002. *Beyond the Pale: The Jewish Encounter with Late Imperial Russia*. Berkeley.

Plesskaya-Zebol'd, E.G. 1999. *Odesskie Nemtsy 1808–1920*. Göttingen.

Rjéoutski, V. 2007. 'Les Français dans la Franc-maconnerie russe au Siècle des Lumières: Hypothèses et Pistes de Recherche', *Slavica Occitania* 24: 91–136.

Robbins, Bruce. 1998. 'Introduction Part 1: Actually Existing Cosmopolitanism', in Pheng Cheah and Bruce Robbins (eds), *Cosmopolitics: Thinking and Feeling Beyond the Nation*. Minnesota, pp. 1–19.

Rothschild, E. 2005. 'Language and Empire, c. 1800', *Historical Research* 78: 208–29.

Rothstein, R.A. 2001. 'How It Was Sung in Odessa: At the Intersection of Russian and Yiddish Folk Culture', *Slavic Review* 60(4): 781–801.

Savchenko, V. 2007. *Odessa masonskaia*. Odessa.

Sekundant, S. 2005. 'Effekt bumerang: yevreiskie pogromy i sud'by liberal'noi idei v Rossii (1905g.)', *Moriia* 4: 17–41.

Serkov, A.I. 2000. *Istoriia Russkogo masonstva XIX veka*. St Petersburg.

Sifneos, E. 2005. '"Cosmopolitanism" as a Feature of the Greek Commercial Diaspora', *History and Anthropology* 16(1): 97–111.

Skinner, Frederick W. 1986. 'Odessa and the Problem of Urban Modernisation', in Michael F. Hamm (ed.), *The City in Late Imperial Russia*. Bloomington, pp. 209–48.

Slezkine, Y. 2004. *The Jewish Century*. Princeton.

Smith, Douglas. 1998. 'Freemasonry and the Public in Eighteenth-Century Russia', in Jane Burbank and David L. Ransel (eds), *Imperial Russia: New Histories for the Empire*. Bloomington and Indianapolis, pp. 281–304.

Spencer, J. 1990. 'Collective Violence and Everyday Practice in Sri Lanka', *Modern Asian Studies* 24(3): 603–23.

Sylvester, R.P. 2000. 'Making an Appearance: Urban "Types" and the Creation of Respectability in Odessa's Popular Press, 1912–1914; *Slavic Review* 59(4): 802–24.

———. 2005. *Tales of Old Odessa: Crime and Civility in a City of Thieves.* DeKalb Illinois.

Tarde, Gabriel. 1969. *On Communication and Social Influence.* Selected papers edited and with an introduction by Terry N. Clark. Chicago.

Taussig, M. 1993. *Mimesis and Alterity: A Particular History of the Senses.* New York and London.

Weinberg, R. 1987. 'Workers, Pogroms and the 1905 Revolution in Odessa; *The Russian Review* 46: 53–75.

Weinberg, R. 1990. 'The Politicisation of Labor in 1905: The Case of Odessa Salesclerks; *Slavic Review* 49 (3): 427–45.

———. 1993. *The Revolution of 1905 in Odessa: Blood on the Steps.* Bloomington.

Werbner, Pnina. 2008. 'Introduction: Towards a new Cosmopolitan Anthropology; in P. Werbner (ed.), *Anthropology and the New Cosmopolitanism.* Oxford and New York.

Zagoruiko, V. 1960. *Po stranitsam istorii Odessy i Odesshchiny.* 2nd edn. Odessa.

Zipperstein, S.J. 1985. *The Jews of Odessa: A Cultural History 1794–1881.* Stanford.

⊰ Chapter 2 ⊱

Negotiating Cosmopolitanism: Migration, Religious Education and Shifting Jewish Orientations in Post-Soviet Odessa

MARINA SAPRITSKY

It was the most 'un-Jewish' of Jewish cities from the traditional point of view, and the most Jewish from the perspective of non-traditional Jewish life and attitudes.
(Klier 2002: 173 describing Odessa through much of its history)

The city of Odessa, sprawling along the coast of the Black Sea, is commonly recognised as 'cosmopolitan', 'unique' and 'Jewish'.[1] Behind this is a complex reality: although there was a mass out-migration of Jews in the late 1980s–1990s, today some returnees as well as international Jewish organisations are taking root. Such post-Soviet transformations have created new arenas of Jewish practice in the city. For some Jewish Odessans, the emergence of present-day religious forms of Jewish expression can be incorporated within the city's long-standing ethos of tolerance. For them, the current development of Jewish life is thus interpreted as a means of rebuilding the Jewishness of Odessa, which stands as one of the defining elements of the city's cosmopolitanism. However, for others – especially in the light of mass Jewish emigration – these changes in the orientation of Jewish practice, together with the increasing pressure of state Ukrainisation policies, signal a sad decline in the city's cosmopolitan virtues.[2]

Through the discourses and activities of religious, Zionist and other foreign Jewish emissaries, Odessa's remaining Jews and returnees have been exposed to an assortment of competing cultural and religious models, various definitions of who is a Jew, and new ideas about individual and communal Jewish values that challenge both the Soviet-informed classifications of Jewish 'nationality' and local perceptions of Jewish identity.[3] This chapter examines the various ways in which these new social norms are negotiated, partially appropriated and, at times, contested by Odessa's Jewry, using as its main source local understandings of Jewishness informed by (somewhat idealised) pictures of the city's historical cosmopolitan orientations (see Humphrey, this volume) and of the Soviet era.

It is important to appreciate that Odessa, historically an international port, has had a multi-ethnic and multi-confessional population from its early days until the beginning of the Soviet regime. According to the 1897 census, the city was home to speakers of some fifty-five languages, who came from over thirty countries and adhered to a wide variety of religious beliefs (Herlihy 1986: 241–43).[4] Equally, the city's Jewish population has a long history of exposure to competing ideologies and external points of reference. As Klier highlights, 'Odessa was a town without "native" Jewish traditions, where new Jewish traditions had to be created' (2002: 175). At the beginning of the nineteenth century, newly arrived Jews, mostly from Germany and Austrian Galicia, as well as newcomers from other areas of the Pale of Settlement,[5] were instrumental in setting up Odessa's most influential religious congregations.[6] This background is central to understanding both Odessa's famed cosmopolitanism and current religious activity.

In both the literature on contemporary Judaism and academic engagements with religious phenomena in the FSU, the issue of revival is hotly debated (Gruber 2002; Pelkmans 2009: 2; Broz 2009: 2; Solomon 1994: 87, 97; Jessa 2006: 169). Researchers of religious life in the FSU question the extent to which we can speak of a revival when describing the current situation in ex-Soviet states.[7] The term assumes that what is being revived was, in fact, previously part of the cultural milieu of the population; in other words, that it is actually a new vitalisation, the re-production of an old phenomenon. Revival implies historical roots that can grow and be nourished: a revival rejuvenates and restores the forgotten and abandoned elements of life, a returning to traditions. Yet, in many instances, ethnic, national and religious revivals include significant innovation and new inventions rather than a return to a past. In the case of Odessa, one might say, ironically, that the current wave of revival is, indeed, replicating a tradition – a 'tradition' of external interventions that Odessa's Jewry experienced historically. Among some local and newly arrived Jews there is a sentiment that Odessa's rich Jewish history makes the city particularly open to the current religious development. Many Jewish leaders and activists involved in organised Jewish life envision themselves as actively rebuilding the lost and forgotten world of pre-Soviet Odessan Jewry. Indeed, nineteenth-century Odessa was home to a number of vibrant traditional communities, including the large congregation of the *Glavnaia* (Main) Synagogue and approximately seventy smaller prayer houses, including followers of Hasidism. The city was perhaps most famous for its impressive Reform congregation organised around the Brody Synagogue. Odessa also served as a centre of Zionist activity, Jewish press, Jewish education and Jewish philanthropy.

Today some of this activity has been reinstated in the city through the efforts of local and foreign Jews; a number of Odessa's current organisations even appear with their pre-Revolutionary names, including the Jewish learning centre and publication Moria, the Jewish sports community Makkabi and the Jewish literary club Beseda (Conversation). The Odessa local City Council has contributed to the project of renewal by handing over three Jewish synagogue buildings for the use of Jewish organisations. Today the former butchers' synagogue houses the Jewish community/cultural centre, Migdal, while the other two buildings, the *Glavnaia* (Main) Synagogue and the former tailors' synagogue, are once again being used for their original purpose. So, at least in some senses, a revival of religious phenomena is undoubtedly occurring.

However, what marks the current wider religious developments is that many of the new organisations can hardly be described as historically Odessan. The Soviet system destroyed pre-Revolutionary Odessan Jewish institutions: in this sense there are few roots left to revitalise. Equally, the Soviet era produced *secular* rather than religious markers of Jewish identity. As Richardson recounts, the current wave of religiosity is alien 'for some Odessan Jews who grew up in the Soviet era and who did not emigrate'; for them, 'the deeply religious communal life that is becoming increasingly dominant is in fact foreign to the city and to their own idea of what it means to be Jewish' (2008: 189). Speaking of the observant Jews he saw gathered outside of the synagogue, one Odessan told me:

> Those are not real Odessan Jews. They are all *priezjie* [newcomers]. Real Odessan Jews do not need any of that ... These *priezjie* are all diplomats, for them it's just business. Odessa Jews never went to the synagogue, they ate *salo* [pig's fat, a traditional Ukrainian delicacy] and entertained more than they prayed.

While this Odessan assumed that the religiously dressed Jews he saw were all religious emissaries from abroad, many of the congregants were actually local Jews who had become active members of the city's religious life and who regularly attended prayer service. At the core of this man's hostility was not so much the literal foreignness of new religious and ethnic solidarities and institutions as their inappropriateness in Odessa, a city that, according to local perception, lacks the taste for ethnic purity and prides itself on the mixing of people from different nationalities.[8]

By contrast to the past, Odessa's Reform Jews now occupy a relatively weak status. The dominant position of the two Orthodox congregations, especially the stronghold of Chabad Lubavitch[9] in the city, has led some scholars to point out the 'ironic renewal of Hasidism in a city that was always better known as a centre for liberal Jewish traditions.'[10] Thus, it can be argued that present-day missions of world Jewry are creating and teaching variants of their own understandings of Jewishness rather than reviving traditions locally recognised as Odessan or cosmopolitan.[11]

In Odessa, as in other places in the FSU, the foreign Jewish institutions, with their policies of Jewish membership and identity, have cultivated new, often international, alliances while, at the same time, heightening ethnoreligious boundaries previously flattened by the rhetoric and practice of assimilation (see Cooper 1988; Goluboff 2003). Odessa's local population is engaged with divergent understandings of what it means to be Jewish today. I argue that these new constellations and ambiguities have, on some levels, widened the social distance both among Jews themselves and between Jews and others. The contestations described here are connected to the larger process of cultural transformation in Odessa and elsewhere in the FSU, where new systems of meanings are pitted against existing rubrics of moral standing, solidarity and material wealth deriving from the specific history of Soviet socialisation. However, in the case of Odessa specifically, the local cosmopolitan characteristics of the city, including its Jewishness, also play a role in the negotiation of current values, practices and orientations.

Odessa and Jewish migration

> If a Jew from the Pale of Settlement does not dream about
> America or Palestine, then you know he'll be in Odessa.
> Svirskii (1904: 169) quoted in Weinberg (1993: 9)

The city of Odessa was founded under Catherine the Great in the wake of the second Russo–Turkish war in 1794. Six Jews were officially registered in the territory of this new settlement when it became part of the Russian Empire. Eager to develop the sparsely settled lands and attract labour, Catherine offered a number of valuable incentives to attract new settlers. As a result, many new migrants arrived, including communities of Russians, Ukrainians, Greeks, Albanians, Moldavians, Armenians, Jews, Bulgarians, and Germans, who chose to settle on the shores of the Black Sea. The empress's commercial policies actively promoted trade, and foreign merchants from Greece, Italy, Galicia and other parts of the world established brokerage houses in Odessa, contributing to the international and bustling aura of the city. The subsequent administration further stimulated migration to the region: Odessa experienced one of the most dynamic growth rates in nineteenth-century Russia – comparable only to the American cities of Chicago and San Francisco: 'In the period of 1800–92 alone, the population [of Odessa] increased by an astonishing 3,677 per cent compared to rates of 220 per cent for Moscow, 323 per cent for St Petersburg' (Skinner 1986: 209–11). During this time, the second largest group of immigrants, surpassed only by the Russians, was the Jews. By 1897, nearly 100 years after its birth, Odessa was home to 138,935 Jews, accounting for one third of the total population (Herlihy 1986: 251; Rozenboim 2007: 33). For the Jews, Odessa quickly turned into a little heaven just inside the border of the Pale where they could experience an equality of rights unattainable in other areas of the country. Its status as a *Porto Franco* (free port) (1819–1859) further secured Odessa's pre-eminent commercial position (Richardson 2004: 11) and prosperity in grain and other export goods, which were exempt from the otherwise heavy burden of tax. By the end of the nineteenth century, 'Odessa was ranked as Russia's number one port for foreign trade … handling the shipment of nearly all the wheat and more than half of the other grains exported from Russia' (Weinberg 1993: 2). Unlike other areas in the territory of the Pale, where competition in trade and industry led to anti-Jewish sentiment, Odessa's ruling elite during this period welcomed competition in trade and labour and thrived on the city's lucrative achievements. This is not to say that Jews did not suffer from violent attacks during later years of their residency in Odessa. Outbreaks of pogroms occurred in 1821, 1849, 1859, 1871, 1881, 1900 and 1905 (Weinberg 1992: 248–89; see Humphrey, this volume). Despite these eruptions of anti-Jewish violence, the economic opportunities in Odessa continued to attract new Jewish migrants to the city.

The migration of Galician Jews (mostly from the city of Brody) further diversified Odessa's Jewish population. Brody Jews were by far the wealthiest of all of Odessa's Jewry, strongly oriented toward trade, and more liberal and progressive in their religious observance. Taking a leading part in the functions of middlemen, factory owners, managers and agents in the grain trade, Brody Jews worked closely with the Greek and Italian merchants, who at the time still controlled most of the export trade (Zipperstein 1986: 42). Within a few years of their arrival in the city, Brody Jews dominated most of the important positions within the Jewish population and had taken over many of the local community organisations and thus all major community decisions. Among them were many adherents of the German-based eighteenth-century Jewish Enlightenment movement known as *Haskalah*. The followers of *Haskalah* (*maskilim*) in Odessa were eager to connect their city's Jewish population with the greater world without abandoning their

Jewish identity. As early as 1826, immigrants from Galicia had opened a modern Jewish school, the first of its kind in all of Russia, where education was provided in both secular and Jewish subjects (Zipperstein 1986: 43, 45; Gubar and Rozenboim 2003: 91). Fifteen years later, Odessa became home to the first Reform Synagogue in the Russian Empire – the Brody synagogue – and, by the turn of the century, services were accompanied by organ music; seats were individually sold to members of the congregation.

A number of other developments were important in setting Jewish Odessa apart from the greater circumference of the Pale and the Russian Empire. Unlike the majority of Russian, Ukrainian and Polish cities, where Jews primarily lived in segregated areas, early Jewish settlers arriving in Odessa were not restricted. Rather, they settled freely throughout the city and thus were exposed to an array of cultural practices by their Italian, Greek, Romanian, Bulgarian, Russian, Ukrainian and other neighbours (Zipperstein 1986: 39). While Odessa enjoyed what many scholars describe as a cosmopolitan sociality from the outset, historians debate whether it is appropriate to describe it as a 'melting pot', due to the relatively limited interaction between different ethnic groups except in the market place (Mazis 2004: 25).

Nonetheless, the high level of integration that Jews found in trade, the geographical location of Odessa (far from any major centre of Judaism), the city's openness to varied ethnic and religious practices, and its mercantile ethos had all started to have an effect in eroding the traditional values experienced by Odessa's Jewish contingent (Zipperstein 1986: 36–37). All these processes reinforced popular Yiddish sayings that associated the city with indifference to religion: 'Seven miles around Odessa burn the fires of Hell' and, referring to their life of comfort, 'To live like God in Odessa' (Zipperstein 1986: 1).

Jewish activity in the city was periodically curbed by internal disputes that erupted in anti-Jewish violence. Pogroms, which ravaged Odessa's Jewish life, were rooted in various socioeconomic, political, and cultural realities, and presented Jews as dangerous to the society, overly successful in trade or too prominent for their minority status in Russia. Such actions and sentiments not only spoiled relations between Jews and non-Jews in the city but also led to early waves of Jewish emigration. By 1904 the percentage of Jews in the city had dropped from 35 per cent to 30.5 per cent and, in the aftermath of the 1905 pogrom alone, nearly 50,000 Jews left Odessa (Herlihy 1986: 258). Despite the outflow of Jews from the city and from the rest of the Russian Empire, Odessa's Jewish population quickly recovered its losses and, mainly due to immigration, continued to grow. This growth continued well into the twentieth century.

Historically, emigration from Odessa reflected the pattern visible across the Russian Empire and the Soviet Union. The pogroms and other forms of social persecution and discrimination were the cause of earlier waves of out-migration from the city. The events of the First World War, the Communist Revolution of 1917 and the Second World War also served as 'push factors' in the emigration of Odessa's Jews. In more recent times, Odessa experienced large swathes of Jewish emigration from the city in the 1970s, late 1980s and the early 1990s when Soviet authorities, under much international pressure, relaxed quotas on Jewish exit visas. Jewish emigration from the city continued well into the early years of Ukraine's independence. While for most of the nineteenth and early twentieth century Odessa's Jewish population benefited from immigration alongside emigration, the recent history of Odessa's Jews has been overshadowed by this mass emigration. During the last years of Soviet rule and after the break-up of the USSR, Odessa experienced some of the largest outflows of its Jewish population.

Since the early 1990s, however, Jewish emigration from Odessa has slowed down considerably, in part due to improved conditions at home but also due to tighter immigration policies of receiving countries (with the exception of Israel). According to the (somewhat varying) statistics, in 1989 Odessa was home to some 65–90,000 Jews whereas today – present-day figures also vary widely – the city's Jewish inhabitants number anywhere between 12,000 and 30,000 out of the total city population of 1,010,298.[12]

The 'one-way ticket' that characterised emigration, and attitudes to it, in the late 1980s and early 1990s no longer defines the patterns of border crossings. Since the breakup of the USSR, individuals may (and do) choose to return, permanently or temporarily, to their countries of origin, which was impossible under Soviet rule. It is notable that, compared to other former Soviet cities that experienced mass Jewish emigration, Odessa still has a relatively large 'stay behind' Jewish population of continuous residents.

Projects of Jewish revival

In the years since Ukrainian independence in 1991, Odessa has experienced a large influx of Jewish international organisations and emissaries whose efforts and economic resources are focused on reviving Jewish traditions and providing support for the local Jewish population. These projects are mainly sponsored and spearheaded by international Jewish organisations and private donors primarily from the United States and Israel. Many earlier local initiatives that sprang up at the end of Soviet rule were not able to sustain themselves individually and have been incorporated into the larger apparatus of foreign Jewish development. Contemporary international interventions can be traced back to the mass initiatives to 'save' Soviet Jewry launched during the 1970s: pressure from American Jewry and others lobbying to 'Let Our People Go' eventually forced Soviet leaders to allow some of their Jewish citizens and their families to emigrate (see Friedman and Chernin 1999; Altshuler 2005). The mission to save Soviet Jewry also focused on the way of life of those who chose to stay on after the fall of the USSR, seeking to restore what was taken to be long-forgotten and forbidden elements of Jewish life, such as Jewish education, religious institutions and cultural activities. These initiatives can be neatly summarised as attempts to help Jews leave or to help them live.

Odessa is not unique in being the recipient of such religious and national initiatives to save, rejuvenate, relocate, or redress the loss of a Jewish way of life. Since the decline and ultimate break-up of the USSR, countries such as Russia, Ukraine generally and neighbouring FSU states have all become active arenas for foreign initiatives among the local Jewish population, who may have forgotten, may have never learned or may have abandoned their Jewish traditions under the Soviet modernisation project. As Golbert has observed of Jewish youth in Kiev, Ukraine's capital, the effect has been the 'remaking of cultural identities and allegiances from a wide range of old

Figure 2.1. Jewish men carrying Torah scrolls on Pushkin Street during the holiday of Lag B'Omer. Photo by the author.

and new cultural models emanating both from within and outside the geo-historical borders of Ukraine' (2001: 713).

Today Jewish life is a visible part of the city's identity, from Odessa's kosher restaurants to the sight of traditionally dressed religious families, readily available Jewish newspapers, street signs along the main road directing drivers to the city's two main synagogues and public manifestations of Jewish religious festivals and life cycle ceremonies.

During important Jewish holidays religious objects such as *sukkah*[13] and *hanukkiyah*[14] can be seen in prominent areas of the city. As Hann points out, the visible display of religion and its openness to transnational influences, now seen across post-Soviet states, is very much a new phenomenon (2006: 2).[15] In Odessa, the public display of Jewish culture and the visibility of Jewish religious practices constitute one of the major transformations in the Jewish life of the city. Yet the altered conditions of organised Jewish life are at times met with mixed emotions by Odessan Jews, some of whom fear that the Jewish character of their city is not being revived but instead altered in a way that is detrimentally shifting the forms of sociality between Jews themselves and between Jews and others.

The role of Jewish religious organisations

At present, Odessa is home to three Jewish religious congregations: the two most prominent communities, Shomrey Shabos (part of the Hasidic Chabad Lubavitch movement) and Tikva Or Sameach (a branch of Lithuanian Orthodoxy known as Litvaks),[16] are affiliated with Orthodox Judaism and are led by Israeli-born rabbis. The third and the smallest of the three, Temple Emanu–El, is affiliated with Reform Judaism and is led by a Ukrainian rabbi.[17] Relations between all three religious leaders are strained. Both Orthodox rabbis claim the status of Chief Rabbi of the city; they interact on very few occasions and take no part in joint projects with the Reform congregation. A common joke that circulates among observant Jews goes like this: 'How many synagogues does one Jew need? Three. One that is his, one that is not his and one that he will never go to.'

Each of the three synagogues holds Shabbat services and celebrations of Jewish holidays and life cycle rituals. They each sponsor their own youth clubs and a range of social activities and *Shabatons* (communal Shabbats), usually organised on the former premises of Soviet-built *dom otdykha* (holiday retreat centres). Among the programmes offered are Jewish summer camps where Jewish history and traditions are taught in an informal manner as part of daily activities. Additionally, the two Orthodox synagogues have their own (female and male) schools, a children's orphanage, a *heder* (junior rabbinic study), a *yeshiva* (senior rabbinic study), a *kollel* (postgraduate rabbinic study for married men), a *mikvah* (purifying bath) and a university whose curriculum includes a combination of religious and secular subjects. Other formal education programmes, sponsored by Student Union of Torah Alliance for Russian Speakers (STARS), are organised on the premises or in private homes of Israeli emissaries where enrolment in and attendance at STARS is encouraged by a monthly stipend of US$75 paid to the students. The two orthodox synagogues each publish a weekly newspaper (in Russian), distributed at no cost at the synagogue or through subscription, and sponsor an hour-long television programme dedicated to Jewish lessons, which runs weekly on two different local channels.

Despite the historical stronghold of Reform Judaism associated predominantly with the Brody Synagogue in pre-Revolutionary Odessa, today the Reform religious movement represents the smallest segment of religiously affiliated Jews. The people I met at the Reform congregation Emanu–El were just as new to Judaism as those who I met in Orthodox settings. A recently opened kindergarten, located on the outskirts of the city, is the community's first attempt to organise formal education facilities.[18]

In line with the rest of the services supported by religious leadership, local Jews are invited to dine in one of the two kosher restaurants in the city and shop in the adjacent kosher grocery stores, which carry an inventory of Israeli and local products. On occasions when members of the local Jewry decide to have a kosher meal for a life celebration, I was told that reduced-cost catering was provided by the rabbis as a reward for their good deed. Advertisements for Jewish (not necessarily kosher) cuisine can also be found displayed around the city centre. The local Chevra Kadisha (burial society) affiliated with the two Orthodox communities owns a separate plot of land where only *halakhic* Jews (see section below) are allowed burial conducted in accordance with the traditional Jewish procedure.

Jewish schools are regarded by Jews and non-Jews alike as having a strong academic curriculum, with proper meals and pastoral care for their students. Similarly the Jewish universities are considered good academic institutions. Jewish summer camps are also attractive because of their extremely low cost and high level of organisation and activity, as well as the opportunity to encounter a foreign (usually Israeli) culture. Other resources provided by Jewish religious organisations go some way towards meeting the daily needs of those who cannot secure them independently, offering subsidised food, medicine and home care, which cannot be guaranteed by the state. Other means of assistance, particularly to the elderly, include a social agenda of organised events, cultural gatherings and groups. All these highly valued amenities are conditional on membership of the relevant religious organisation. For the middle and younger generations, privilege is also embedded in rites of passage ceremonies and the teaching of a sacred history, Hebrew language and rituals, which are guaranteed to community members only. This sense of exclusivity is a 'perk' that young people sometimes mentioned. Affordable, often free, travel abroad (usually to Israel and sometimes the United States) was also considered a bonus.[19]

Many of these benefits (although not travel) were previously part of the Soviet state welfare programme, which has not been fully replaced with a Ukrainian state system of social services, thus leaving many ex-Soviet citizens without essential or appropriate resources. Faith-based organisations (especially those linked to the West) have played a paramount role in this transition as they secure specific benefits for their congregants and a general sense of security.[20]

One of the unfortunate by-products of this generous provision of resources to Jews under the auspices of international Jewish organisations is that it has arguably contributed to a new wave of anti-Jewish sentiments and even grass-roots anti-Semitic slurs.[21] Evidently this is part of a wider phenomenon in which economic and social distinctions and imbalances within Odessan society are demarcating ethnic differences and social hierarchies. I did myself occasionally hear non-Jewish Odessans express envy of Jews' travel and emigration opportunities, even the possibility of European or Israeli citizenship. An important legacy from the Soviet era is the socialist assumption of social justice in which the welfare system provided for all on equal terms (Kotkin 1995: 152). Consciously or not, this functions as a backdrop of expectations and everyday reality that conditions today's sense of inequality. It seems that being a Jew has become a privileged status, no longer an undesirable identity that one has whether or not one wants it (Markowitz 1993: 159).

The rule of *halakhah*

The *halakhah* definition of being a Jew was virtually unknown in the Soviet Union. For the most part, religious associations played little, if any, part in one's Jewish orientation and Jewish identity carried a secular definition as being the ethnicity/nationality inscribed in one's Soviet internal passport (Chlenov 1994: 133).[22] While acceptance into the Orthodox community and institutions is strictly defined by the *halakhah*, which recognises a Jew as one born to a Jewish mother (or properly converted to Judaism), Jewish 'nationality' under the Soviet definition recognised descent through either parent. So the introduction of a religiously derived Jewish identity by Odessa's Orthodox leadership has brought an unfamiliar twist to local perceptions of Jewishness, and a new sense of uncertainty. Many people's self-identification as Jewish is now under question or at least seen as requiring proof. Given previous state manipulation of ethnic, religious and national categories in the USSR, religious emissaries feel it necessary to check who is 'really' Jewish. *Halakhic* status is usually affirmed by one's passport and birth certificate or the appropriate documents of one's mother or maternal grandmother, where Jewish 'nationality' would be shown. The old Jewish passport identification is reviewed carefully in each case to avoid cases of forged documents. Personal dossiers, compiled in cases where a person has no documents at all (usually as a result of the Second World War events, including evacuation), are scrupulously checked and sometimes even sent to Israel for final consultation. Documents showing one's Jewish descent are essential for emigration, admission to religious Jewish schools and many Jewish clubs, social and economic benefits, subsidised travel to Israel and more.

Many elderly informants spoke to me of their distaste at having to present their documents in order to prove themselves as Jewish. However, Israeli emissaries insisted that such checks were essential and told me of cases where documents had been forged in applications to their schools and universities. In fact, such stories were often presented in a positive light and described as 'the best advertisements for the Jewish community'. As one congregant of the Tikva Or Sameach Jewish school explained, 'Back in the old days, people tried to forge their documents to hide their Jewish identity and now they forge them to create one'.

Jewish education

Education has become a sensitive topic among Odessa's Jewish population. Here are the issues as seen through the eyes of Viacheslav, a man in his early sixties who, during the late Soviet period and in the early 1990s, ran a youth club, which he started as a public mathematics tutorial but later saw evolve, with his support, into a 'hang out of intellectual youth'. It has been some ten years since his club ceased to operate and Viacheslav proudly identifies himself as the only member left. (Currently, he gives private maths lessons to students and does a number of odd jobs that keep him entertained.)

Viacheslav seldom initiated discussions of his own or other people's Jewishness, although he responded to my many questions about Jewish life in the city. On the many occasions when we discussed the education system in Odessa – a topic that interested him very much – he despaired of the general level of schooling in the city, which he described as 'shameful', a system riddled with bribes and corruption and underfunded by the state. It was in that context that Viacheslav talked about Jewish schools that provided separate education for Jews. For all their high educational standards, he saw such segregation in Odessa's schools as undermining fair competition among children from different backgrounds and reducing diversity among students. 'It used to be the case that everyone in Odessa had at least one Jew in their class, they knew what Jews looked like and who they were through either close or even distant interaction with them.' Describing his own classroom as a child, Viacheslav spoke of his Ukrainian, Albanian and Greek friends.[23] 'Today,' he continued, 'Russian and Ukrainian children grow up distanced from Jewish children as the tendency of sending Jewish children to Jewish schools rises in the city.' According to Viacheslav, both Jews and non-Jews will suffer from this mutual lack of contact. Eroding the city's multinational character will ultimately lead to these children seeing each other as fundamentally 'different.' 'In my club,' he continued, 'no one asked each other and no one cared if the others were Jewish. We were all interested in maths and problem solving. We came together because of our interests, not because of a superficial tie based on our nationality.' He was also worried about the curriculum in Jewish schools, where, he believed, there was little teaching on *Odesika* (Odessan history and culture).[24] 'What matters in these schools,' he proclaimed, 'is that Jews are living as religious Jews, be it here or elsewhere – to them it's all the same.'

Viacheslav's account of the past, with its atmosphere of classroom cohesion between students of mixed background, may be somewhat romanticised. Certainly, as an account of secular education in contemporary Odessa, it did not match what I was told by a number of younger people who explained that they had chosen to move to a Jewish school because they had been harassed as Jews whilst studying elsewhere (whether in state or private schools). Igor, a twenty-two-year-old computer engineer, told me that in one classroom discussion of religion, his teacher had not even mentioned Judaism and refused to do so even after he raised the subject. A number of other young people recalled being called *zhid* or *zhidovka* (a derogatory name for a Jew, male and female respectively) by their non-Jewish classmates in schools they had previously attended.

Aside from such conflict-related reasons for attending Jewish schools, Jewish students whom I met described their educational experiences at the Jewish schools as 'interesting,' 'new' and 'exciting.' Karina, a seventeen-year-old student at the Chabad girls' school, spoke of the excitement of learning a new language (Hebrew), of being in a milieu that often included foreign teachers and of interacting with other students from abroad on their visits to Odessa. She welcomed the chance to learn about her religion and heritage and proudly spoke of herself as a Jew. While Viacheslav never mentioned the new transnational relations and solidarities forged in the classrooms of religious Jewish schools, for Karina and a number of other students I met, these were the features they especially valued. Living and studying in Odessa, many students at Jewish religious schools were engaging in communication with a large network of Jews overseas. Like the Ukrainian Jewish youth in Kiev, as described by Golbert, they were experiencing 'transnational orientations from home', linked into transnational networks, relationships, institutions, experiences and lifestyles and without ever leaving home (2001: 713, 715). Beyond the transnational connections sustained by youths at home, an increasing number of Jewish students in Odessa are also taking part in various organised travel and education programs offered in Israel. These opportunities allow young Jewish Odessans to familiarise themselves with Israeli culture first hand.

Shifting Jewish values

Despite the enthusiasm of children attending the recently established Jewish schools, the feelings of their parents were sometimes at odds with the new ethos. I did not have a chance to interview Karina's parents but a number of the local Jewry whose children or grandchildren attended Jewish schools, or were involved in other Jewish religiously based organisations, expressed mixed feelings, and at times concern, over the fact that – in the name of being Jewish – their children were being exposed to a quite different set of values from their own. The new focus of young Jews on principles of faith and religious practice was a not entirely welcome change. Some of the parents spoke of their children's home life and their Jewish education environments (including schools, camps, Jewish organised travel and other social programmes) as two different worlds. Major life choices concerning intermarriage, dietary laws, dress and other elements of Jewish self-expression were understood and dealt with in quite different, at times opposing, ways.

On one occasion my friend David took me to meet his grandmother for their regular tea. David, a newly observant Jew, did his best to evade her persistent questioning about his marriage plans but eventually said that he was waiting to meet a nice Jewish girl. In response, his grandmother said:

> You should want to marry someone because they are a good person, an intelligent person, a kind person but to marry someone just because they are Jewish, it's silly. Our family has so many nationalities in it, so many wonderful people who have helped me throughout my days. Must you upset me by this type of talk? ... and why do you walk around with that funny hat [a *kippah*]? Must you tell everyone you're Jewish? 'That is exactly the point', David answered.

Prior to becoming observant of the Jewish religious laws, David told me, he had similar views to his grandmother but he has since realised the importance of marrying someone Jewish and raising his children in a Jewish family.

The increasing isolation of contemporary Jewish life in Odessa from the wider social environments of the city was a point regularly made by Sveta, a local historian who had been involved in various Jewish projects since the early days of *perestroika*. She made an interesting analogy between the new ways of learning to be Jewish and learning a language:

> When people are fluent in a language, they can make up words, speak incorrectly, but they know when it becomes nonsense. When you're learning a new language you don't have the same comfort and security in your understanding of what you can and cannot say. This type of 'disloyalty' [to the rules] is unknown to many people today. A non-fluent speaker or a novice, similar to the newly observant Jews, is not as secure in his or her language skills and thus often relies on other authorities, such as books and the advice of the assumed-to-be-experts, to make their judgement. Previously, when Jews were exposed to various ways of being Jewish, they understood that their mischief did not take away their Jewishness. In other words, they were not any less Jewish having stepped outside Jewish Orthodox law – especially in Odessa, where Jews lived in a relatively liberal manner. Today, when Jewish education is for most part directed at bringing Jews out of assimilation into the religious Jewish world – thus stripping them of all that is condemned as non-Jewish – a stronger trend of strict observance follows.

Sveta cited many examples of young Jewish people whom she had met in her years of working for different Jewish initiatives, who now judged and valued their Jewishness on the basis of religious or traditional Jewish principles. She mocked the ostentatious behaviour that newly 'literate', rule-bound young Jews were sometimes prone to display, such as refusing ever to step foot inside a church. Yet, Zeev Jabotinsky, a prominent Odessan Jewish writer and Zionist, had been happy to act as a witness at the Russian Orthodox wedding of one of his friends. For Sveta, it was obvious that a Jew does not lose his Jewishness by entering a church or gain it by entering a synagogue. Newly observant Jews, like new language learners, did not feel as comfortable in making such judgements, having only recently learnt of their Jewishness or finding their sense of Jewishness now abundant with new terminology, symbols and laws in which they were not yet fully fluent; they still lacked the authority of 'just knowing'. Herbert Gans observes similar contrasts between first- and second-generation Jews in the United States: 'The first-generation Jew had no need to decorate his house with Stars of David or hang pictures of a rabbi on the wall in order to give a Jewish "feel" to his world, as many second-generation Jews do' (1956: 427).

Odessan Jews who adopt the new symbols and traditions frequently find themselves facing dilemmas about practices they had previously taken for granted. For one young Jewish family I often stayed with during my shorter visits to Odessa, the problem was whether to put up a New Year's tree, a Russian tradition they had both grown up with. According to Israeli teachers advising Seregya in his weekly classes at the synagogue on proper Jewish conduct at home, this tradition was 'Christian and Soviet' but definitely 'not Jewish'. Lika thought that it would be strange not to follow a family tradition and could not understand Seregya's interpretation that it was 'wrong'. They spent many late nights in their kitchen debating the issues. At the point when I left Odessa, they had decided against the tree – but that they would nonetheless celebrate the holiday.

Sveta emphasised that the Jewish values prized and practised by today's Jewish youth are not embedded in knowing local Jewish history, art, literature and music, the works of Odessan Jewish artists who wrote in Russian, Yiddish and Hebrew and sought wider recognition of their talents. The notions of belonging to the Russian-speaking intelligentsia, of having an open orientation to the world and seeking to attain the highest level of education were no longer obvious secular markers of Jewish identity, as they were for self-aware Jews of her generation. This was not to say that contemporary Jewish youth in Odessa no longer espouse these values and aspirations but, she explained, they are no longer seen as markers of being a Jew. This old 'cosmopolitan' way of 'being' a Jew was now being displaced by the new, more potent associations between being Jewish and identifying with Judaism as a religion. However, it is also an inescapable fact that the cosmopolitan basis of Jewish identity was itself already radically undermined during the major period of Soviet rule when most of the Jewish religious, cultural, educational and Zionist institutions were closed, destroyed or banned.

In fact, Sveta expressed both approval of and concern about Jewish education. Whilst she welcomed the openness to learning and being able to explore explicitly Jewish topics in the post-Soviet environment, she was worried that such teachings would have an adverse effect on the way in which Jews related both to other Jews and to non-Jews. Odessa's present-day narrowing of inter-ethnic contact was another departure from the historical accomplishments of the city's unique cosmopolitan way of life. With the boundaries between ethno-religious groups becoming more concrete and, more importantly, with the rise in Ukrainian nationalism, Sveta believed that there was a perceptible increase in intolerance, as witnessed by outbreaks of anti-Semitism, such as the flyers that sometimes appeared in the city that blamed Jews for all the troubles of the country or the spray-painted swastikas sometimes found on the walls of old Odessan buildings.

It was notable that many Jewish Odessans of the Soviet era spoke in perhaps surprisingly favourable terms about the regime's policies of secularisation and assimilation. These were accepted by many Jews and others as a modernising process that represented a move forward from the once segregated and backward Jewish way of life under the Russian Empire. From this perspective, the present-day religious revival appeared to be a step backwards. Also, in contrast to the usual image of the suppressed subjects of the Soviet regime, they valued the principles of equality and morality that they recognised in their Soviet days. Many Soviet inhabitants, as Kotkin notes, recognised the righteousness of socialist values even if they did not see them always actually applied in state practices (1995: 228).

Tatiana, a retired librarian and prominent member of the local intelligentsia whom I met in the last year of her life, claimed that Jews of her generation voluntarily and enthusiastically accepted Russification and assimilation, viewing these as the 'way forward' in their self-development. Slezkine explains that in the Soviet Union:

> Young Jews were not just learning Russian the same way they were learning Hebrew: they were learning Russian in order to replace Hebrew, as well as Yiddish, for good. Like German, Polish, or Hungarian in other high-culture areas, Russian had become the Hebrew of the secular world … If the Russian world stood for speech, knowledge, freedom and light, then the Jewish world represented silence, ignorance, bondage, and darkness. (2004: 128, 136)

Tatiana acknowledged the role of state authorities in these processes but in her opinion this was secondary to the opportunities provided to the greater Jewish population to pursue a self-chosen path.[25] Speaking of Odessa, her home, she claimed that the city's distinctive history had played a significant role in the speed and degree to which Russian language and culture was absorbed by Jews and non-Jews alike. Tatiana argued that Jews in Odessa were historically much closer to Russian culture than to Jewish culture. Russian was 'the language that they spoke, the books that they read, the theatre they attended, the food they ate, the clothes they wore, and, on the whole, their philosophy of life or *mentalitet* [mentality]'. In her view, their identification with being Russian and Jewish (legally exclusive categories in the Soviet Union) was combined in their identification with the larger social class of Russian-speaking intelligentsia. As was the case for Viacheslav and his club, a 'hang out of intellectual youth', the ideal of belonging to the 'intelligentsia' was, Rapoport and Lomsky-Feder argue, central to the construction of the ethnic identity of many Russian Jews, a 'prism through which Jews consider and evaluate both themselves and others' (2002: 233). For Tatiana, members of the Jewish intelligentsia were 'cosmopolitan' almost by definition since their circle of friends included many different nationalities and not only Jews. In such groups, relationships were based on purely personal interests and not loyalty to a specific religious or national group. Friendships formed in Soviet times, as she recalled, carried moral value and were not driven by economic interests, unlike today.[26] Sveta's comments represent a rather extreme version Soviet idealism that ignores much of the state-promoted anti-Jewish sentiments expressed in quotas and other means of discrimination that some Soviet Jews were exposed to. Yet other Odessans of her generation, who were more balanced in their view of the Soviet state, similarly lamented Soviet values and expressed a concern for the religious revival witnessed in their city.

Tatiana definitively rejected the claim of contemporary Jewish activists that they were restoring the lost or stolen treasures of Jewish life in Odessa. On the contrary, by speaking and acting against assimilation, these Jewish religious leaders were undoing the sophisticated past accomplishments of the city. She felt that today's Jewish religious leaders were moving the local Jewish population toward a religiously oriented Jewish identity and history based on values and processes foreign to their world (attending and making donations to the synagogue, observing Jewish traditions and rituals, the importance of marrying a Jewish spouse, learning Hebrew, receiving religious education, disaffiliation from Soviet secular holidays, etc.). However, reflecting on the new Jewish visibility Tatiana did acknowledge that the state of harmony she so admired in Soviet Odessa was perhaps based more on hiding differences between ethno-religious groups than on true mutual acceptance.

The type of concerns expressed by Tatiana, Sveta and Viacheslav was found more frequently among the elderly and, to some degree, among the middle-aged. However, I also came across a number of young Jewish people who were opposed to contemporary Jewish community building because of the problem of ethnic separatism. Alex, a nineteen-year-old graphic designer, said that, despite his Jewish origins, he would not feel comfortable attending activities in a place especially created for Jews: 'I never ask my friends if they are Jewish or not and never really talk to them about my Jewish roots. If I suggested to them that we might attend something at the Jewish Cultural Centre, we would all start thinking about who is and who is not Jewish. No one has time for that in Odessa.' Katia, a student at Odessa University, chimed in, agreeing that Jewish programmes divide Jews from others. She described how, after attending a Jewish youth camp, she had returned feeling closer to her Jewish friends than others in her social network.

In contrast, others said that they automatically gravitated towards other Jews. Vitali, a recent returnee from Israel, said that Jewish institutions were a natural part of his life. They served the important purpose of bringing Jews together to guarantee their survival as an ethnicity, a religion and a people, and they offered good opportunities to meet a Jewish partner and later build a Jewish family.

Jewish Odessa in the view of returnees

Vitali was one of the migrants I met who, after spending four years in Israel, had returned to live in Odessa. After many visits home, he was now setting up his own agricultural business together with his father, who had previous experience in the sector. Despite this commitment, Vitali described his stay in Odessa as 'indefinite'. Other Israeli returnees had a variety of reasons for choosing to return to the city, whether on a permanent, undefined or temporary basis, such as family loyalties, career development, the danger of living in the Middle East, and the improving economic and social prospects in the Ukraine. Opportunities attracting Israelis to Odessa also included the availability of posts in education or forms of community service.[27] For the most part, returnees come back from Israel, although some return from the United States, Germany, Australia and other locations.[28] The presence of returnees in Odessa, as elsewhere in the FSU, is a relatively new phenomenon but one that is gaining momentum and not only among immigrants who had difficulty adjusting to Israeli life or those who had seen Israel merely as a stepping stone to another, perhaps unreached, destination. Even those who had been well integrated into Israeli society are now seeking opportunities back home that will utilise the skills and knowledge gained abroad (Sapritsky 2006).

Throughout my interviews, meetings and interactions with returnees, I was keen to find out how their time abroad had shaped their views of Odessa's new ethnic and religious diversity and whether their sojourns abroad had had an effect on the type of relationships they forged with local Odessan Jews and others on their return. Whilst Vitali's time abroad clearly defined his perception of solidarity with other Jews in the city, other returnees had very different attitudes towards Odessa's new sense of itself as a place of Jewish belonging. For some, it took returning to Odessa, rather than moving to Israel, to develop a desire and a need to be in an organised Jewish community. Kostia, for instance, told me that it was not until a few years after his return to Odessa that he started to become more observant of Jewish religious laws and began regularly attending the synagogue, neither of which had been part of his daily routine in Israel. On his return, however, he found himself wanting to battle against Odessa's 'assimilationism': by observing the Jewish commandments (which he had not observed in Israel) he formed a link between his experience in Israel and his everyday life in Odessa. Other returnees made the same kind of point, although with a less observant pattern of affiliation. As Marat explained, 'In Israel I did not do anything Jewish, you don't need to. But when I came back I started doing little things with the community. Here I felt that it was nice to keep traditions.'

In some cases, however, returnees had a difficult time relating to the heightened sense of religiosity they now found in Odessa. Dina, a twenty-six-year-old engineer who had recently moved back to Odessa to be closer to her family, spoke of her inability to reconnect with her Jewish friends who were now involved in Jewish organisations in the city: 'They became too Jewish for me. Although I am Jewish, we don't understand that to be the same thing. I think of myself as an Israeli, as an Odessan and then as Jewish. For them it's the other way around.' At the age of fifteen she had emigrated to Israel, leaving her sister and parents behind in Odessa. Before the move, she had been very involved in the Jewish life of the city. However, during her time in Israel, her passion for being an active Jew had slowly faded. As Dina saw it, when you move to 'Zion', acting out your Jewishness no longer seems important. Returning to Odessa, she had not opted to rekindle her old connections with Odessa's Jewish circles. Nothing about the religious world struck a chord with her present Jewish identification. The new outlook she had adopted abroad now made 'stay back' Jews seem 'too Jewish', 'narrow and old fashioned'.[29] Similarly, many other returnees describe Odessa as a place known and at the same time unknown. Writing about the experience of homecomings more generally, Stephansson (2004: 4) points out how, for many returnees, in the course of their protracted absence their home had inevitably undergone changes and they too had been exposed to new realities and adopted new habits. In the case of Odessa's returnees, for some this made living in Odessa interesting, for others difficult to cope with.

Genady, a business entrepreneur who moved back to Odessa with his wife and two children after spending eleven years in the city of Ashdot in Israel, is someone I was introduced to at the Jewish Cultural Centre Migdal, where a number of returnees came to practise their Hebrew and find out about programmes for their children. When we met some two months into his stay, Genady told me about an incident in which a teacher on the after-school programme had complained about his children's lack of attention in the Jewish traditions and religion class. Genady's response to the teacher had been that, in Israel, many immigrants do not interact with the religious community, from which, as he described it, they are often ostracised. Although his children had grown up in Israel celebrating the Jewish calendar as a state-initiated agenda, he did not accept that Judaism had to become a crucial part of their Jewish identity. In his view, Odessa, his native place, had never been a religious city and he found the recent changes in local Jewish attitudes altogether out of character. Jewish educators seeking to ensure the survival of a Jewish culture and perpetuating traditional Judaism embodied in religious form were committed to an endeavour that is of little importance to him or his children. He is happy for his children to be raised in a secular Jewish environment, such as he had come to know in Israel but he saw the imposition of more religious codes as infringing his level of accepted Jewish practices.

Another effect of spending time in Israel was that some returnees had new views about Odessa's Arab minority. A number of the Israeli students I met at the Odessa Medical Institute felt a close connection with their Arab classmates, being fellow international students and sharing a partiality for Turkish cuisine as the next best thing to their Middle Eastern favourite dishes. Such close relations with Arab students was something many had not experienced in their previous Russian or Israeli environments but now were able to build in the context of an international group of foreign students in Odessa. Some returnees, however, found it difficult to work with local Arab residents. Nathaniel attributed his reservations to personal issues with locals in Ramat Gan, Israel, and his experience of a terrorist attack. 'Before going to Israel,' he explained, 'my best friend in Odessa was a young Arab boy. They used to come here and bring back a lot of goods that I would buy and sell on for better prices. I knew them all. Now if you ask me to do something with Arabs, I would think twice.' Working as a director of a construction company, Nathaniel said that he was more at ease dealing with a 'European mentality' rather than a 'Middle Eastern' one, which, according to him, meant a lack of punctuality, reliability and trust.

While some returnees arrive back in Odessa with a heightened sense of Jewishness or develop stronger attachments to Jewish life on their return, others prefer to remain on the periphery of Jewish activity in the city. The issue of Jewish and Arab relations remains in question. Some of the scenarios of sociality that I witnessed in Odessa offer some hope, while other cases are less promising.

Conclusion

This chapter has described some of the changed orientations of post-Soviet Odessa's Jewish population as it has been affected by mass emigration, the influx of international Jewish religious emissaries, primarily from the United States and Israel, and the presence of returnees. It has focused especially on the phenomena of Jewish religious revival in Odessa, manifest in the new visibility of Judaism throughout the city, the mushrooming of new Jewish religious institutions and interventions, not least in the field of education, and a sharpening of boundaries between Jews and non-Jews. This involves both social ruptures and new solidarities and networks.

The ethnographic material presented here has revealed a significantly varied range of ways that Odessan Jews, young and old, negotiate a path through competing definitions of what it is to be a Jew. Religious practices were contested, welcomed by some as offering certainty and support, while rejected by others as alien to the ethos of the city.

The backdrop to all these interactions is Odessa's past as a famously cosmopolitan city, a cosmopolitanism that stretches back to its days as a free port, includes a rich history of local Jewish and non-Jewish artists and writers and, for some at least, also encompasses the Soviet era with its Russian intellectuals, modernisation and principles (and at least partial provision) of equal welfare for all. Even if this cosmopolitanism has been assaulted at times by anti-Semitic outbursts in the city's history, for many of the city's Jewish inhabitants its heritage frames the issues surrounding contemporary developments. For the most 'cosmopolitan' aspect of Odessa has always been, precisely, its Jewishness – a distinctive non-exclusive Jewishness evinced most strongly in adopting values, ideals and a way of life that was largely liberal, culturally eclectic and open to mixing between Jews and others.

Can the new religious mentality be in turn absorbed within that evocation of cosmopolitan tolerance and liberalism? For some, especially children and young people, the new religiosity offers the excitement of international links with Jews in other countries. It means crossing borders (even without leaving home), which might indeed be seen as partaking in the openness so valued in the notion of cosmopolitanism. Or is this very border-crossing merely a transnational parochialism, to be viewed as a sad decline in the city's cosmopolitan heritage? From this perspective, largely expressed by the older generations, the new models of Jewishness adopted by many of Odessa's Jewry under the auspices of the international religious emissaries are narrow and isolationist. Religiously based Jewish identity segments Jews from the wider social and cultural environment of the city and divides the Jewish population itself as to who is a 'real' Jew. Current projects of Jewish revival are, in this view, extinguishing what remains of Odessa's distinctive and Jewish cosmopolitan past by their aspirations to make Jews feel and act more Jewish and by their efforts to selectively strengthen their ties with other Jews. What is indisputable is that altogether new modes of sociality are emerging, quite different from the pre-Revolutionary and Soviet Odessan practices whose loss is lamented by the older generations of Jews.

At the same time Odessa is being transformed in other ways. Economic and employment opportunities are expanding, while the state struggles, so far unsuccessfully, to replace the levels of welfare and educational provision provided in the Soviet era. The way in which separate Jewish schools are seen is, in part, affected by their high academic quality compared to the available state or private facilities. Equally, elderly Jews cannot but appreciate the services provided to them as members of religious organisations. And, in the face of the state's relentless Ukrainisation policy (only alluded to here), Jewish identity provides a point of resistance. On a more fearful note, the new visibility and benefits accruing to Odessa's Jews risks the envious attention of re-emerging anti-Semitism.

Writing about Odessa's Jews, I have made an attempt to capture the complexities and ambiguities that arise within one of the city's ethno-religious groups confronted with changes in their identification, education, social status and system of beliefs and practices. Like other ethnic and religious minorities in the city, Jews are redefining themselves in their new socioeconomic and political environs both as individuals and as members of a distinct group whose boundaries have become more pronounced. This challenge may possibly set off further intra- and inter-group conflict or it may lead to a new phase in Odessa's ethnic and religious coexistence, with different urban groups accepting one another on the basis of their distinct traits and all sharing a sense of belonging to the highly distinctive place that is Odessa. I suspect that improved economic and political conditions in Odessa and Ukraine more widely would be a determining factor in enhancing social cohesion and that the reverse would cause further social turmoil. Within the Jewish community it is apparent that new Jewish religious orientations have been partially absorbed into Odessa's social fabric but it is possibly too early to tell how influential they will be for the future generations and whether their direction will continue to be set by Orthodox Judaism and foreign-based sponsorship.

NOTES

1. I want to suggest that the term 'Jewish', as used by most Odessans to describe their city, does not literally mean that only Jews live there or that Jews dominate the place in any significant shape or form (see Karakina 2007: 7). Rather, this seeming stereotype stands in for other ways of expressing what distinguishes Odessa, notably 'cosmopolitan', 'tolerant' and 'international' – which the historic and continuing presence of Jews (as an accepted ethnic and religious minority) guarantees and, to some degree, stands to define. Understood this way, as a metonym of the city's famous attributes, the stereotype of Odessa as a 'Jewish' city does not abolish or overwrite its other characteristics (or inhabitants).

2. The ethnographic material presented in this chapter was collected in Odessa during fieldwork carried out from October 2005 to January 2007 and again in September 2007. The methods used ranged from participant observation and informal interviews to focus groups with Odessa's youth and life histories gathered among the elderly Jewish population. This research was funded by the Title VIII Research Scholar Program from the American Councils for International Education and the Memorial Foundation for Jewish Culture.

3. Although various Jewish institutions are involved in Odessa's contemporary development, this chapter will mainly focus on religious congregations, organisations and religious doctrine.

4. Herlihy (1986: 241–42) notes that, according to the 1897 city census, over 40 per cent of the city's population adhered to non-Orthodox faiths. This division of Odessa's population by religious belief clearly represented its cosmopolitan character.

5. An area designated for Jewish residence in the Russian Empire, which was officially constituted in 1835 and lasted until 1917.

6. As Zipperstein (1986: 86) highlights, Odessa's Jewish affairs from 1860 to 1888 were for the most part controlled by the city's Chief Rabbi, Aryeh Schwabacher, a German Jew who did not speak Russian or Yiddish.

7. Mathijs Pelkmans' edited volume, *Conversion After Socialism*, focused predominantly on Christian and Muslim conversions, similarly challenges the 'problematic notion that religious life after socialism can be characterized as a revival of repressed religious tradition' (Pelkmans 2009: 2). As Pelkmans rightly points out, 'Religion served new needs and was linked to new imaginaries' (2009: 2).

8. Richardson points out that Odessans consider the distinctiveness of their city and its citizens to be partially the result of the mixing of people of different nationalities. This 'is viewed as the source of the beauty of the city's women, the tolerance among its citizens, its tasty cuisine and its dialect, which combines aspects of Russian, Ukrainian, Yiddish as well as other European languages' (2004: 3).

9. Chabad Lubavitch is a transnational Hasidic movement engaged in worldwide outreach, dispatching thousands of *shlihim* (emissaries) to university campuses, major cities and some of the most remote places in the world. Among others, see Fishkoff (2003) for an entertaining and in-depth description of the Chabad Lubavitch movement.

10. http://epyc.yivo.org/content/19_3.php, YIVO Institute for Jewish Research.

11. I am aware that the Jewish population in Odessa is by no means undivided in its views on the developments said to represent them or in their understandings of what is recognised as 'Odessan' today. Indeed, it is questionable how far one can generalise about any continuing Soviet imprint on the thought and behaviour of Odessa's Jews when talking about the youth and children who have grown up influenced not only by the history and experience of their parents and grandparents but also amidst new trends of post-Soviet culture. As Horwitz notes, '[t]he growth of at least two generations of Jewish youth who have experienced open celebrations of Jewish holidays, attendance at Jewish schools, and an environment of open, public Jewish activity has produced a Jewish youth quite different in attitudes and sensibilities from its parents' (2003: 124).

12. The Museum of History of Odessa's Jews states that there were 65,000 Jews in the city in 1989, while statistics provided by the city's mayor, Eduard Gurvits, give the figure as 90,000 for the same year. These official statistics are highly debated (as are the figures on the numbers of Jews in Ukraine as a whole, where

estimates vary from 250,000 to 500,000). A mere 12,380 Jews are registered as such on the official city census collected in 2005: see http://www.misto.odessa. ua/index.php?u=gorod/stat (last viewed on 25 February 2011). However, Jewish scholars and leaders of various communities argue that the actual figures are two or even three times more than that figure: see http://tikvaodessa.org/Page/Content.aspx?page=about/odessa_community (last viewed on 25 February 2011). In their view, many of the city's Jews do not want to be registered as Jews any longer, or regard Jewishness as one of their identifications but choose to mark their allegiance with their nation state or their language. I myself met a number of Jewish residents who, despite their self-proclaimed Jewish identity, felt it more 'appropriate' to label themselves as Ukrainian or Russian in official documents.

13. Constructed for the seven-day holiday of *Sukkoth*, a *sukkah* is a ritual outdoor dwelling (booth or hut) in which Jews take meals and occasionally sleep.

14. A *hanukkiyah*, also known as a *menorah*, is a special candelabra used for the lighting of the candles during the festival of *Hanukhah*.

15. In the Marxist-Leninist ideology, religion was the 'opiate of the people' and approached as irrational superstition and potentially dangerous. 'Proselytizing and religious education in schools were prohibited and any display of religious commitment could prejudice not only one's own job but also the position and prospects of a wider circle of relatives and friends' (Hann 2006: 2).

16. Litvaks are traditionally followers of Lithuanian Jewish Orthodoxy, which can be traced to the late thirteenth century. Historically, Lithuanian Orthodoxy was marked by concentration on highly intellectual *Talmud* study. Litvaks are characterised as being more dogmatic and authoritarian than other branches of Ashkenazi Jewry. The movement is often closely related to the teachings of Rabbi Elijah ben Shlomo Zalman of Vilnius, known as the 'Vilna Goan', who strongly opposed the development of Hasidim in Eastern Europe.

17. In addition, the leaders of the organisation Jews for Jesus – which operates mostly underground – claim that it is officially registered as an institution of Jewish activity, although it is not recognised as such by other Jewish religious leaders.

18. Possibly due to the late arrival of the Reform Congregation in post-Soviet Odessa (2001), insufficient funds, less aggressive tactics, and a weaker infrastructure of services and programmes, Reform Judaism is not nearly as widespread today in the city as is Jewish Orthodoxy.

19. Odessa also has a number of Jewish secular and Zionist organisations, which provide programmes and aid to the local Jewish population. Among the most popular are The Jewish Agency (otherwise known as Sokhnut) and the Israeli Cultural Centre, both of which function as education centres for potential Israeli immigrants and also those interested in Israeli culture, political affairs, study abroad programmes or free Hebrew lessons. The Israeli Cultural Centre also bears the responsibility for reviewing the documentation of Jewish descent necessary for emigration or subsidised travel to Israel. Unlike the religiously oriented centres, these institutions hold Israel, rather than religious observance, at the heart of a person's Jewish identification – this is expressed most

vividly in the act of *aliyah* (emigration to Israel). Other organisations include the American Jewish Joint Distribution Committee (Joint), which sponsors the Club for Elderly Jews, Gmilus Hessed (recently renamed Shaarey Zion), the Jewish Community Centre Migdal (and all of its programmes, including the Early Child Development Centre, Mazl Tov, and the Museum of History of Odessa Jews), World ORT (which finances the public Jewish school number 94), the Jewish Library, the Association of Former Ghetto Prisoners, the Jewish Learning Centre and Publication Moria, the athletic organisation Makkabi-Pivden, a Student Cultural Centre, Hillel, and a new Jewish cultural centre, Beit Grand.

20. See Caldwell (2008) for a comparative discussion of Christian-based welfare in the FSU.

21. On a few occasions I heard Odessans of non-Jewish descent complaining about their Jewish neighbours receiving food and clothes packages and also financial support from Jewish centres where no such benefits would be available to them. Similarly, non-Jewish concentration camp survivors (whom I met under different circumstances when I was working as a translator) were highly aggrieved by the fact that Jewish ex-prisoners were receiving higher reparations from the German government than they were themselves.

22. A child born to two Jewish parents was automatically registered as a Jew in his or her documents. For children of mixed marriages, the option of being registered as a Jew remained open as they could choose to take up either their mother's or father's nationality. Gizwitz (2001: 4) points out that, due to the high percentage of intermarriage among Soviet Jews (estimated at 70–80 per cent), the number of 'full' Jews in relation to the overall Jewish population is relatively small. As one of the Orthodox rabbis told me, 'If you meet a Jew whose parents are both Jewish it is probably an accident'.

23. Viacheslav's account echoed many other stories that lament the loss of the cosmopolitan character of the city.

24. Odessa currently has three different Jewish school structures, two of which are sponsored by the Orthodox congregations; the third is a state school run by World ORT. In our conversation Viacheslav primarily concentrated on the synagogue-sponsored schools in which he knew a number of students.

25. Terry Martin (2001: 428) draws attention to the fact that the Russian language was also promoted as 'public propaganda' in a series of Soviet newspaper articles, one of which reads 'The great and mighty Russian language, the language of Lenin and Stalin, Pushkin and Gorky, Tolstoi and Belinskii, is profoundly dear to all citizens of the USSR, and is studied with love by children and adults … [which shows] the exclusive interest of all nationalities to the study of the language of the great Russian people, first among equals in the fraternity family of the peoples of the USSR'.

26. See Patico (2005: 484) where she provides a similar account of how local residents of St Petersburg in the late 1990s felt the decline of sociality and the increasing power of money in their personal affairs.

27. A small number of returnees are affiliated with one of the two Orthodox movements in the city and the local branch of Sokhnut. Employed by their respec-

tive organisations, they usually relocate to the city for a limited duration of one or two years.

28. This trend can possibly be explained by the fact that migration to the United States and Germany usually involved inter-generational families rather than individual Jewish young people or young couples, as was frequently the case with migration to Israel (Goldbert 2001: 716–17). The low frequency of returns from the United States and Australia can also partially be explained by the distance and the cost of travel. While visits from Germany are very common, permanent returns occur less frequently with European citizens.

29. Similarly Long and Oxfeld point out that 'as the act of returning unfolds, the specific experiences often contrast with the returnee's original dreams' (2004: 10). In the same book Gmelch describes how Barbadian returnees 'feel that their own interests are more cosmopolitan and transcend [those of] the local community; the place now appears as "narrow"' (2004: 213).

REFERENCES

Altshuler, S. 2005. *From Exodus to Freedom: A History of the Soviet Jewry Movement*. Lanham.

Broz, Ludek. 2009. 'Conversion to Religion? Negotiating Continuity and Discontinuity in Contemporary Altai', in Mathijs Pelkmans (ed.), *Conversion After Socialism*. New York, pp. 17–37.

Caldwell, L.M. 2008. 'Social Welfare and Christian Welfare: Who Gets Saved in Post-Soviet Russian Charity Work?', in Mark D. Steinberg and Catherine Wanner (eds), *Religion, Morality and Community in Post Soviet Societies*. Bloomington, pp. 179–214.

Chlenov, M. 1994. 'Jewish Communities and Jewish Identities in the Former Soviet Union', in Jonathan Webber (ed.), *Jewish Identities in the New Europe*. London, pp. 127–38.

Cooper, A.E. 1988. 'The Bukharan Jews in Post Soviet Uzbekistan: A Case of Fractured Identity', *Anthropology of East Europe Review* 16(2): 27–33.

Fishkoff, S. 2003. *The Rebbe's Army: Inside the World of Chabad Lubavitch*. New York.

Freidman, M. and A. Chernin. 1999. *A Second Exodus: The American Movement to Free Soviet Jews*. Hanover.

Gans, H.J. 1956. 'American Jewry: Present and Future: Part One', *Commentary* 21(1): 422–30.

Gizwitz, B. 2001. 'Jewish Life in Ukraine at the Dawn of the Twenty-First Century: Part One', *Jerusalem Letter* 451: 1–14.

Gmelch, George. 2004. 'West Indian Migrants and their Rediscovery of Barbados', in Lynellyn D. Long and Ellen Oxfeld (eds), *Coming Home? Refugees, Migrants, and Those Who Stayed Behind*. Philadelphia, pp. 206–23.

Golbert, R. 2001. 'Transnational Orientations from Home: Constructions of Israel and Transnational Space among Ukrainian Jewish Youth', *Journal of Ethnic and Migration Studies* 27(4): 713–31.

Goluboff, S. 2003. *Jewish Russians: Upheavals in a Moscow Synagogue.* Philadelphia.

Gruber, R.E. 2002. *Virtually Jewish: Reinventing Jewish Culture in Europe.* Berkeley.

Gubar, O. and A. Rozenboim. 2003. 'Daily Life in Odessa', in Nicolas V. Iljine (ed.), *Odessa Memories.* Seattle, pp. 49–122.

Hann, C. 2006. 'Introduction: Faith, Power, and Civility after Socialism', in C. Hann (ed.), *The Postsocialist Religious Question: Faith and Power in Central Asia and East Central Europe.* Berlin, pp. 1–26.

Herlihy, P. 1986. *Odessa: A History, 1794-1914.* Cambridge.

Horwitz, Martin. 2003. 'The Widening Gap between Our Model of Russian Jewry and the Reality (1989–99)', in Zvi Gitelman, Musya Glants and Marshall I. Goldman (eds), *Jewish Life after the USSR.* Bloomington, pp. 117–26.

Jessa, P. 2006. 'Religious Renewal in Kazakhstan: Redefining Unofficial Islam', in Chris Hann and the 'Civil Religion' Group (eds), *The Postsocialist Religious Question: Faith and Power in Central Asia and East–Central Europe.* Berlin, pp. 169–90.

Karakina, E. 2007. 'Jews Always...', in E. Karakina et al. (eds), *City Guide of Jewish Odessa.* Odessa, pp. 6–13.

Klier, J.D. 2002. 'A Port, Not a Shtetl: Reflections on the Distinctiveness of Odessa', in David Cesarani (ed.), *Port Jews: Jewish Communities in Cosmopolitan Maritime Trading Centres, 1550–1950.* London, pp. 173–79.

Kotkin, S. 1995. *Magnetic Mountain: Stalinism as a Civilization.* Berkeley.

Long, L.D. and E. Oxfeld. 2004. 'Introduction: An Ethnography of Return', in Lynellyn D. Long and Ellen Oxfeld (eds), *Coming Home? Refugees, Migrants and Those who Stayed Behind.* Philadelphia, pp. 1–15.

Markowitz, F. 1993. *A Community in Spite of Itself: Soviet Jewish Emigrés in New York.* Washington.

Martin, T. 2001. *The Affirmative Action Empire: Nations and Nationalism in the Soviet Union, 1923-1939.* Ithaca.

Mazis, J.A. 2004. *The Greeks of Odessa: Diaspora Leadership in Late Imperial Russia.* Boulder.

Patico, J. 2005. 'To Be Happy in a Mercedes: Tropes of Value and Ambivalent Visions of Marketization', *American Ethnologist* 32(3): 479–96.

Pelkmans, M. 2009. 'Introduction: Post-Soviet Space and the Unexpected Turns of Religious Life', in Mathijs Pelkmans (ed.), *Conversion After Socialism.* New York, pp. 1–16.

Rapoport, T. and E. Lomsky-Feder. 2002. 'Intelligentsia as an Ethnic Habitus: The Inculcation and Restructuring of Intelligentsia among Russian Jews', *British Journal of Sociology of Education* 23(2): 233–48.

Richardson, T. 2004. 'Odessa, Ukraine: History, Place and Nation-Building in a Post Soviet City' (Ph.D. diss., Cambridge University).

———. 2008. *Kaleidoscopic Odessa: History and Place in Contemporary Ukraine.* Toronto.

Rozenboim, A. 2007. 'Old Odessa: Community and City Life', in E. Karakina et al. (eds), *City Guide of Jewish Odessa.* Odessa, pp. 33–37.

Sapritsky, M. 2006. 'Tuda ili Obratno?', *Moriia* 6: 12–20.

Skinner, F.W. 1986. 'Odessa and the Problem of Urban Modernization', in Michael F. Hamm (ed.), *The City in Late Imperial Russia*. Bloomington, pp. 209–49.

Slezkine, Y. 2004. *The Jewish Century*. Princeton.

Solomon, N. 1994. 'Judaism in the New Europe: Discovery or Invention?', in Jonathan Webber (ed.), *Jewish Identities in the New Europe*. London, pp. 86–98.

Stefansson, A.H. 2004. 'Homecomings to the Future: From Diasporic Mythographies to Social Projects of Return', in F. Markowitz and A.H. Stefansson (eds), *Homecomings: Unsettled Paths of Return*. Lanham, pp. 2–20.

Weinberg, R. 1992. 'The Pogrom of 1905 in Odessa: A Case Study', in John Klier and Shlomo Lambroza (eds), *Pogroms: Anti-Jewish Violence in Modern Russian History*. Cambridge, pp. 248–89.

———. 1993. *The Revolution of 1905 in Odessa: Blood on the Steps*. Bloomington.

Zipperstein, S.J. 1986. *The Jews of Odessa: A Cultural History, 1794–1881*. Stanford.

％ Chapter 3 ｛

At the City's Social Margins: Selective Cosmopolitans in Odessa

VERA SKVIRSKAJA

In anthropology there is a tendency to conceptualise notions that once claimed universal singularity in the plural: there are alternative modernities, different capitalisms and 'discrepant cosmopolitanisms' (Clifford 1992). Following the latter idea that there are different, plural cosmopolitan practices and attitudes, this chapter looks at cosmopolitanisms present in contemporary Odessa and represented by two different communities – post-Soviet Afghan (im)migrants and native Ukrainian Roma (also known by the ethnonym Servy). In the city, the ethnic worlds of these groups are far apart and they have little to do with one other in their everyday lives. What they have in common is the experience of marginality (both in terms of numbers, social-cultural positioning and racial categorisation) in a city that is an important commercial crossroads in the Black Sea region and widely praised for its traditional and post-Soviet tolerance in public discourse (literature, films, political speeches, cultural events and so on).[1] These two groups have been chosen for a discussion of cosmopolitan dynamics in the city because they illustrate two different modalities of marginality: the marginality of a historically local (or 'internal') Other, the Gypsy; and the marginality of the recent foreign migrants who have become omnipresent in Odessa's market places but less so in other public realms. Although Afghanis have come to Ukraine via particular routes, and they occupy specific trading niches and have a unique diasporic organisation in Odessa, when it comes to coexistence with wider society, they are, in many respects, representative of new migrants from Turkey, the Arab world, China and Central Asian states.

Since Ukraine's independence in 1991, Odessa's authorities have promoted the city as a centre for trade, international commerce and cooperation.[2] An increasing number of 'native' Odessans and recent Ukrainian newcomers have developed first-hand familiarity with international practices and foreign languages through labour migration, employment in foreign shipping industries and long-distance trade (China and Turkey being the most common destinations in the first decade of the 2000s). This does not prevent many of these urban dwellers – whom I refer as to 'wider society' and who represent the city's predominantly Slav majority (see also the Introduction to this volume) – from keeping clear of various 'others' (be they local Gypsies or new migrants from China, Africa and Afghanistan) or from keeping them at bay. This wider society may or may not engage with, open up to or befriend 'others' in the city, and it can operate with negative racist labelling or simply resort to indifferent 'tolerance' to keep the image of a hospitable city alive (Skvirskaja and Humphrey 2007). Both the Roma and Afghanis, by contrast, and despite their recognised tendency towards insularity, do not seem to consider avoidance and indifference as viable options. For them, as we shall see, avoidance of wider society is not really an option. The aim of this chapter is to initiate an open-ended enquiry into the nature of the mutuality, openness and closures pertaining to these distinctive ethnic worlds. I suggest that the individual's and the group's well-being is predicated on actual cosmopolitan skills and capabilities and their mastery is taken (almost) for granted as an instance of cultural competence.

This chapter, then, explores the tales of coexistence shared with me by male Afghan migrants and mainly Servy women. While people's narratives and abrupt remarks expressed individual sensibilities, their commentary was constantly dialogised with reference to their ethnic worlds and to wider society, including the anthropologist. In their dialogues and interactions, neither my Afghan nor my Servy interlocutors fashioned themselves in terms of abstract universal models or individual destinies. Instead they considered their individualities as capable of saying something, and producing representations, about their communities.

My Servy hosts expected that their individual stories would place them on the city map and would be able to counteract the repressive power of the popular myths and stereotypes about Gypsies that made them eternal outsiders.[3] By the same token, Afghan migrants were very cautious and insecure about what they could say to an anthropologist, a stranger. Although most of my Afghan acquaintances have secure legal status in Ukraine, their life-stories were told in patches and 'flashes'; conscious attempts at self-censorship often shaped their representations of themselves. They were reserved about their lives and experiences in Odessa because they were concerned with how public knowledge of their individual lives might affect the images, as well as the prospects, of their diaspora (e.g. applications of Afghan asylum seekers, engagement in semi-legal activities, etc.).

In what follows, I shall first situate ideas about cosmopolitan subjectivity in anthropological debates and introduce the Afghan and Gypsy communities in Odessa. I then consider the ways in which they are habitually stigmatised as 'aliens' and 'blacks' (*chernye*) and their responses to this form of marginalisation. Finally, I discuss the ethnic worlds of my interlocutors as simultaneously arenas for cosmopolitan engagement and inward-looking sensibilities.

Situating cosmopolitan subjectivity theoretically

Who is 'entitled' to be called cosmopolitan? The question of entitlement is not accidental here: referring to the age of empire, cosmopolitanism is often considered an attribute of the commercial and political elites who shared a common lifestyle (if not a common high culture) spanning different countries or ethnicities. Among these elites, interethnic cooperation, residential cohabitation and mingling took place even at times when the poor and socially underprivileged in the same urban environment organised violent riots against other ethnic or religious groups.[4] Certain well-to-do but marginalised religious groups have also, however, been 'discovered' to be agents of global urban cosmopolitanism by virtue of their connections to multiple locales and their ability to use these connections to channel modern views and new practices to numerous sites.[5] Visions of cosmopolitanism as an elitist phenomenon have travelled well into anthropological discussions of present-day transnational diasporas and global mobility. It is imputed to those who have wealth and multiples homes and for whom flexible capital accumulation is linked to 'flexible citizenship' (Ong 1999; Hannerz 1992) as well as to the minority elites who defend their cultures while being tolerant, liberal and well-educated world travellers (Werbner 2006: 497).

Some alternative theorising attempts to disrupt the 'long history of arrogance' (Malcomson 1999: 241) associated with cosmopolitanism, and challenges the homology between privileged class position and cosmopolitan outlook (see also Werbner 1999: 18). This revision argues that at lower social levels there are fewer entry requirements (Malcomson 1999: 239), hence putting greater emphasis on the openness to the world of labour migrants, factory workers, refugees, poor settlers and the like. Yet, when the class bias is turned upside down, celebrations of 'bottom-up' cosmopolitanism necessarily raise the issue of the homogeneity of people's experiences, desires and cultural loyalties.

Cosmopolitanism is a matter of attitudes, skills and the enjoyment of difference, and working-class migrants, petty merchants and the destitute (i.e. people from lower down the socioeconomic ladder) do not necessarily share them uniformly. Different dispositions can cohabit within one and the same milieu, producing somewhat different subjectivities. Ferguson's (1999) study of what he calls 'localist' and 'cosmopolitan' styles practised among Copperbelt mineworkers in Zambia is a case in point. Cultural styles, as Ferguson argues, need not map onto a set of shared values and views of the world, nor do they refer to traditional and modern orientations (1999: 97–102). Instead, cultural styles designate performative competences that require an internalised capacity acquired over time and motivated by the structures of the political economy and the logic of social relations (in the case of urban mineworkers, rural-urban relations). On the Copperbelt, cosmopolitan style is dominated by international cultural forms (e.g. fashionable dress, speaking English, tastes in music and drinks, etc.); it signals the mineworkers' unwillingness to comply with their rural relatives' expectations and their desire to reach out 'beyond the local', to the outside world (1999: 212). In brief, stylistic differences among working-class people exemplify that cosmopolitanism (any particular variety of it) cannot simply be collapsed into the category of class.

More recently, Rapport (2007) highlighted yet another dimension to these debates by postulating cosmopolitanism as a universal human truth available to an individual through introspection. Challenging anthropology's 'collectivist orthodoxy', he argued for 'the global individual'. In this perspective, cosmopolitanism is (the universal) ontology that underlies the singularity of human beings and makes commensurate individuality possible. Rapport's call to recognise individuality as if situated outside power relations and historically produced freedom (see Laidlaw 2002) might set him apart from class/social group-focused theorisations. At the same time, his anti-collectivism is in line with those implicit and explicit trends in anthropological thinking that situate cosmopolitan subjectivity in contradistinction to the vernacular, i.e. culturally-specific forms of sociality and imaginary (with the exception of cosmopolitan culture itself).[6]

Cosmopolitanism and culture, I suggest, should not be approached as mutually irreducible reifications. A move in this direction has been undertaken by the historian Sheldon Pollock (2000), who highlighted the imprisoning aspects of our terminology and urged us not to fill the categories of the cosmopolitan and vernacular 'with any particular social or political content' (2000: 20) in advance. His point – that some people in the past could avoid 'making either their particularity ineluctable or their universalism compulsory' (2000: 48) – warns against approaches that would situate cosmopolitanism as a characteristic of class or a performative style or individuality, in Rapport's sense. The challenge is not to sort out people's experiences into 'cosmopolitan' or 'localist' variants or to resort to the vocabulary of 'hybridity', but to elucidate the enabling force of culture (understood broadly as a host of practices and values) that underlies the different ways in which people make cosmopolitanism possible.

Contours of Odessa's Roma and Afghan communities

Ukrainian old-timers

Some artistic Roma families in Odessa trace their genealogies to the city's beginnings in the late eighteenth century.[7] For the majority, the connection to Odessa is more recent. Throughout the twentieth century, the geographical movements of Ukrainian Roma, just like Roma elsewhere in the USSR, were entangled with processes of Soviet resettlement, evacuation during the Second World War and sedentarisation. Since the implementation of Khrushchev's 'Gypsy decree' in the late 1950s, Soviet Roma have been ascribed to fixed addresses. In the words of one of my Roma acquaintances in his late forties: 'Khrushchev gave us land plots to build houses in exchange for our horses'. For many, however, mobility has remained important, but now people can go on long-term trips and trading expeditions without changing their places of residence or moving houses.

In independent Ukraine, the issue of the number of Servy and the very notion of the Roma 'diaspora' have become politicised. For activists and intelligentsia representing the Roma's cultural interests and rights, census data and the official status of Roma population are the main points of controversy in their engagement with the state. Like other groups that experienced discrimination or persecution during different periods in Soviet history (e.g. Jews, Germans and Greeks), some Roma have disguised their ethnicity by manipulating ethnic labels and declaring themselves to be non-Gypsies in Soviet censuses (Udovenko 2005; Kondenko 2006). According to the census of 2001 more than 47,000 Roma are recorded as living in Ukraine, including around 4,000 in the Odessa region,[8] but activists in Kiev and Odessa claim that the actual figures are much higher.[9] They also challenge the 'minority' status of Ukrainian Roma, arguing that Servy should be legally recognised as indigenous (*korennye*) inhabitants of Ukraine, alongside Ukrainians, Crimean Tatars and Gagauz, rather than only as an ethnic minority.[10]

My Servy acquaintances, who live in the village of N., approximately half an hour from the city centre by public transport, were not particularly interested in debates about official status categories; they envisioned themselves as native to Ukraine in spite of their supposedly ancient roots in India. While wider society seems to be generally unaware of differences between local Roma, these distinctions are prominent in Roma's images of themselves. In the families of my hosts, the demarcation lines between Gypsies in the locality were drawn with reference to different groups' places of 'origin', reflected in the names of these groups. People singled out Russian Gypsy, Moldovan Gypsies, Central Asian Gypsies ('Chinese gypsies') and *Krymchaki* or Gypsies who were said to have migrated from Crimea.

My Servy hosts contrasted themselves with these other Gypsies, as they did with *gazhje* (i.e. Russians and Ukrainians). I was told that the language of Moldovan Gypsies was unintelligible to Servy, that their dress style, featuring wide skirts and multi-coloured shawls, was too 'theatrical' or 'ethnic', their main economic pursuits (such as dealing in scrap metal) were very different and their custom of arranging marriages between children was truly backward. Russian Gypsies, by contrast, were seen as culturally similar to Servy, but they were not really able to understand or use the Servy's language properly and for polite forms of address the two groups used different Russian idioms. The Krymchaki were Muslims, and they were also said to comprise the majority of so-called 'urban' Gypsies (*gorodskie tsygane*) whose women dressed in trousers or short skirts and dated Russians and Armenians freely, without showing any concerns for (customary) female modesty and the honour of their families.

A certain contempt for the 'urban' Gypsies indicated an axis of differentiation that was not only focused on modes of conduct or female dress code. The census statistics might be skewed, but they provide some idea of the Roma's spatial distribution in the locality, showing that the majority live outside the regional capital: only 842 Roma are registered in Odessa.[11] There is, of course, a long history of Gypsies being excluded from major (post-)Soviet cities (see e.g. Lemon 2000:111–12), but people's own preferences also play an important role. My Servy hosts enjoyed living in proper houses with spacious courtyards and did not aspire to move to city apartments; they spoke of 'urban flats' (*gorodskie kvartiry*) as inferior places of residence, as 'birdhouses' (*skvorechnik*).

Until recently, living in the city's outskirts was also seen as convenient from the point of view of jobs on the state and collective farms. During the late Soviet period, the men worked mainly with horses on the farms and dealt in horses on the side; through their key business partners, Odessan Jews, they supplied horses to racetrack courses and for tourist entertainment. Roma women had a range of occupations: some were ordinary blue-collar workers employed in ethnically mixed work collectives in Odessa, others were engaged in trade, moving goods between different regions, often selling wares produced in Odessa's illegal workshops and smuggled by sailors from abroad and bringing deficit goods from other regions of Ukraine and the USSR.

With the post-Soviet decline of state farms, many Servy men have reoriented themselves to city-based occupations, working as taxi drivers, manual workers, butchers, dealers in various merchandise, etc. while women have turned mainly to commerce, both seasonal long-distance door-to-door trade and trade in Odessa's numerous markets. The days of employment on a par with other city's residents (e.g. as clerks, laboratory assistants, medical personnel and so on) seemed to them to be gone for good; these jobs were now hardly available and those that were available were not particularly desirable due to the meagre salaries. My acquaintances shared with me their aspirations of setting up their own shops or divination salons in the city, and so joining the ranks of recognised entrepreneurs (*predprinimateli*). Over the years of our acquaintanceship, a shop in the city still remained a distant dream, as any spare cash was quickly consumed by the house: an ever bigger plasma TV, a new karaoke and stereo system, a good quality washing machine, and so on.

A proper house – the bigger the better – embodies a host of important values for Servy, such as modernity, rootedness and economic prosperity. It is a material statement that differentiates modern sedentarised Servy from the 'nomadic' Servy of the past, as well as from the present-day 'street' (*ulichnye*) Gypsy beggars and the 'camp' (*tabornye*) Gypsies represented by some other Roma groups. It is a token of economic success, for those without houses are often disdained and seen as poor or destitute, 'living like refugees'. House-less Roma were also portrayed as simply having misplaced their cultural values, as caring more for superficial manifestations of material well-being in the form of shiny cars, expensive clothes and jewellery than for long-term investment in the family's prosperity. 'We make money to build houses, to buy good furniture, china, and everything for the house ... to leave something to our children', a Servy woman told me when explaining the importance of setting aside money for 'stone' (*kamen'*, i.e. 'bricks and mortar) whenever the family's budget allows.

In the scholarly literature, this emphasis on houses as the preferable form of residence is linked to Romas' desire to sustain family members' proximity by accommodating large kinship groups (cf. Fraser 1992). Over the last two decades, Servy living in the outskirts of Odessa have striven to build individual houses for each nuclear family, but the geographical proximity of related family houses remains important. In this way, people's kinship networks have become rooted in particular places/neighbourhoods and articulated as familial clusters among the ethnically diverse population of the city's suburbs. In the village of N., Servy families live side by side with Moldovan and Chinese Gypsies, Russians, Ukrainians and Koreans.

Despite my Servy hosts' preference for countryside houses and their socio-cultural distancing from 'urban' Gypsies, they are integrated into Odessa not only economically, but also affectively and often talk about it as 'their' city. 'I would not like to live in any other city', one of my well-travelled hostesses told me. 'Here, there are many cunning people. It is particularly nice to deal with real old Odessans. They would always have a joke to hand.... And when you say elsewhere that you are from Odessa, people understand that they are dealing with a smart person.'

Figure 3.1. A Roma grandmother in her courtyard. Photo by the author.

Odessa's new diaspora

Unlike the Servy, who see themselves as native to Ukraine and integral to Odessa, the city's Afghans form a new, post-Soviet diaspora with firm links to their homeland. One aspect of Afghan migrants' sensibility developed in the context of late Soviet modernity as it was experienced both in Afghanistan and via the provisioning of higher education in the USSR.[12] As Roy (1989) pointed out, 'Sovietisation' in Afghanistan put great emphasis on the modern way of life set off against traditional society. Modern (western) dress, dancing, drinking alcohol and less restricted relations between the sexes were stressed as pleasurable elements of Soviet modernisation, but the limits of Soviet influence were also omnipresent: they were notable in the Afghan family, the relations of patronage, the revival of religious practices and in the Afghan economy with its thriving private trade. In Soviet cities, Afghan students were a largely transient population; graduates were encouraged to return to Afghanistan where they were given political and professional posts or good jobs in the administration (Roy 1989: 49–52). These arrangements came to an end in 1992 when President Najibullah, formerly supported by the Soviets, was forced to resign and a civil war broke out in the country. Despite the rupture in political cooperation, those Afghan students who commenced their education in Ukraine before 1992 were allowed to finish their degrees for free, i.e. they were not charged for courses and lodging.

Former Afghan students as well as former Soviet allies and sympathisers comprise the core of the Afghan diaspora in Odessa.[13] There are also ongoing flows of Afghan refugees and illegal migrants; some pass through Ukraine on their way to the West; others arrive to join their relatives for a period of time and/or in the hope of eventually obtaining Ukrainian citizenship. And some are serial migrants, having prior experience of living in Russia, Pakistan, Dubai and so on. None of these are mutually exclusive categories. From the 1990s and, at least until the early 2000s, Afghans represented more than half of all refugees and asylum seekers in Ukraine from the non-CIS countries, concentrating mainly in Kiev and Odessa.[14] By 2009, Afghan asylum seekers and refugees were still the largest group registered in the Odessa refugee centre situated in the suburb of Chernomorka. Since asylum seekers are legally allowed to work in Ukraine, and the refugee centre has a limited capacity to provide accommodation, many Afghan asylum seekers cater for themselves and live in rented apartments.

Like many other ethnic groups in Odessa, the Afghan diaspora has its own 'ethno-cultural' organisation called the 'Afghan community' (*Afganskaia obshchina*). The community cooperates with the city council's department of internal affairs and the Odessa refugee centre and periodically organises high-profile cultural events in the city. For instance, in 2006 Navrus (New Year) celebrations organised by the diaspora featured Afghan musicians from Germany and were attended by Afghan diplomats from Kiev, as well as by representatives of the city authorities and the heads of other ethno-cultural centres registered in the city. In 2007, the head of the 'Afghan community' was elected chairman of the council representing the ethno-cultural organisations of all of Odessa's ethnic minorities.

By Odessan Afghans' own estimates there are at least 1,300 Afghans including children in the city; almost everyone knows everybody else in the community. Social networks of Afghans are predicated on kinship, a shared history of study in the USSR, and political and familial alliances back in Afghanistan. Although former Afghan students come from different social backgrounds (e.g. from the urban pro-Soviet elites and intelligentsia to ordinary rural families), friendships in Odessa are often established across status hierarchies. The vitality of networks is maintained and reproduced by work relationships at the 7th km market located just outside Odessa, the largest outdoor commodity market in Ukraine (see Humphrey and Skvirskaja 2009). More than ninety per cent of Afghan men in Odessa are said to work on the 7th km market. Some have businesses in the wholesale trade with branches in Kiev, Moscow and Dubai; others, especially those who cannot travel abroad freely due to the absence of Ukrainian passports or foreign visas, specialise in retail, often depending on Afghan wholesalers for their supply of goods; yet others, more recent migrants, work as salesmen and assistants in the shops or stalls of their relatives and friends. 'This market feeds all Afghanis', an Afghan wholesaler told me. The former students can also seek employment according to their qualifications, and some were offered jobs by their Ukrainian colleagues in Odessa's hospitals and clinics, but few, if any, seemed to consider formal employment to be economically worthwhile. A proven way to success is trade.

Whilst the 'Afghan community' is a formal body representing the Afghan diaspora[15] and has real power to sort out things with the local authorities and police, a mosque located at the industrial outskirts of Odessa functions as a locus of communal life. For the majority of male migrants, Friday is the only day off work at the 7th km market and people come regularly to the mosque to 'manifest' their belonging to the diaspora. The issue of piety seems to be rather secondary for many, for even those of my interlocutors who drank alcohol and did not consider themselves to be particularly religious would make an effort not to miss Friday prayers two weeks in a row. Various happenings in the life of the diaspora, even events such as the death of a family member in Afghanistan, require the attendance of community members. In private, people sometimes expressed discontent with what they saw as the community's excessive claims on their very limited free time, but they participated nonetheless. Despite, or because of, differences in migrants' economic resources and legal status (refugees, asylum seekers, Ukrainian citizens), they comprise a tight-knit group of mutual

Figure 3.2. The 7th km market at closing time. Photo by the author.

help and trust; internal tensions and controversies tend to be resolved by internal means – the local police and courts are not called upon.

Not unlike my Roma friends, those of my Afghan interlocutors who had travelled widely in Ukraine (and indeed elsewhere in the former Soviet Union) singled out Odessa as the most agreeable city in the country. The focus was not only on Odessa's commercial potential, but also on its diversity and relative tolerance to 'dark-skinned' foreigners in comparison to other Ukrainian (and Russian) cities. Odessa was perceived as being more accustomed to foreign-looking faces and therefore less hostile to newcomers. An extra bonus was its Russian-speaking milieu, for former Soviet students have been taught exclusively in Russian.

'Blacks' and social marginalisation

Although my Servy and Afghani interlocutors emphasised their attachment to Odessa, these same people were also highly conscious of the negative attitudes of wider society towards them. The idea of a plural city is invoked publicly as a matter of course to celebrate Odessa's diversity, but visible forms of difference also evoke an alternative popular imaginary. In Odessa, as in many parts of Russia and Ukraine, Eastern and Southern-looking ethnicities are habitually referred to by the racist slur 'blacks' (*chernye*). The term *nerusskie* (non-Russians) can also be heard as a more 'politically correct' or ironic gloss for 'blacks'. That is to say, *nerusskie* does not designate any particular ethnicity (simply meaning those who are not 'Slavs', or non-Russians) – and in Odessa, the 'native' population is very mixed – but indicates a category of 'aliens' *(chuzhie)*, those who are 'not us' or 'not like us'. Gypsies and Afghans may be visually differentiated on the street as different types of 'blacks', and they both challenge and live with the implications of being perceived as 'blacks'.

Before I turn to people's narratives of marginalisation, let me briefly introduce my own observations of wider society's attitudes. To start with, there are various Internet forums and chat rooms where Odessans and other Ukrainians actively attack 'unpatriotic' Jewish emigrants, 'Gypsy-criminals' and Asian immigrants.[16] There are also visible signs of intolerance of different 'others' in the city itself, such as offensive graffiti or anti-Russian demonstrations (some of which were organised by Ukrainian Cossacks in protest against the reconstruction of the monument to the Russian Empress Catherine the Great, see Skvirskaja and Humphrey 2007). These are often readily dismissed by 'native' Odessans as provocations by outsiders or the city's few madmen *(gorodskie sumashedshie)*. Yet, at the same time there are firm associations between particular people and places that nourish urban anxieties. For instance, one neighbourhood on the outskirts of the city that since the late 1980s/early 1990s has become known as 'Palermo' due to its drug trade, is also an area where many Roma live. 'Palermo', drug dealing and Gypsies have become an integral chain of associations. For many urbanites, 'Palermo' has simply become a 'Gypsy district'. This association does not remain unchallenged, but sometimes these challenges only go so far as to say that 'normal people [*normal'nye liudi*], non-Gypsy also live in Palermo'.

It is not just neighbourhoods that are surrounded by an air of suspicion coded by difference – buildings may be suspect as well. The Arab Cultural centre and mosque built in the city centre by a Syrian businessman (and a former student in Odessa) in 2002, is a good example, not unique to Odessa. (Public protests against 'minarets' have now become commonplace in many Western European cities.)[17] The plan to build a mosque adorned by minarets in the city's centre provoked a series of protests, both from Russian Orthodox clergymen and the ordinary public, claiming that Odessa had always been an Orthodox (*pravoslavnyi*) city. As a result, a compromise was found in a mosque cum 'Arab centre' design that excluded a minaret, but this strategy did not fail to generate a host of conspiracy theories. Some of my acquaintances among elderly 'native' Odessans speculated that a cache of arms and explosives might be hidden in the catacombs under the Arab Cultural centre. And from a middle-aged man, a former sailor turned journalist, I heard that there might be something even more uncanny going on, for the mosque is surrounded by several big churches in such a way that it seems to be at the centre of some geometrical figure marked by these churches; he could not or did not want to explain what this central positioning might entail or imply.

The mass media, both local and international, plays a role in generating negative public associations. Many Odessans have first-hand 'Gypsy-stories', but some of my non-Roma interlocutors referred me to local press and TV, pointing out that there was 'no smoke without fire'. Indeed, in recent newspaper archives, one comes across articles with headings like 'The specificities of ethnic rape', presenting the story of a teenager raped by a Gypsy man.[18] In summer 2007, a number of incidents involving Roma were reported on Odessa TV with the emphasis placed on ethnicity as the explanation of disturbances and people's antisocial behaviour. Likewise, many Odessans' attitudes towards Muslims, especially those arriving from abroad as students and entrepreneurs, were influenced by Western representations of 'the war on terror'.

Complete strangers in a shop or travelling by public transport occasionally shared with me a discourse of straightforward racial prejudice. As a summary of several voices, the argument runs as follows:

> Hitler was right in targeting the Gypsies and it is a pity that he did not manage to kill all of them. Tell me, who needs a nation [*natsionalnost'* – i.e. ethnic group] like that? They do not work, they do not serve in the army. They are thieves and tricksters. Some are dressed like us and live in houses like us, but they are drug dealers and swindlers.... Hitler should also have targeted other blacks, the Muslims. He should have moved in that direction, further east, to kill the blacks.

This Hitler-discourse was shared by people of different ages but from similar working-class backgrounds, some of whom had never had an encounter with a Gypsy whilst others lived in the same area as my Servy hosts. Such comments were not, however, heard in the circles of Odessa's 'polite society', among its intelligentsia, who were keen proponents of urban harmony. Indeed, even raising the question of other people's or one's own ethnicity might be considered bad form – 'in Odessa we do not care about ethnicity; here we have people of "Odessan nationality"' – but then the intelligentsia's social and professional space in the city more often than not remained remote and withdrawn from the worlds of ordinary 'blacks'. Some of my interlocutors among the 'native' Odessan intelligentsia even claimed that they had never been to the 7th km market (a place where all Odessa's newcomers are visibly exposed to visitors) and referred to 'foreign' or 'unfamiliar' looking people as 'some incomprehensible personalities' (*neponiatnye lichnosti*) they could not clearly identify.

The subjects of these racialised representations have, of course, their own stories to tell and accommodations to make. My Servy interlocutors dwelled on the long history of their marginalisation as a trading minority and as 'speculators'[19] during the Soviet period. Marina, in her late thirties, told me that she was born in prison, because her pregnant mother received a jail sentence for selling knitwear she used to bring from Latvia, commenting that 'now everybody is engaged in the same kind of speculation, but they just call it business and it is fine'. Today, Marina's own small-scale, sporadic trade in clothing is what marks her commonality with many of her Russian and Ukrainian neighbours. Yet, this conformity with what have become mainstream pursuits does not undermine the ease with which Servy can be 'denied' both moral parity with wider society and the few social entitlements provided by the state. This became particularly evident during Marina's two-year-long attempts to receive the plots of land from the administration of N. to which Servy and all other official residents in the neighbourhood were entitled.

The local authorities did not dispute the family's legal claims; they were open about their fear of losing the support of their electorate were they 'to give land to the Gypsies'. Not being acknowledged as a part of the local electorate and having failed as individual claimants, the Servy families decided to resort to a collective action. They eventually succeeded in receiving their plots of land by playing up their 'Gypsiness': a group of Servy relatives and friends had registered a Gypsy 'commune' (*obshchina*) and sought support from the Odessa Roma Congress. Instead of exercising their right to land as ordinary Ukrainian citizens, they could succeed only by performing difference and by being the first among the local Roma to do so. Marina's prognosis was that 'after we have gotten the land, and now that the administration can always claim that Roma are allocated land, other Gypsies here have no chance for years to come'.

Meanwhile, in Afghan migrants' view of the urban landscape, their 'black-ness' makes them a visible target for local bandits, hooligans and police whom they see as being motivated by the possibility of some easy money. Unlike the Gypsies, who might be avoided on the street for they are seen as possessing a cunning ability to extract money from the public, Afghans (and other 'foreigners' directly associated with market activities) are often approached on the street. Their experiences of marginalisation are first of all related to physical and verbal violence in public places. Aamir, a refugee in his early twenties, told me that he was regularly accosted with the expression 'Hey Blacks! Hand over the money'.

My Afghan acquaintances admitted that to avoid unpleasant or dangerous confrontations in the city they had to ignore racist appellations or pretend that they did not understand Russian. A range of safety precautions was also in place. People rented apartments close to one another so that they could travel to and from the market as a group. Some always carried a stun device, which caused an electric shock, for self-protection. Many, especially recent arrivals, tended to spend a substantial amount of their free time at home watching Afghan TV run by the worldwide diaspora (mainly the US-based one) and browsing the Internet.

The city was perceived as a segregated social space where it was important to know where and when one could venture as a 'black' person. But even some supposedly established relations in the immediate neighbourhood could not always be taken for granted. Aamir told me about an incident in a shop where he was sold a defective mobile phone. When he tried to exchange the phone, a shop assistant insulted him and pushed him away. What upset Aamir was that he was treated so rudely in his local shop where people knew him well and where many Afghans used to shop regularly. He decided not to mention the incident to his brothers and friends in order not to provoke any further confrontations.

But my Afghan and Servy interlocutors did not only retreat in the face of social exclusion and banal racism in the city. Aamir would turn a blind eye to humiliating comments on the street or in a corner shop, but he was firm about not giving in to police extortion. Once he spent several hours in the police station refusing to pay for an imaginary stamp in his passport and not allowing his Afghan friends to 'buy him out': 'After a while they just had to let me go. If you pay them once, they will never leave the Afghans in peace. One should not be afraid.' Like ordinary 'native' Odessans, the Afghans (and Servy) fully participate in the bribe-based local economy, but they also draw a fine line between bribes aimed at achieving desired ends and bribes that could lead to ever greater humiliation of, and extortion from, the 'blacks'.

People's responses to being stigmatised as 'blacks' take a variety of forms. As they were unable to control negative representations of themselves, Servy often used a strategy of straightforward verbal shaming. Maria, in her mid thirties, told me proudly how she managed to persuade a Slav goldsmith in Odessa to accept her nephew as an apprentice in his workshop:

> He [the goldsmith] seemed very surprised and displeased that a Gypsy boy was sent to him for training by the college. 'What kind of internationalism am I going to have here with a Gypsy?' he asked me. 'We are honest people', I told him. 'It is hurtful to hear such things. Do you think that my boy is a thief because he is born a Gypsy? He has studied, he wants to become a professional jeweller, like you are, not a thief.' He had nothing to say to that and accepted my nephew.[20]

One way of dealing with racist labelling can be traced in discursive inversions of received popular images and categories by 'blacks'. On the 7th km market, I observed how the term *nerusskie* (non-Russians) was appropriated by 'black' traders to address obviously 'local' men of paler complexion. This passing on of the *nerusskii* attribute took place within the single social setting of a food stall. 'Hey, non-Russians, two beers, please', was the initial address by a Slav-looking man to an Arab bartender, and a few minutes later, the Arab bartender asked the next 'white' customers in line: 'So, non-Russians, what would you like?' This circulation of the *nerusskii* label provoked smiles from the few people present and effectively defused the exclusionary nature of the attribute. In a similar mode, my Servy hosts' stories often exhibited a transfer of Gypsy stereotypes onto non-Roma. Thus Marina, who was born in prison, suspected that her twin brother had not died in childbirth as her mother had been told, but was stolen by a childless Ukrainian prison guard. Nobody in the family saw the boy's body, no death certificate was ever issued, and the family was truly concerned as to what had happened to the boy. In this narrative of the family's history, the stereotype of 'the baby-stealing Gypsies' is projected onto the figure of the Ukrainian woman.

These stereotypes are often rhetorically deployed in a reverse manner: Servy women's stories were peppered with episodes of them doing 'non-Gypsy things' from the point of view of wider society. If beggars on the street or in public transport are often identified as Gypsies, Gypsies giving money to beggars, especially to the 'white' ones, is described as a gesture of compassion that undermines ethnic stereotypes. Maria's younger sister, Olga, recounted the shock of an elderly Russian woman to whom she once gave money for a taxi: 'The old one (*starushka*) was almost crying. She was so grateful, she said she would have never expected to get money from a Gypsy in her life!'

These discursive inversions of stereotypes are certainly aimed at mocking and/or challenging some forms of stigmatisation. However, people who deploy these inversions are equally steadfast in maintaining and accentuating their difference in encounters with others, simultaneously producing and entertaining a plurality of self-images (cf. Mageo and Knauft 2002). A well-to-do Afghan trader, now a Ukrainian citizen, mentioned to me his intention to send his nephew to study at a university in China or Dubai (rather than to the West or Ukraine), because 'The East should remain the East. We are the East' (*Vostok dolzhen ostavat'sa Vostokom. My eto Vostok*). Likewise, Servy could postulate their affinity with other 'blacks' in Odessa, such as Caucasians, whereby 'blackness' serves as a source of moral solidarity, however illusory. When an Armenian trader cheated Maria on a bazaar, her response appealed to a sense of betrayed affinity: 'You are black and we are black. Do not you have enough mugs (*lokhi*) around [to cheat]?'

In relationships with the (Slav) majority, mockery and inversions of racial stereotypes as well as affirmations of difference highlight ethnic-diasporic experiences of imagined 'anticommunity' (to borrow Lemon's (2000: 78) reversal of Benedict Anderson's formulation). The perception of one's 'otherness' in these 'anticommunities' does not entirely dominate the consciousness of those thus marginalised. Rather, as we shall see below, it is concomitant with the different registers of cosmopolitanism present within specific structures of power and cultural practices. If we recognise that any cosmopolitan register is itself culturally and politically conditioned, we can then address the question of the parameters (and ambiguities) of cosmopolitan subjectivity in each particular case.

Endogamous and selective cosmopolitans

The individual life histories of both my Afghan and Servy acquaintances often bring into focus the dilemmas posed by marriage and marriage strategies, foregrounding people's vision of interethnic mixing in the intimate sphere. Among Servy, marriage celebrations are also opportunities to search for potential suitors for the younger generation and divorcees within the dispersed Roma community. Marriages with Ukrainian and Russian neighbours, usually from similar, working-class backgrounds, are not uncommon, but they are tainted with disapproval or expectations of failure. The unattractiveness of a mixed marriage is explained by the inability or unwillingness of a non-Roma spouse to uphold the values and attitudes that Roma consider important.

From a Servy perspective, a working-class Slav man is more likely to drink heavily and live off unstable income rather than investing time and effort in securing prosperity for his family. Marina's sister's first husband was Russian and Marina did not have a good word to say about him:

> He was a cool guy who rode a motorbike. My sister fell in love with him and although our father did not approve of her choice, she married him. Then he stole something and went to prison. She waited for him. When he came back he did not want to work with her father and continued to hang out with his guys. They had a life of sheer poverty for years. Second time she married a Gypsy, and look at her now – she has a big house, she has everything, her Gypsy husband is a real master (*khoziain*).

For my Servy hosts, when Roma men married Slav girls, it was seen as a loss of potential marriage partners for 'our' girls. Roma women were also concerned with Slav women's unwillingness to adopt Gypsy ways and show some 'cultural' flexibility. Tatiana complained to me at length about her Russian sister-in-law:

> The forbidden fruit is always sweet, so my brother married his high-school sweetheart. That Russian has a temper on her ... I try to teach her our ways, how to serve tea our way when the guests are in the house: not to fill the glass completely and to add a slice of apple. She listens and always does it her way. Now she told my brother that she does not want to live with our mother and they moved out. But he is the only son, he has to take care of our parents. My only hope is that he will eventually grow up and divorce her. Who needs an in-law like that!

This Servy woman's disapproval of mixed marriages was not simply about the preservation of some essential Gypsy-ness within the family. For a minority group that is seen as 'alien' at home (in their own country and city) but that strives to articulate its normality (its 'being like everybody else'), the lack of versatility on the part of their Slav in-laws is interpreted as a token of disrespect and cultural arrogance. My unmarried hosts claimed that they would rather stay single or marry a different type of Roma (i.e. non-Servy) than consider the possibility of starting a family with a *gazhje*.

If marriage is one instance where cosmopolitan openness to the world is negotiated, for Afghan migrants it poses a set of issues somewhat different from those of the Servy. The mosque, as I mentioned, functions as a social centre for the diaspora in Odessa, but it is the natal household in Afghanistan that is the locus of 'managerial' power and male migrants' emotional attachments. The majority of migrants are young and middle-aged men whose parents continue to live in Afghanistan, receive remittances from their children and make strategic decisions regarding the reallocation of accumulated funds. Parental decisions and money often stand behind the type of education their children receive, the migration routes they choose and the people they can marry. Complex negotiations within the family group take into account children's own inclinations and preferences, but parental wishes that place family interests and well-being above individual concerns are rarely overturned or challenged directly.

One's reputation and extended family connections function as an entry pass into the Afghan community, be it in Odessa or elsewhere in the world; such 'an entry pass' is indispensable because the migrants' ability to make a living, find a job or set up their own business is largely dependent on relations of mutual help in a tight-knit transnational diaspora. Abdul, a successful entrepreneur on the 7th km market, with siblings living in Norway, Denmark and Dubai, put it bluntly:

> The father is like the law. He can make one phone call to our people to say that you are a bad person and that it is it. One phone call can ruin your life forever and everywhere – in Odessa, in Dubai… You can lose everything – your mother, because she is with your father; your relatives on all continents; your business; your place in paradise; and all respect.

In the realm of marriage, familial practices of discipline and control are of great importance. Like the majority of Odessa's married Afghan men, Abdul has a wife from Afghanistan. Prior to his marriage, he had a local Slav girlfriend. This was a serious, long-term relationship; Abdul was ready to buy his own apartment and marry the Ukrainian woman, when his father found him a bride in Afghanistan and informed him about this alternative marriage arrangement. When I met Abdul he had already been married for several years and seemed rather content.

> After all it is easier to make a good family with a person from your own culture. Had I married my Ukrainian woman, she would have wanted to bring up our children in one way and I would have wanted to do it differ-

ently. Our women are also less controlling in everyday life. I can tell my
wife that I am going on business and she never asks me any questions.
Anyway, after ten years or so, love just turns into a habit.

In contrast to male migrants, who follow Western dress code, drink and
sometimes enjoy the city's night life, their Afghan spouses tend to wear
shalwar kameez or long skirts and are rarely visible in public and economic
life: there are no Afghan female traders or sales assistants on the market,
and no Afghan women were present during the celebrations of Navrus
organised by the 'Afghan community' in 2006. That said, although marriages continue to be arranged with brides from Afghanistan and Afghan
diasporas elsewhere, marriages with Slav women do take place and many
men, both married and bachelors, have relationships and liaisons with local women. Familial obligations and conformity do not shut men off from
romantic and sexual engagements with Russian, Ukrainian, Bulgarian
women, etc. and the maintenance of 'traditional' gender roles in the diaspora cannot be attributed solely to some cultural 'stubbornness' in a new
environment or the far-reaching power of family patriarchs. At least for
some migrants, cultural compliance is an inherently political, long-sighted
strategy and works as a way of securing a smooth return to Afghanistan if
the need or opportunity should arise.[21] Abdul, who has spent more than
twenty years in Ukraine, speaks fluent Russian and has become a Ukrainian citizen, still entertains the idea that one day he will be able to run his
business in Odessa from his hometown of Kandahar: 'I see this place in my
dreams. Many of our people want to go back. I do not want to spend all my
life in Odessa.'

A strong preference for endogamy and close economic cooperation in
both the Afghan and Roma communities helps to fashion them as distinct
corporate groups. At the same time, these communities are far from being
'closed', because knowledge of the traditions and ways of various 'others', as
well as friendships, and commercial and professional relationships across
'ethnic/cultural boundaries', define what it is to be an Afghan migrant or a
Servy. Whereas for an ordinary Slav Odessan, engagement with difference
may largely be a matter of individual dispositions or preferences, for these
marginalised groups, their economic success and the very possibility of
making a living is predicated on their ability to master the cultural diversity
of commercial structures and social networks. The cosmopolitan subjectivity of the marginalised-groups-cum-imagined-anticommunities is articulated not so much as an awareness of the equal validity of other cultures
and values (e.g. Werbner 2006: 498), still less as an idea of a common moral
community (Parry 2008), but as the ability to forge networks of trustworthy
partners and friends based on one's fluency in several languages, knowl-

edge of the international and/or local markets and first-hand experience of other cultures. Wide networks that cut across different occupational and ethnic groups are ever more essential given the corrupt institutional environment in Ukraine; 'There is no law; there is no state in Ukraine. There is only money', as Abdul's friend once put it.

Afghan migrants place great weight on the comparability of the other's entrepreneurial culture and cosmopolitan skills when applying criteria of inclusion/exclusion in their far-reaching networks. Chinese, for instance, who work the 'next container' to these Afghans on the 7th km market and rent apartments next door in the cheaper neighbourhoods, are excluded from the Afghans' circles of sociality and commercial relations because they are seen as deprived of any cultural openness, only honouring deals with their compatriots and leading particularly secluded lives. Central Asian Muslims and people from the Caucasus (Azeri, Georgians, Chechens, etc.) are, in turn, said to have lost their commercial culture and civility under the Soviets. 'They carry knives on the market! They used to have great traders in the past but do not have this culture anymore – now they are "neither fish nor fowl"', was the opinion of Mustafa's, an Afghani in his late twenties. One exception among the post-Soviet Muslims is reserved for the Tajik-speaking population of Uzbekistan and Tajikistan who are seen as having belonged to the same geopolitical space as the Afghanis. Abdul (a Pashtun), who had a young Tajik man working with him on the market, put it this way: 'My grandparents are buried in Samarqand. Before it was a single country; we understand each other well'.

Arabs, Iranians, Indians and Pakistanis are, in turn, set apart from the discredited post-Soviets and considered, in the main, to be sound and reliable partners. Knowledge of these diverse peoples is based on encounters that take place not only in Odessa, but also in Russia, Dubai, Pakistan and elsewhere, where many Odessan Afghans have previously lived and worked. The attitudes of these serial migrants do not suggest, as some theorists of subaltern cosmopolitanism have claimed, that global migrant 'highways' necessarily pose fewer entry requirements or forge cross-national social relations in the intimate context of working side-by-side (Malcomson 1998; Werbner 1999). The case of Odessan Afghanis shows that knowledge and cosmopolitan skills can be used to exclude and 'select' not only in circles of transnational elites, but also lower down the social hierarchy.

Being less global in their scale of commercial relations, local Servy cultivate their cosmopolitan sensibilities by incorporating local 'others' into their domestic and business realms. Switching linguistic codes is a common strategy used to establish a sense of affinity both with the strangers encountered on the long-distance trade expeditions and with their Ukrainophone and Russophone neighbours. At home, my hosts spoke either

Roma Servy dialect or Ukrainian mixed with Servy words, but they would effortlessly switch into Russian when talking to me or into Ukrainian when, for instance, negotiating prices with a Ukrainian-speaking seamstress. This might appear insignificant, but Servy's linguistic strategy is noticeably different from the non-reciprocal bilingualism of wider society whereby each partner carries on in her preferred language (Russian or Ukrainian) that is common in Odessa and other parts of Ukraine (see Bilaniuk 2005; Skvirskaja 2009). Maria told me that it was equally important to master regional linguistic variations and that when she went to trade in West Ukraine, it took her only a couple of days to pick up a different Ukrainian dialect and talk 'like the locals'. Maria was visibly pleased with her competent shifting between different linguistic registers; her multilingualism was a way of establishing friendly relations with non-Roma, and friends are very important for Roma: 'Many friends means a lot of money' (*Mnogo druzei, mnogo deneg*). Maria told me that this was an Armenian saying and that she fully endorsed it.

In their everyday and professional lives, Servy are both dependent on and enjoy having a range of contacts and friends. Odessan Jews are held in particular esteem; cooperation and close relations between these peoples stretched as far back as my Servy interlocutors could remember. In the Soviet times, Jews supplied Roma with counterfeit goods produced in back yards and 'underground' workshops and functioned as middlemen in the Odessan horse trade. These relations produced respect for one another and some long-lasting friendships. People sometimes attended each other's celebrations and funerals. Although the new economic situation and the mass emigration of Odessan Jews (see Sapritsky, this volume) have modified the scope of Servy-Jewish cooperation, some links still remain in place. When Maria's sister's family decided to bring up their children as professional goldsmiths, they entrusted the children's private training to an 'old Jew' in Odessa.

Servy families may not welcome non-Servy as marriage partners, but they include them in their circles of sociality as domestic helpers in residence, and the institution of godparenthood is used to cement particularly close or valuable friendships with other Christian groups. Even the poorest in the Servy community would not provide services to other Roma households, such as care for the elderly, babysitting, cooking and cleaning. Instead, for such tasks Servy take on young girls and boys from poor Slav households (and female Slav helpers are treated very similarly to female Servy in-laws who are expected to do a great deal of domestic work under the supervision of the family's matriarch). Over the years, Servy families may host several members of the same household as domestic help. In these arrangements, Roma women seem to enjoy the role of patrons of their helpers and their families, seeing them as a pool of affordable labour, but also helping with advice and money when the need arises. Through this domestic workforce, Servy gain first-hand knowledge of how the less privileged live in other communities.

Godparenthood, in turn, tends to frame relations with people of equal standing or from even more prosperous families, both in the immediate neighbourhood, the city, and in far-away places. Godparents are first of all chosen from among kin, but given the Servy 'norm' of having up to four sets of godparents for one child, godparenthood also creates and maintains relations with other Christians who are not relatives but who are business partners, neighbours and friends representing different ethnicities, e.g. the Russians, Ukrainians and Armenians. As a result of all these arrangements that seek to engage with non-Roma, an ordinary Servy claims, and indeed takes pride in, having deep insights into the affairs and cultural particularities of their non-Roma compatriots.

Conclusion

There are multiple forms of coexistence at play in post-Soviet Odessa. The racist Soviet construct of 'blacks' (*chernye*) and more recent suspicions of 'otherness' nourished by widespread economic insecurity and images generated by post-9/11 politics coexist with cherished public images of the historically diverse and still tolerant city. In considering two distinct types of Odessa's 'aliens', representing old local and new immigrant groups, I have attempted to make a point about the less obvious aspects of urban coexistence that can be deemed 'post-cosmopolitan' (see the Introduction to this volume). On the one hand, the city's marginalised communities now tend to live up to their reputation as closed and inward-looking corporate groups. Where the former Soviet work collectives (factories, collective farms, kindergartens, hospitals, offices and so on) were an inescapable social space of mixing and engagement, in post-Soviet Ukraine, the unattractiveness or inaccessibility of jobs in formal establishments (factories, schools, hospitals, firms) has led to the proliferation of largely ethnic networks of trust and commerce where strict 'entry requirements' often apply.

Yet, both externally imposed and internally generated social boundaries coexist with particular cosmopolitan dynamics. What the examples of Afghan migrants and Servy families show us is that inclusive thinking and practices must not be considered in opposition to, or as distinct from, people's ethnic worlds. Afghanis and Servy can, each in their own specific way, be seen as 'selective' and 'endogamous' cosmopolitans. In other words, cosmopolitanism does not have to be exercised as personal autonomy from one's own culture (cf. Hannerz 1990).

The same cultural repertoire that postulates endogamy as a culturally appropriate practice puts great value on the mastery of cultural differences and diversity in everyday and commercial life.

Strathern's (1991) observation on cosmopolitanism in relation to scholarly habits helps to highlight a key aspect of the 'endogamous' and 'selective' cosmopolitan subjectivity of my interlocutors. She writes: 'the cosmopolitan is more than the consumer, ... and more than the tourist, for she or he *works* to keep active this sense of complexity in claiming it as a source of personal and professional identity' (1991: 20, emphasis added). On the margins of Odessa's wider society, people's mastery of and pride in dealing with complexity often offsets their experiences of local hostilities and indifference. Cosmopolitan competences and openness are cultivated with, and without, expectations of reciprocity because these competences are recognised cultural values and a source of identity. While wider society often eagerly claims urban cosmopolitanism for itself, it is those at the margins who have to actively work to keep cosmopolitanism alive in the post-Soviet city.

NOTES

I am grateful to Matthew Carey for his companionship during my fieldwork in Odessa and his insightful comments on this chapter.

1. Odessa's reputation as a tolerant multiethnic city reaches far beyond national boundaries. In December 2006, Thomas Hammerberg, the EU's human right's commissioner, stated that the Odessa region was a very interesting model for the peaceful coexistence of people of different nationalities and religious beliefs, and that the region could serve as an example to all European countries.
2. Odessa is a special city in this respect, for while the political elites of other major Ukrainian cities have focused on the struggle for political influence at the centre (Kiev), Odessa's political elites have mainly been engaged in the promotion of their city as an international centre and have kept aloof from this struggle (cf. Bukkvoll 2001: 101).
3. Cf. Humphrey (1996/7) on myth-making and narratives of the disposed in post-Soviet Russia.
4. See e.g. Sifneos (2005) on the Greek diaspora in Odessa in the eighteenth and nineteenth centuries.
5. See Baer's (2007) discussion of the Dönme religious minority (i.e. Jews converted to Islam in the seventeenth century) in Ottoman Salonica and Istanbul.
6. The idea of 'vernacular cosmopolitism' suggested by Bhabha (1996) centres on the coexistence of two distinct registers – local or cultural loyalties ('rootedness') on the one hand, and the translocal, transcendent, universal or modernist, etc., on the other.
7. See also Golubovskii and Markina (2005).
8. http://ukrcensus.gov.ua.

9. See, for example, 'Development communities and improved social conditions for Ukrainian Roma' report of 5 November 2003, available on http://www. hartford-hwp.com/archives/63/380.html.

10. The first issue of the 'Roma legal newspaper' (*Pomani tlarmenvadeski patrin*), published in February 2003 by the Roma Congress of Odessa region, criticised depictions of India as the 'great-fatherland' that Roma should consider as their actual homeland. As the argument runs, since Roma have never had, and do not have, a nation state, they can hardly be considered a diasporic population. (The Roma Congress of Odessa region was founded in 1998, and includes both individual Roma and independent Roma organisations.) In contrast to 'minority' status, categorisation as an indigenous people entails protection according to the international conventions.

11. http://www.misto.odessa.ua/index.php?u=gorod/stat, accessed on 15 January 2010.

12. In the late 1980s, there were about 10,000 full-time Afghan students in the USSR (Roy 1989: 56).

13. For instance, a prominent member of the Afghan pro-communist government, and a defence minister under Najibullah, General Mohammad Aslam Watanjar, was in exile in Odessa until his death in 2000. http://news.bbc.co.uk/1/hi/world/south_asia/1037290.stm.

14. 'A review of the refugees' needs in Ukraine. Capacity Assessment', 2001. http://www.uames.org.ua/index.php?option=com_content&view=article&id=9:a-review-of-the-refugee-needs-in-ukraine-and-local-capacity-assessment-&catid=3:2010-05-23-14-51-23&Itemid=18, accessed on 11 March 2008.

15. The 'Afghan community' is not free from internal conflicts. In 2009 it was on the verge of dividing into 'Pashtun' and 'Tajik' segments.

16. See, for example, Forum '*Tsygane i kak s nimi borot'sia*', active in 2006, http://www.muz-prosvet.com/vb/showthread.php?p=8854#post8933, accessed on 13 October 2010.

17. See, for example, David Charter's article in *The Times*, 11 February 2010, p. 41.

18. 'Osobennosti natsional'nogo iznasilovania', *Vremia Ch* (2002), 3 August, no. 29:12.

19. The activity of reselling 'deficit' goods for profit was considered a criminal offence in the Soviet period and people engaged in this activity, called 'speculators' (*spekulianty*), were widely despised.

20. The jeweller here apparently mocks the Soviet discourse on 'internationalism' that implies (working class-based) 'friendship between peoples'.

21. Cf. Ferguson (1999) on Copperbelt miners.

REFERENCES

Baer, M. 2007. 'Globalisation, Cosmopolitanism, and the Dönme in Ottoman Salonica and Turkish Istanbul', *Journal of World History* 18(2): 141–70.

Bhabha, Homi. 1996. 'Unsatisfied Notes on Vernacular Cosmopolitanism', in P.C. Pfeiffer and L. Garcia-Moreno (eds), *Text and Narration*. Columbia, S.C., pp. 191–207.

Bilaniuk, L. 2005. *Contested Tongues. Language Politics and Cultural Correction in Ukraine*. Ithaca and London.

Bukkvoll, Tor. 2001. 'Ukraine and the Black Sea Region', in T. Aybak (ed.), *Politics of the Black Sea, Dynamics of Cooperation and Conflict*. London and New York, pp. 85–114.

Charter, D. 2010. 'Steel Town Divided over Mosque Minaret amid Fears of Islamic Quest for Power', *The Times*, 11 February, p. 41.

Clifford, James. 1992. 'Travelling Cultures', in L. Grossberg, C. Nelson, P. Treichler (eds), *Cultural Studies*. London and New York, pp. 96–116.

Ferguson, J. 1999. *Expectations of Modernity: Myths and Meanings of Urban Life on the Zambian Copperbelt*. Berkeley.

Fraser, A. 1992. *The Gypsies*. Oxford.

Golubovskii, E. and V. Markina. 2005. 'Poi, moia gitara, poi..', *Passazh*, May: 42–43.

Hannerz, U. 1990. 'Cosmopolitans and Locals in World Culture', *Theory, Culture and Society* 7: 237–51.

———. 1992. *Cultural Complexity, Studies in the Social Organisation of Meaning*. New York.

Humphrey, C. 1996/7. 'Myth-Making, Narratives, and the Dispossessed in Russia', *Cambridge Anthropology* 19(2): 70–92.

Humphrey, C. and V. Skvirskaja. 2009. 'Trading Places: Post-socialist Container Markets and the City', *Focaal* 55: 61–73.

Kondenko, M. 2006. 'The Opinion of the Initiative Group "Roma of Ukraine" on the Second National Report submitted by Ukraine Pursuant to Article 25, Paragraph 1 of the Framework Convention for the Protection of National Minorities', The Initiative Group 'Roma of Ukraine'. Available on: http://www. minelres.lv/reports/ukraine/PDF_Roma_of_Ukraine_eng.pdf.

Laidlaw, J. 2002. 'For an Anthropology of Ethics and Freedom', *JRAI* 8(2): 311–32.

Lemon, A. 2000. *Between Two Fires: Gypsy Performance and Romani Memory from Pushkin to Postsocialism*. Durham and London.

Mageo, Jeannette Marie, and Bruce M. Knauft. 2002. 'Introduction: Theorizing Power and the Self', in J.M. Mageo (ed.), *Power and the Self*. Cambridge, pp. 1–25.

Malcomson, Scott L. 1999. 'The Varieties of Cosmopolitan Experience', in Ph. Cheah and B. Robbins (eds), *Cosmopolitics: Thinking and Feeling Beyond the Nation*. Minneapolis, pp. 233–45.

Ong, A. 1999. *Flexible Citizenship: The Cultural Logics of Transnationality*. Durham and London.

Parry, Jonathan. 2008. 'Cosmopolitan Values in a Central Indian Steel Town', in P. Werbner (ed.), *Anthropology and the New Cosmopolitanism: Rooted, Feminist and Vernacular Perspectives*. Oxford, pp. 325–44.

Pollock, Sheldon. 2002. 'Cosmopolitan and Vernacular in History', in *Cosmopolitanism*. Durham and London, pp. 15–53.

Rapport, N. 2007. 'An Outline for Cosmopolitan Study', *Current Anthropology* 48(2): 257–83.

Roy, Oliver. 1989. 'The Sovietization of Afghanistan', in M. Hauner and R.L. Canfield (eds), *Afghanistan and the Soviet Union. Collision and Transformation*. Boulder, San Francisco, London, pp. 48–60.

Sifneos, E. 2005. '"Cosmopolitanism" as a Feature of the Greek Commercial Diaspora', *History and Anthropology* 16(1): 97–111.

Skvirskaja, Vera. '"Language is a Political Weapon" or on Language Troubles in Post-Soviet Odessa', in Juliane Besters-Dilger (ed.), *Language Policy and Language Situation in Ukraine. Analysis and Recommendations*. Frankfurt am Main and Berlin, pp. 175–200.

Skvirskaja, Vera and C. Humphrey. 2007. 'Odessa: skol'zskii gorod i uskol'zaiushchii kosmopolitizm', *Acta Eurasica* 1(35): 87–116.

Strathern, M. 1991. *Partial Connections*. Lanham and New York.

Udovenko, G. 2005. 'Suchastny prolemy zakhistu prav ta interesiv romiv Ukrainy', in *Pro suchastne stanovyshche romiv v Ukraini. Zbornik materialiv za pidsumkamy slukhan'*. Kiev.

Werbner, P. 1999. 'Global Pathways. Working Class Cosmopolitans and the Creation of Transnational Ethnic Worlds', *Social Anthropology* 7: 17–35.

———. 2006. 'Vernacular Cosmopolitanism', *Theory, Culture & Society* 23(2–3): 496–98.

Chapter 4

'A Gate, but Leading Where?' In Search of Actually Existing Cosmopolitanism in Post-Soviet Tbilisi

MARTIN DEMANT FREDERIKSEN

Introduction

In his novel *Ali and Nino* (2000) Kurban Said paints a vivid picture of Georgia's capital Tbilisi at the turn of the twentieth century as a culturally varied and multi-religious city. Imagine a bustling city with cobbled streets, wooden houses with wide balconies and intricate carvings, all lying along the Mtkvari River and climbing the surrounding hills, with a blend of a wide variety of churches, synagogues, mosques and a lively bazaar: 'This town with its eighty different peoples, each with their own language ... Armenian peddlers, Kurdish fortune-tellers, Persian cooks, Ossetian priests, Russians, Arabs, Ingush, Indians: all the peoples of Asia meet in the bazaar of Tiflis' (Said 2000 [1937]: 118). This is a literary evocation of Tbilisi when the city was a melting pot centrally located on the Silk Route connecting Asia with Europe. In his description, however, Kurban Said also touches upon the ambivalence of this location in the middle of the Caucasus: between the Caspian and Black seas, between East and West. As the Muslim protagonist Ali notes upon a visit to Tbilisi: 'Was this the gate to Europe? No, of course not. This was part of us, and yet so very different from the rest of us. A gate, but leading where?' (2000: 109).

Today, international guidebooks as well as local tourist information publications continue to highlight the cosmopolitan atmosphere in Tbilisi. As one government sponsored tourist brochure states: 'a wide variety of nationalities [have], down through the ages, made their home in Tbilisi. The old town still has its Jewish, Azeri and Armenian quarters. The mosque, synagogue, Armenian and Georgian orthodox churches are all within a stones throw' (Department of Tourism and Resorts 2007). Yet, although it is still a bustling city, seventy years of Soviet rule and almost twenty years of post-independence turmoil and societal changes have in many ways altered Tbilisi. At present, what could actually be seen as cosmopolitan is often taken locally as intrusions rather than natural parts of the city. Further, since the gaining of independence in 1991, nationalism has been an increasing part of political life in Georgia. Interestingly, while promoting Tbilisi as a cosmopolitan city, the current government has at the same time promoted the Rose Revolution, after which it came to power, as a 'rebirth of the Georgian nation' (Shatirishvili 2009). Moreover, we see today issues of sharp ethnic and territorial segregation, and wars politically legitimised through ethnic lines of reasoning (van der Zande 2009: iii). In this chapter I follow Bruce Robbins' notion of 'actually existing cosmopolitanism' in order to examine this situation. Cosmopolitanism, Robbins argues, has to be understood as a 'fundamental devotion to the interest of humanity as a whole'; a detachment from the ordinary commitments and affiliations of the nation (Robbins 1998: 1). Interdependence and acknowledgement, then, between different people(s) seems to be at the root of the cosmopolitan. In order for cosmopolitanism to 'actually exist' a sense of coherence between the social actors within a given social world is thus necessary. If cosmopolitanism is to exist within the confines of a nation, the ability to think and feel beyond the nation is a prerequisite (Cheah and Robbins 1998).

In what follows I explore how in Tbilisi today some types of 'difference' continue to be seen as a natural part of the city whereas others are seen as intrusions, making it questionable whether cosmopolitanism actually exists. I take my point of departure in a seemingly banal love story, which is *Ali and Nino*, and compare this early twentieth-century description of the Caucasus and specifically the cosmopolitan atmosphere in Tbilisi at this time to the situation I know first hand from my own field experience in the city within recent years.[1] I pursue Ali's statement quoted above and use this as a window to explore what – if anything – could be called cosmopolitan in Tbilisi today. Central to this exploration is the image of the gate. I argue that whereas Tbilisi at the time of *Ali and Nino* was seen as a gate through which people from everywhere could enter and leave, it has today become a contested image mainly between the West on the one side and Russia and Asia on the other. In this sense, the all-inclusive image that 'the gate' represented previously has today become both a political battleground and the cause of great ambiguity in the everyday lives of people living in Tbilisi.

After presenting a brief overview of the influences that have shaped Tbilisi since its founding in the fourth century AD, I focus on two historical periods. First I describe the late nineteenth and early twentieth century when Tbilisi was commonly seen as a juncture between East and West. I then look into the city's recent political and socioeconomic situation, focusing specifically on the manifold influences that have affected both politics and daily lives in the post-Soviet period. In this latter section I present three interrelated examples that describe respectively perceptions of historical, material legacies, issues of consumption and finally recent foreign intrusions in terms of war, development work and oil pipelines. In doing so, I discuss the similarities and differences of the two mentioned periods and the tensions experienced locally in the city at present in terms of differences and influences that do and do not disturb the coherence in people's everyday lives. These differences can be traced to what Manning and Uplisashvili have aptly described as the country's position on 'the uncomfortable shifting border of an imagined geographic opposition between Europe and Asia' (Manning and Uplisashvili 2007: 637).

In the city of perpetual change

Tbilisi is truly an ancient city. Legend tells us that it was founded by King Vakhtang 1 Gorgasali in the middle of the fourth century AD. Allegedly, the King's falcon injured a pheasant during a hunting trip that afterwards fell into a hot spring and died ('Tbilisi' is said to derive from the old Georgian word *tpili*, meaning warm). Impressed by what he had seen, the King decided to cut down the forest covering the area and build a city.

Tbilisi was made capital of Eastern Georgia around the beginning of the sixth century AD and soon became a strategic location due to trade routes between Europe and Asia. Although the city steadily grew, its central location also made it prone to the rivalry between the major powers surrounding the Caucasus region, namely the Byzantine Empire, the Persians, and the Seljuk Turks. Only in 1122 did the city become capital of a unified Georgia under King David the Builder and later his daughter Tamara. However, this 'Golden Age' lasted for little more than a century. Although it was semi-independent, the country was from this period onwards under shifting foreign domination and Tbilisi was burned to the ground on two occasions. In 1795 King Erekle turned to Russia for help against the Turks and in 1801 the country joined the Russian Empire. Although this has probably been experienced as an intrusion by local Georgians, coming under Russian administration actually provided the city with a stability that ensured a significant economic growth and the influx of a variety of foreign traders and artists. As historian Ronald Suny notes on this period, for example, Armenian merchants and craftsmen from other places in the Caucasus region benefited greatly from the new security provided by Russian arms. Further, whereas before much trade had been oriented towards the Middle East, local traders now began to focus equally on the markets of Russia and Europe (Suny 1994: 63).

Since the early Middle Ages, Tbilisi had been a junction on the Great Silk Route. Between four and five different routes made their way through the city (Gotsiridze 2003: 100). Although everyday products such as grains, wine, wool, vegetables, meat and milk where brought from nearby villages and exported onwards, it was still necessary to import goods that were not produced locally, such as sugar, coffee and spices (2003: 101). The Russian administrative presence meant that such trade became easier as the different regions within the country became connected by means of roads (Suny 1994: 66). The building of roads and railways was part of maintaining Tbilisi as a main connecting point between cities such as Batumi, Poti, Yerevan and Baku in the Caucasus region as well as a number of important cities both in Russia and further East. Hence, by the mid-nineteenth century Tbilisi had become a major centre of trade as well as a temporary residence for passing writers and artists such as Tolstoy, Pushkin, Tchaikovsky, Lermontov and Alexander Dumas.[2] In the 1840s the Russian viceroy and field marshal Mikhail Vorontsov undertook a mayor rebuilding of the city. Golovinskii Prospekt (the main thoroughfare through the city today known as Rustaveli Avenue) was laid and a number of important buildings were raised; Tbilisi Opera House (1847–1851), the 'Artist Society' (1879, today the Rustaveli Theatre), a public library and a Russian theatre (1846), as well as a number of other official buildings (Suny 1994: 93). The city was by now a lively place and numerous ethnic groups had made it their home. It is this setting that serves as a background in Kurban Said's novel.

Figure 4.1. View from the Maidan over the Mtkvari River running through Tbilisi, January 2007. Photo by the author.

'Ali and Nino' and the ambiguous gate

Said's novel is the Caucasus version of Romeo and Juliet – the story of an unlikely couple; Nino, a Georgian Christian, and Ali, an Azeri Muslim. They meet in the streets of Baku in Azerbaijan and embark on a journey through the Caucasus to secure their love. But the novel is much more than a mere love story; it is a description of two people in search of their own identities while trying to make sense of the rapid societal changes occurring around them. They arrive in Tbilisi in order for Ali to be introduced to Nino's family. Here they meet a melting pot of the different peoples of the Caucasus, where even 'each tree has its own name' (Said 2000 [1937]: 106). Walking along Golovinskii Prospekt and through the Maidan[3] – the heart of the city at the time – they take in the mixture of influences that seems to linger in the air they breathe (2000: 112).

Although Said subsequently has been criticised for his at times romanticised and slightly exaggerated use of history in his writings (Reiss 2005), his description of Tbilisi in *Ali and Nino* corresponds to later analyses of the city and its cosmopolitan past (e.g. Suny 2009, van Assche 2009). Elin Suleymanov has pointed out in a review of the book that 'the union of Ali and Nino is not a union of Europe and Asia, as an outsider might rush to conclude, but a union of the many distinct and yet related cultures of the Caucasus' (Suleymanov 2000: 2). As mentioned, Ali notes upon his arrival to Tbilisi that it is both part of him and different from him. *Ali and Nino* could too easily be seen as an example of the 'clash' of cultures – Europe meets Asia, West meets the Orient. What is important to note is that the novel actually describes the opposite; when the central characters – and Tbilisi – are described, it is done not in terms of an either/or, but rather as a both/and. The differences they experience in Tbilisi are somehow connected to each other, as everyone there is dependent on everyone else. This is a central point that I shall return to later. Hovering over the novel, however, is the sensation that something is coming to an end. As Said writes, the country, and the entire region in fact, is 'being squeezed to death between two claws of a red-hot pair of thongs' namely the Ottomans and the Russian Tsar, the latter strengthening his grip on the country. What in the end came to squeeze Georgia was in fact neither, but a new force, the Bolshevik army, entering the region. In the wake of the February Revolution in Russia in 1917 the Russian influence in the Caucasus diminished. The Turks were advancing on the country and in 1918 Georgian leaders declared the country independent while Russia was embroiled in war (Suny 1994: 192). Independence lasted until 1921 where the Bolshevik army incorporated Georgia into the burgeoning Soviet empire wherein it was to remain until 1991.

Among many other deep-felt changes, the Soviet period closed off Georgia from the world outside the USSR and the country was put on a socialist path towards a communist future. Erivansky Moedani,[4] the square at one end of Rustaveli Avenue, was renamed Lenin Square and concrete apartment blocks started to surround the city. Trade was limited to import and export to and from the other Soviet republics and the Soviet politics of empire closed off nationalities to individual nations (Hirsch 2005). The different republics were made to produce single parts to the Soviet whole, and as for instance Uzbekistan became a main producer of cotton (Louw 2007: 71), Georgia became a main producer of tea, tobacco and wine as well as the home of various heavy industry. When the Soviet system collapsed in 1991 a swift transition from communism to market economy was widely expected, in Georgia as elsewhere. There was among the general popula-tion a widespread hope that things were going to improve, and that they were going to do so rapidly. As time came to show this would not be the case. In Georgia – as well as in large parts of the post-Soviet space – civil war, economic stagnation, insecurity and corruption replaced the freedom and the growth that had been expected to emerge. The only swift transition was from positive to negative feelings concerning future prospects, what Svašek has termed 'the morning after effect' (2006: 12) – waking up to a world less desirable than it was thought to be the day before. For numerous Georgians these negative feelings, along with recurrent instability, became part of everyday life during the 1990s, and for some it remains so today (Frederiksen 2007b, 2011; Dudwick 2004).

Roses and renewals

In the early 1990s civil war broke out in newly independent Georgia. After only a few years in power, the country's first president Zviad Gamsakhurdia was replaced by the former Soviet foreign minister Eduard Shevardnadze. With continuous problems in basic infrastructural spheres such as electric-ity supply, ongoing problems in the breakaway regions of Abkhazia and South Ossetia, and corruption prevalent at many levels of political life, She-vardnadze's period of presidency was a prime example of the tumultuous changes that constituted the so-called transition in the post-Soviet region. On 23 November 2003 accusations of ballot fraud in the governmental elections ignited the Rose Revolution. Led by the young lawyer Mikhail Saakashvili, thousands of people demonstrated in front of the parliament building in Tbilisi. After twelve years of political instability people were looking for change. Following success at the January 2004 elections, win-ning with a staggering 92.6 per cent of the votes, the 'National Movement

Party' of Mikhail Saakashvili put themselves at the forefront of creating this change. In a speech given on 4 February 2004, nine days after his inauguration, President Saakashvili said that:

> The Georgia of the past was a nation where neither leaders nor the people could believe in the future. I believe we have succeeded in changing that perception. I believe we have succeeded in offering hope. I believe we have succeeded in showing strength in the face of enormous challenges. And I believe that we have a vision that can transform a nation and an entire region. (Saakashvili 2004a)

In the speeches delivered by the new president at this time 'the future', and visions of the future, played a central role. Saakashvili strongly distanced himself and his government from the previous 'regime' and declared the Rose Revolution to be a sign of the country having finally escaped the instability of the transitional period. As he stated: 'Georgia has matured, and the State weakened during the previous era does not exist' (Saakashvili 2004b). Further he claimed that the 'democratic revolution' had proved Georgians to be 'members of Europe and the European family' and had shown a 'special relationship with the United States of America'.[5] Of the many ambitions and visions the new government had for the country, he accentuated the restoring of territorial integrity[6] by peaceful means, stabilising the economy, eliminating corruption and reforming civil society (Saakashvili 2004a). These were, according to the president, essential elements in 'safeguarding the future' in order for Georgia to 'prosper' (Saakashvili 2004c).

However, the post-independence turmoil and the socioeconomic changes of the 1990s had left their mark on Tbilisi; the emergence of street children, prostitutes and beggars came to serve as visual reminders that worked against the visions and promises made by the new government. A poignant example is the main hotel 'Iveria', centrally located by Resp'ublikis Moedani, which was used from the mid-1990s to host internally displaced persons (henceforth IDP): Georgians that had been driven from their homes in Abkhazia due to war. As with hotels, schools and sports facilities in many other cities in the country, the Iveria became a residence for these IDPs for well over a decade and the Iveria soon became a continuous reminder that the war in Abkhazia remained unsolved. Many of the IDPs who ended up in Tbilisi supported themselves by trade in the markets and streets. Yet, as Dudwick (2003) notes, the residents of Tbilisi did not altogether welcome this and accused the IDPs of 'taking over the market, buying local produce cheaply and then establishing a single price among themselves'. IDPs felt they were often taken for Megrelian traders,[7] who have a similar regional accent and are locally viewed with suspicion as swindlers.

One IDP complained, 'They call us speculators and accuse us of causing all their problems!' (Dudwick 2003: 246). During an interview in early 2006, a middle-aged Georgian woman from Abkhazia told me how she as an IDP in Tbilisi was 'feeling like a prisoner of her own nation'. As she explained, she had no possibility of getting back to her old home. And even though Georgia was her home, her life in Tbilisi was marked by confinements. Although she and many others had ended up in their current situation due to being Georgian, they were often looked upon as not belonging in the city. Discussing the presence of IDPs at a dinner party with some local Tbilisuri friends, one man aggressively stated to me that 'they should all just fuck off! What are they doing here? Nothing but taking our jobs, making our home into their home! Why don't they just go back?' There were certainly tensions, and the promises of change made by the new government clashed with the everyday experiences of Tbilisi residents, tensions that have not become smaller as new IDPs have come to the city in the wake of the recent war with Russia in and around South Ossetia.

Presently, the city is being 'cleaned up' in the sense that political measures have been taken in order to remove unwanted residents (Manning 2009a, 2009b). This is especially the case in the parts of the city centre that figure in tourist brochures such as Rustaveli Avenue and the Maidan mentioned earlier.[8] In the late summer of 2004 the IDPs living at the Iveria Hotel were relocated by the government, who gave them a small amount of money to buy a flat in the outskirts of town. Other visual changes include the removal of small traders who had resided in underground passageways and large bazaar areas in the centre of town. However, the changes made by the Rose Revolution government reflect not only the desire to remove those individuals that highlight social problems such as beggars and IDPs, but also the wish to establish the country as distinctly Georgian. I am thinking here of the renaming of Russian street names as Georgian ones, and the introduction of a new anthem and flag, the latter featuring the cross of St George in a five-cross constellation used in the thirteenth century, known as the Golden Age of independent Georgia previously mentioned (see also Shatirishvili 2009). Further, these changes have been made with the explicit aim of presenting Georgia not only as an independent nation, but as an independent European nation, as shown for instance in the rhetoric of President Saakashvili quoted earlier.

The quarter of Tbilisi that has been the main focus of alterations is the Old Town, Maidan.[9] This part of town blossomed in the nineteenth century and is still accentuated in tourist brochures as the cosmopolitan centre of the city. Further, it is the quarter in which Ali and Nino stroll in their visit in Tbilisi. The question is, given the public alterations mentioned, what do you see when you walk through the Maidan today? And more importantly, which role do the historical remnants of previous periods have to play in the everyday lives of residents in this particular urban area?

Ateshga – a temple absorbed by the city

In the spring of 2007 I set out to explore the parts of Tbilisi I was not familiar with yet. Believing myself to be fairly acquainted with the city, I wanted to seek out some of its historical gems. By looking through guidebooks and local tourist brochures I had been surprised to find descriptions of an old fire worshippers' temple built by the Persians, Ateshga. In various writings on Georgia the presence of such ancient Zoroastrian shrines was mentioned but I had never actually seen them and only rarely heard talk of them. The Zion temple in Tbilisi was also mentioned in *Ali and Nino*. Nino goes into the 'dark damp room' to pray at a cross made from the vine St Nino had brought when 'she came to announce to Georgia that the Saviour of the world had arrived' (Said 2000 [1037]: 115). So, one morning I set out to find Ateshga. The maps mentioning the temple located it in different parts of Tbilisi's old town. Most descriptions placed it on the hillside between Maidan and the Narikala fortress overlooking the city, a description fitting that given by Said.

With its winding and dwindling roads Maidan is always a good place to get lost in. I had lived in two apartments near Maidan for extensive periods and felt I knew where to look for the Ateshga temple based on the differing descriptions. Yet, after having walked up and down the small street for a couple of hours unable to find any sign of the temple, I was forced to give up. A few days later I met up with a local friend who was equally interested in finding Ateshga and had agreed to help me. Again we had no luck. We began asking everyone we passed whether they could help us: '*Ateshga sad aris?*' – Where is Ateshga? But few knew of the temple and those who had heard of it were not sure where exactly it was to be found. We were, however, continuously sent up the same street with nothing but classic, seemingly fragile, intermingling wooden balconies around us. Finally we were successful; after having approached an elderly man standing on his balcony, he yelled down to us: 'you're standing right in it'. We were both confused. 'They're not home' he continued, 'but if you wait a few hours they'll be back'. He was referring to his neighbours whose house had apparently simply absorbed the temple, using its foundation to build upon. The Ateshga in itself was a square construction of crumbling red bricks easy to overlook in between the newer housing constructions that had been built around it. The residents were well aware of the fact that they were living in or besides an old Zoroastrian temple, but did not seem to grant this much

Figure 4.2. The Ateshga temple with parts turned into residential buildings, October 2008. Photo by the author.

importance, as this was their home above anything else. Hence, although they lived in a building that was officially taken as being a sign of a cosmopolitan past (and, in a sense also a cosmopolitan present), this did not seem to seem to link the current residents to that past.

Too strange to be a part of – consumption and ambiguity

That historical remnants over time have been slowly absorbed by new residents who have used the foundations to build a new life for themselves is hardly surprising.[10] Further, although the historical heritage inherent in buildings such as the Ateshga temple might have been appreciated by the people living in or around them, on a daily level the present was of far greater importance than the past. This was certainly the case for the family with whom I lived near the Maidan. As was true of many other families they had lived there for generations, in an old historical building. The family consisted of three generations of women: a grandmother, a mother and a daughter. They shared a relatively large apartment with another family, each family owning every other room along a long hallway. However, the proposed renovation taxes of historical buildings threatened to force them out. Further, it was well known to the family that the government

had evicted whole buildings of apartment owners elsewhere in the neighbourhood. Paul Manning, writing on the same issue, has noted how this
was done on behalf of investors who wished to transform the buildings
into modernised private homes (Manning 2009b: 86). Proposed taxes and
possible eviction posed a serious threat to the family who had great difficulty in making ends meet financially. Their only income was what the
mother, Manana, earned working two jobs. Added to this was the grandmother's modest pension. This barely sufficed to pay for their daily living
and the expenses for the daughter's education. The prospect of having to
pay extra taxes was devastating. Manana and I spent many evenings in the
kitchen, smoking and drinking tea, and grumbling over the situation. Manana was certain that moving her mother from the apartment where she
had lived her entire life would surely kill her. Meanwhile, the grandmother
was grumbling in the living room over the price of our cigarettes.

Making ends meet was a constant worry for Manana, with a mother
who continuously believed her to be spending too much money on nothing
and a daughter pushing to buy more in order to be 'up-to-date'. Going to
the market with Manana on weekends was therefore an intricate excursion
with its goal of how to reconcile economic sensibility with an eye for quality; both price and product had to be just right. The purchase of meat and
dairy products was done directly in their backyard where a farmer came
now and then. The selection was usually limited, but the grandmother insisted that the family ate meat and scorned the granddaughter and me if
we had leftovers of tongue and calf brain on our plates; there was no room
for waste. Fruit, vegetables and grains where bought at *basroba*, Tbilisi's
main market. At the time prices seemed to be continually rising but as
most products were locally produced Manana believed that they were
the best buy. The purchase of non-food products on the other hand often
proved a more difficult quest as these were usually produced abroad. For
Manana there were two options: the 'one-dollar shop' near the main market
and *daniuris sakhli*, 'The Danish House'. For Manana these places held the
promise that the quality was to be trusted as the products one bought there
would surely be either American or Danish and thus 'Western', for her a
sign of quality. She was very disappointed to discover that I, being Danish,
knew very few of the products from the Danish House, and even more so
when I, with some guilt, had to admit that I believed most of the products
in both stores were manufactured in Turkey or Southeast Asia. Manana
was hesitant to believe me.

As Pelkmans (2006: 188) has noted, based on his work in Western Georgia, foreign goods in Georgia are often articulated into hierarchies of value
that place European goods above Russian (the latter being cheaper albeit
uglier), and Russian above Turkish (the latter here being of poorer quality).[11]

This is highly reminiscent of the situation in Tbilisi. Hence, when a cable was overheated in my room because I had turned on the electric heater too high, melting the wire and the socket, Manana hastened to buy a new one. When the new device also succumbed to the heater, her explanation was that the new cable was made in Turkey. By looking at the melted remnants I found that the two broken cables had in fact been made in Germany and Japan respectively, the problem probably being the state of the electric instalments which no cable ever managed to survive while I stayed in the apartment. Manana, however, was firm in her conviction that if it broke it would surely have been made in Turkey, and if Danish House sold Turkish and Chinese products a case of mismanagement or corruption was at stake.

When observing in Manana's consumer practices it seemed to me as if she was caught between the unattainable and the inferior. She was not really part of either, and although she strove towards the former, in practice she was unable to attain it. Although Manana believed Western influences to be primarily positive, they also often disappointed her, which was not limited to the fact that some 'Western products' were not Western at all. One evening for example, as I was reading a UNICEF report on their projects in the country, Manana sat next to me and looked at some of the papers. 'The pictures are nice', she said in an ironic voice, 'small children looking in their school books. But what is actually being done? People are still poor'! In many ways, what had come from the West had been highly discouraging for a person such as Manana. Rather than being useful aspects of her everyday life, 'the Western' often presented itself as being either too strange or too unobtainable. This is a situation that has been found in many other post-Soviet countries. As Caroline Humphrey has for instance noted on the situation in Moscow already in 1993, the ability to 'delight unambiguously in the possibility of consumption for self-expression by means of exotic and global signs' was swiftly coming to an end and was being replaced by a growing awareness of what was *ne nashi* – not ours (Humphrey 2002: 40).[12] As shown above, consumption for a woman like Manana was an ambiguous affair. Hers was, paraphrasing Creed (2002), a consumer paradise lost.

The fact that Turkish (and Asian) products were often the ones least valued by my informants might be traced to the aforementioned quest to (re)link Georgia with Europe and the West (a 'place' to which Turkey does not belong in the view of most Georgians).[13] One might ask then where Russia fits into the picture. To be sure, current political attempts to create allegiances with Europe and the US have been part of a deliberate policy of creating distance to Russia and the Soviet past. Interestingly however, despite this and the recent war against Russia ordinary citizens rarely see Russia in its entirety as a foreign influence that is also an intrusion, as will become apparent in what follows.

Pubs, trinket shops, and Russians – friends or foes?

Whereas the Silk Route and after that the railways once enabled a flow of traders to pass through Georgia and its capital, what goes through the country today comes in pipelines: oil from the Caspian Sea. Hence, the most recent influx of new inhabitants in Tbilisi has been oil workers and consultants. There is also a massive presence of international NGOs and aid workers that have come in a steady stream since the early 1990s. From this has grown an ex-pat community whose Irish pubs and Western cafés have become a regular part of the city's physical appearance. Although seen by some – and particularly the younger crowd – as a positive development, I encountered many Tbilisuris who were of two minds when it came to these pubs and cafés as they did not seem to be there for them to use. This was certainly the case for Manana and her friends who came to visit us in the apartment. For them, what was being built to accommodate the NGO crowd was not something they would be able to use mainly because the prices were simply too high. From their point of view, what was being done in the city was being done for someone other than them. As with the Western goods at the market, this was not something that was attainable for them. Furthermore, there were fears that some of the international organisations present in the country would prove to be benevolent colonisers. For example, the presence of the Soros Foundation, which actively supported the Rose Revolution as well as the reform process later enacted by the government, caused several people to ask themselves why the foundation would spend so much money on Georgia if they were not at the same time supporting their own interests (Gotfredsen 2008: 88); there had to be some hidden agenda.

Another recent influx that was generally been less accepted was that of Chinese immigrants. This was a subject of much concern to many of the people I talked to and interviewed in the spring of 2007. Whereas they had hardly been mentioned during my six-month stay the previous year, it seemed as if their presence was beginning to cause worries among locals. Consider the following statement given to me by a local friend: 'I hear that the Chinese government has bought massive amounts of land in Mingrelia – they [the Chinese government] will be sending around 200.000 Chinese here soon!' Not surprisingly, I never had this confirmed. In fact, the only sign I ever personally saw of any Chinese influences were two relatively modest trinket shops located in the centre of town. However, there was certainly aggression towards Chinese immigrants. In mid-2006, following an armed robbery carried out on three Chinese businessmen in central Tbilisi, the Chinese consul, recalling other recent assaults, warned fellow countrymen of the dangers of working and living in Tbilisi in an article in *China Daily* (Qin Jize 2006: 2).

What these examples illustrate is that new waves of influx are looked upon with some degree of anxiety. International NGO workers and Chinese traders have come to represent strangers in the sense of Bauman's allegorical figure, as presented in his *Modernity and Ambivalence* (1991), a present yet unfamiliar person within society who is both enticing but also the object of fear, a thing or a person that does not quite fit in. As I have argued elsewhere, it is difficult to relate to others in a situation where it is difficult to relate to what is happening to oneself (Frederiksen 2007a: 51). Another thing, from the viewpoint of my informants, was the fact that external influences have historically entailed negative outcomes. The positive aspects of foreign influences, such as the invigoration of Tbilisi in the early twentieth century, seem to be lost in the array of foreign conquerors that have set their mark on the country, with the Soviet empire as the most recent and most easily remembered example. But it should be kept in mind that for many of my informants, such as Manana, it was not a matter of all foreign influence being problematic, but rather that there were right and wrong kinds of foreign influences.

The question of Russia illustrates this point. When the Russian army invaded the country in mid-August 2008 it caused widespread anxiety. If anything, this was surely an intrusion. However, people were still speaking to each other interchangeably in Georgian and Russian, in bazaars the price of 2½ was still given as *dva naxevar* ('*dva*' being Russian and '*naxevar*' Georgian). People were annoyed at not being able to watch Russian news on TV as they were used to doing, and many were worried about Russian friends who they could not contact. When at one point during the war I stated to a friend that Russia seemed to be a generally bad influence, he eagerly explained to me that 'Russia' was not one thing but two; there was the Russian *naród* (people) and the Russian *politika* (politics). Whereas the latter was a great threat the former were their friends and part of their lives.[14] At a following dinner party toasts were thus made for the dead Russian soldiers as these were the victims of Russian *politika* as much as the Georgian soldiers were. The Russian people and Russian cultural elements were still acknowledged as part of people's lives rather than an imposition. Further, although universities in Tbilisi only teach in Georgian and no longer in Russian, Russian legacies in terms of theatre and 'high culture' are still greatly esteemed.[15] The strangeness and possible intrusion ascribed to the Chinese trinket shops and Western NGO workers therefore did not apply to ordinary Russians and Russian cultural influences, even at the height of a war against Russia itself.

A gate to where?

In Kurban Said's novel Tbilisi is described as a gate to both East and West, and a gate through which various groups and peoples travel, making Tbilisi a truly cosmopolitan centre both in terms of trade and livelihood. It was a gate that could lead anywhere and through which anyone could pass, an image that has fundamentally changed today.

The Soviet bloc defined itself in opposition to 'the West' (Yurchak 2006: 7). On the Georgian-Turkish border crossing, a massive sign had been put up stating 'The Entire Soviet Nation Guards the Border'. Interestingly, as Pelkmans notes, the sign only faced the Soviet Georgian side and could not be read from across the border (Pelkmans 2006: ix). The post-independence eagerness to create distance from the Soviet period has been prominent in Georgian politics from the 1990s until the present. This has led to what Pelkmans has referred to as the neutralisation of the Soviet period (2006: 209). But although the border that is currently being guarded is that towards Russia, the people on the other side are not strangers in the same sense as were those across the border when it was being protected against Turkey. Further, it is not only the Soviet period that is being neutralised; in some respect it is also many other periods. Hence, in official representation the historical periods where foreign influence has dominated the country have been significantly downplayed – if not overlooked – as opposed to the relatively short periods of independence that are continuously highlighted and used as symbolic references to the current situation, such as the 'Golden Age' mentioned earlier. The inauguration and the concomitant rhetoric of the current president Mikhail Saakashvili was (and is) a striking example of this as it points clearly to two things: the fact that Georgia is a Christian Orthodox nation; and the fact that it is a natural part of Europe. The inauguration itself was carried out at the Bagrationi cathedral where King David the Builder – known for having gathered Georgia under him in the twelfth century – had himself been inaugurated; Saakashvili took an oath at the tomb, claiming it to be a symbol, that he would follow King David's footsteps and bring unity and prosperity to Georgia. In his inauguration speech he stated that 'Georgia is neither "old Europe" or "new Europe". Georgia is one of the oldest parts of Europe' (quoted in Sideri 2006: 1). But in making such statements, Saakashvili did not just create an image of what Georgia was in his opinion; he also created an image of what it certainly was not, namely Russian or Asian.

The linking of the Georgian Orthodox Church to the Georgian state was strongly highlighted by President Saakashvili (Shatirishvili 2009). In her work on conspiracy theories and the intermingling of politics and religion in Georgia, Katrine Gotfredsen (2008) has shown how official attempts to

Figure 4.3. Soldier in tank waving the new national flag on a military parade in central Tbilisi, May 2006. Photo by the author.

link the Georgian Orthodox Church with the nation, thereby seeking to reinforce the idea of Georgia as distinctly European, are contradicted by everyday practices. As she argues, the main question in public debate seems to be whether Georgia, in order to develop in a positive direction, must ally itself with the US and Europe and move away from Russian political influence, or whether this strategy will backfire and undermine Georgian traditions and values (2008: 115). Recurrent in conversations, whether in the local NGO office where I conducted fieldwork in 2006 or among local friends during evening get-togethers, was this theme of Georgia's position between East and West and whether the country was Asian or European. While some praised the European connections advocated by the government, others held that many of the country's traditions where distinctly Asian. It was interesting that such debates almost always circled around the question of either-or rather than both-and.[16] In this sense, it was a question of defining what was Georgian and what was not.

This seems to be totally opposed to the descriptions of Tbilisi found in Kurban Said's novel where the city and the characters of the book are described in terms of both-and; as different yet part of each other. In some respects, the country is still inclusive as it remains extremely varied – Georgia is not one but many things. In political rhetoric and action, however, things have become more simplified as 'cosmopolitanism' has become a difficult practice in a Georgia for Georgians. Hence, the goods and people entering Tbilisi today, such as foreign produce, pubs, trinket-shops and international NGO workers, do not quite fit in. It is unlikely that Ali and Nino would have seen these influences as different but still a part of them had they lived in the city today. The world has undoubtedly grown bigger since Kurban Said wrote his novel, and the connections that created the cosmopolitan atmosphere in the late nineteenth century were maybe more easily incorporated in everyday life than those which leave their mark on the city at present. Being a mixture of East and West was a characteristic of the city a little more than a century ago. When the country became part of the Soviet Union, however, it was suddenly defined in opposition to the West. For the current president Mikhail Saakashvili there was thus a strong symbolic power in seeking a 'return' to Europe, thereby distancing himself from Russia. As a consequence of these developments the question of being both European and Asian has turned into a question of either/or; Georgia today is seen as being one and not both.

There is an interesting parallel to be found here with Oushakine's work on patriotism and despair in post-Soviet Russia. As he writes, post-Soviet society in the Russian Altai region has become marked by palimpsests, that is, things that overwrite each other, which has created a situation of dissonance and disconnectedness. In terms of newly emerging commercial institutions, for example, these 'rarely grew out of existing forms of social life. More often they appeared as a stylistic invasion, a physical rupture in the established social fabric' (Oushakine 2009: 77). Manning has made a similar observation in relation to the evictions and reconstructions taking place in Tbilisi's Old Town. As he notes, new owners have created 'postmodern skyscraper townhouses' behind defensive walls, contradicting the traditional 'openness of the courtyard based communality of Old Tbilisi' (Manning 2009b: 86). The threat of eviction and renovation taxes, the ambiguity of consumption and the experience of foreign intrusion described throughout this chapter all point towards the fact that the kinds of disconnections and ambiguities described by Oushakine are equally at stake present in post-Soviet Tbilisi. As noted earlier, the Georgian government's attempt to promote Tbilisi as a still-cosmopolitan city while at the same time defining it in relation to a distinctly Georgian nation is in itself a contradiction. Residues of the city's cosmopolitan past, such as the Ateshga temple, have over time been absorbed by the city as residential areas, created not in an attempt to hide the shrine, but out of the sheer necessity of making a living, having a place to stay. Should the government choose to renovate the temple in an attempt to make it part of the image of Tbilisi's cosmopolitanism, it would entail the eviction of the current residents.

So can we speak of actually existing cosmopolitanism in Tbilisi today? In the time of Ali and Nino, differences were somehow comprehensible within a known world. One could argue that this was equally the case during the Soviet period in the sense that the differences experienced and encountered by people in their everyday lives were parts of the same overall entity. With the pervasiveness of the current discussions of whether Georgia is part of East or West, foreign influences have become more contested. The new Baumannian strangers that have entered the city – such as NGO workers, oil consultants and Chinese trinket shop owners – have thus become figures in the midst of society who seem to divide people rather than bringing them closer together. It might be that what makes Westerners and Chinese so different and difficult to relate to is the fact that they are non-Soviet. Even in a situation of war Russians are still thought of as a people with a distinct connection to Georgia, as shown with the continuing reverence for Russian high culture and the Russian *narod*.

To conclude, during its history Tbilisi has undergone periods of integration and mixing of ethnic groups as well as more recent periods of segregation. In earlier periods, cosmopolitan culture and practices in Tbilisi often transcended distinctions of ethnicity and religion and the city was an example of a relatively successful multiethnic and multi-religious society (van der Zande 2009: I; van Assche 2009: 7). Because the known worlds in the time of *Ali and Nino* and during the Soviet period were relatively limited, the differences encountered within them were comprehensible and acknowledged as being part of society. This situation is decidedly different than the one found in the city today, where many of the incoming influences are perceived as being either too different, or not quite controllable, or as being too far towards one side of an East-West divide, creating senses of disconnectedness and ambiguity in everyday lives.

NOTES

I owe my thanks to the editors, as well as Maria Louw and Rikke Elisabeth Frederiksen, for their very constructive and helpful comments, critiques and suggestions.

1. I conducted fieldwork in Tbilisi in the first half of 2006 and again in the spring of 2007. At the time of the Georgian-Russian war in August 2008 I was conducting fieldwork in Western Georgia, making a short visit to Tbilisi after the war ended. In this chapter I refer to ethnographic data collected during these three periods.
2. Later also Knut Hamsun and George Gurdjieff.
3. Name of the Old Town in Tbilisi.
4. Georgian for 'square'.

5. It was commonly held that the former president Eduard Shevardnadze, due to his background in Soviet politics, had strong connections with neighbouring Russia.

6. For example, the region of Abkhazia, which had been part of the Kingdom of Georgia in the Middle Ages, and later converted to Islam during the Ottoman invasion, was declared an independent republic when the Bolsheviks arrived in 1921 and was later incorporated into the Georgian SSR. At present three autonomous republics exist within Georgia: Abkhazia and South Ossetia (the reasons for the war with Russia in 2008) and the autonomous republic of Adjara, which functions peacefully with the government in Tbilisi.

7. Megrelian: residents of a region in Western Georgia. As a stereotype they are often the subjects of jokes about wicked cons.

8. For an excellent exploration and overview of recent developments in city planning in Tbilisi, see Van Assche et al. (2009).

9. Also known as the *Kala.*

10. Yael Navaro-Yashin (2009), albeit writing about a different context, has written an interesting account about living in the ruins of a former community.

11. See also Manning and Uplisashvili (2007).

12. In an analysis of the domestication of consumer goods in Russia and Vietnam, Elizabeth Vann (2008: 465) has made a similar argument in her description of what she calls a 'crisis of locality', namely 'the movement of goods between spaces designated as "domestic" and "foreign"'.

13. In her book *Faces of the State* (2002), Yael Navaro-Yashin has shown how state ideologies penetrate deep into the everyday lives of ordinary citizens. In a similar vein, the political quest for Europe promulgated by the current Georgian government might have partaken in the recurrent valorisation of European goods by ordinary Georgians.

14. Note also that the removal of Russian street names previously mentioned was a political statement aimed at removing symbols of the Russian State, not the Russian people. Therefore, the new street names – based on Georgian historical figures – continue to be featured in both the Georgian and Russian language.

15. Remember here the numerous cultural institutions built by the Russian viceroy in the 1840s, previously mentioned, which were part of shaping the city as it is today.

16. The somewhat schizophrenic situation of Georgia as a nation is found not only in local debates but also outside the country. The location of books about Georgia in many university libraries reflects this ambivalence towards the regional location of the country. At my university these books can be found in the sections on Eastern Europe, the Middle East and Central Asia.

REFERENCES

Bauman, Z. 1991. *Modernity and Ambivalence.* New York.

Cheah, P. and B. Robbins. 1998. *Cosmopolitics – Thinking and Feeling Beyond the Nation.* Minneapolis and London.

Creed, G. 2002. '(Consumer) Paradise Lost: Capitalist Dynamics and Disenchantment in rural Bulgaria', *The Anthropology of East Europe Review* 20(2): 119–25.

Department of Tourism and Resorts. 2007. *Georgia: A Fabulous Surprise.* Ministry of Economic Development of Georgia.

Dudwick, Nora. 2003. 'No Guests at Our Table: Social Fragmentation in Georgia', in N. Dudwick, E. Gomart and A. Marc (eds), *When Things Fall Apart – Qualitative Studies of Poverty in the Former Soviet Union.* The World Bank, pp. 213–59.

Frederiksen, M.D. 2007a. 'Invisible Suffering: Mental Illness, Social Annihilation and Violence in Georgia', *KONTUR* 14: 47–53.

———. 2007b. *Managing and Imagining State, Strategy and Instability in a Georgian NGO – Field Report.* The Moesgaard Library.

———. 2008. 'Temporality in Participation and Observation: Perspectives from Albania and Georgia', *Anthropology Matters* 10(2): 1–10.

———. 2011. 'Good Hearts or Big Bellies: *Dzmak'atsoba* and Images of Masculinity in the Republic of Georgia', in V. Amit and N. Dyck (eds), *Young Men in Uncertain Times.* New York and Oxford, pp 165–187.

Gotfredsen, K. 2008. *Dirty Politics in a Glorious Nation – Master's Thesis.* The Moesgaard Library.

Gotsiridze, G. 2003. 'The Great Silk Road and Tbilisi: Trading Relationships and Market in the Nineteenth Century', *International Silk Route Symposium.* Retrieved on 15 March 2008 from www.ibsu.edu.ge.

Hirsch, F. 2005. *Empire of Nations: Ethnographic Knowledge and the Making of the Soviet Union.* London.

Humphrey, C. 2002. *The Unmaking of Soviet Life: Everyday Economics after Socialism.* London.

Louw, M. 2007. *Everyday Islam in Post-Soviet Central Asia.* New York.

Manning, Paul. 2009a. 'The Hotel/Refugee Camp Iveria: Symptom, Monster, Fetish, Home', in K. Van Assche, J. Salukvadze and N. Shavishvili (eds), *City Culture and City Planning in Tbilisi: Where Europe and Asia Meet.* Lewiston, Queenston and Lampeter, pp 375–412.

———. 2009b. 'The City of Balconies: Elite Politics and the Changing Semiotics of the Post-socialist Cityscape', in K. Van Assche, J. Salukvadze and N. Shavishvili (eds), *City Culture and City Planning in Tbilisi: Where Europe and Asia Meet.* Lewiston, Queenston and Lampeter, pp 71–102.

Manning, Paul and A. Uplisashvili. 2007. '"Our Beer": Ethnographic Brands in Postsocialist Georgia', *American Anthropologist* 109(4): 626–41.

Navaro-Yashin, Y. 2002. *Faces of the State: Secularism and Public Life in Turkey.* Princeton and Oxford.

———. 2009. 'Affective Spaces, Melancholic Objects: Ruination and the Production of Anthropological Knowledge', *JRAI* 15: 1–18.

Oushakine, S.A. 2009. *The Patriotism of Despair: Nation, War and Loss in Russia.* London.

Pelkmans, M. 2006. *Defending the Border: Identity, Religion, and Modernity in the Republic of Georgia.* London.

Qin, J. 2006. '3 Chinese Attacked in Georgia', *China Daily*, 15 June, retrieved on 15 March 2008 from www.chinadaily.com.

Reiss, T. 2005. *The Orientalist: In Search of a Man Caught Between East and West.* London.

Robbins, Bruce. 1998. 'Introduction Part 1: Actually Existing Cosmopolitanism', in P. Cheah and B. Robbins (eds), *Cosmopolitics: Thinking and Feeling Beyond the Nation.* Minneapolis and London, pp. 1–30.

Saakashvili, M. 2004a. 'Inauguration Speech by President Mikhail Saakashvili'. Retrieved on 15 November 2006 from www.president.gov.ge.

———. 2004b. 'Georgia is a Breath of Fresh Air for All Freedom Loving People: Speech delivered at John Hopkins University'. Retrieved on 15 November 2006 from www.president.gov.ge.

———. 2004c. 'Speech Delivered by Mikhail Saakashvili at George Washington University'. Retrieved on 15 November 2006 from www.president.gov.ge.

Said, K. 2000 [1937]. *Ali and Nino.* London.

Shatirishvili, Zaza. 2009. 'National Narratives, Realms of Memory and Tbilisi Culture', in K. Van Assche, J. Salukvadze and N. Shavishvili (eds), *City Culture and City Planning in Tbilisi: Where Europe and Asia Meet.* Lewiston, Queenston and Lampeter, pp 59–70.

Sideri, E. 2006. 'In Quest of Eastern Europe: Troubling Encounters in the Post-Cold War Field', *Anthropology Matters* 8(1): 1–9.

Suleymanov, E. 2000. 'Inside the Soul of a Caucasian: "Ali and Nino" by Kurban Said', *Azerbaijan International* 8(2): 1–3.

Suny, Ronald Grigor. 1994 [1988]. *The Making of the Georgian Nation.* 2nd edn. Bloomington and Indianapolis.

———. 2009. 'The Mother of Cities: Tbilisi/Tiflis in the Twilight of Empire', in K. Van Assche, J. Salukvadze and N. Shavishvili (eds), *City Culture and City Planning in Tbilisi: Where Europe and Asia Meet.* Lewiston, Queenston and Lampter, pp 19–58.

Svašek, M. 2006. *Postsocialism: Politics and Emotions in Central and Eastern Europe.* Oxford.

Van Assche, Kristof. 2009. 'City Culture and City Planning in Georgia: Identities and Their Remaking', in K. Van Assche, J. Salukvadze and N. Shavishvili (eds), *City Culture and City Planning in Tbilisi: Where Europe and Asia Meet.* Lewiston, Queenston and Lampeter, pp. 1–18.

Van Assche, Kristof, J. Salukvadze and N. Shavishvili. 2009. *City Culture and City Planning in Tbilisi: Where Europe and Asia Meet.* Lewiston, Queenston and Lampter.

Van der Zande, Andre. 2009. 'Foreword', in K. Van Assche, J. Salukvadze and N. Shavishvili (eds), *City Culture and City Planning in Tbilisi: Where Europe and Asia Meet.* Lewiston, Queenston and Lampter, pp i–iv.

Vann, E. 2008. 'Domesticating Consumer Goods in the Global Economy – Examples from Vietnam and Russia', *Ethnos* 70(4): 465–88.

Yurchak, A. 2006. *Everything Was Forever, Until It Was no More – The Last Soviet Generation.* Princeton and Oxford.

◦） Chapter 5 ｛◦

Cosmopolitan Architecture: 'Deviations' from Stalinist Aesthetics and the Making of Twenty-First-Century Warsaw

G. MICHAŁ MURAWSKI

Introduction: Warsaw's architecture and the cosmopolitan aesthetic

In striking contrast to cities such as Odessa and Dushanbe (as discussed in chapters 3 and 8 respectively), the period of Soviet domination over Warsaw was anything but a time of demographic diversity. The Jewish community, which had comprised around thirty per cent of the city's population throughout the 1930s (Zalewska 1996), was almost entirely decimated during the Holocaust, and thousands more Jews left Warsaw during a government-led 'anti-Zionist' campaign in 1968. Brutal population exchanges between Poland, Germany and the Soviet Union in the first years after the Second World War and the regime's tendency to pursue a 'homogenising' minorities policy (see Hann 1996) ensured that socialist Warsaw remained the most 'Polish' and least cosmopolitan capital of Poland in modern times. During the last two decades, however, the marked rise in the number of Vietnamese schoolchildren, Japanese chefs and Turkish shopkeepers has had an impact on the appearance of Warsaw's streets. Many of the city's inhabitants are proud of this diversity; they treat it as evidence that Warsaw is once again becoming a worldly, cosmopolitan city. For them, Warsaw's 'cosmopolitanisation' is interpreted as the long overdue righting of historical wrongs, a sign that Warsaw is returning to its natural condition as the diverse and dynamic capital of a country positioned at the heart of Europe.

Warsaw's turbulent history has left a powerful imprint on the city's urban landscape, and its inhabitants often claim to be especially sensitive to the role played by the physical presence (or absence) of buildings in defining the realities of the city's past, present and future.[1] I intend, therefore, to explore how some of Warsaw's buildings – in particular, 1950s modernist ones – are said to have expressed the city's re-emerging cosmopolitanisation amid Soviet-style homogeneity. During fieldwork conducted in Warsaw, I participated in the everyday lives of people whose professional and private interests are more or less devoted to thinking about and creating Warsaw's architecture: historians, journalists, artists, architects, amateur enthusiasts as well as property developers. Among many of my informants, I observed a remarkably coherent tendency to celebrate the role of an architectural 'resistance movement', said to have emerged in response to Stalinist cultural policy during the 1950s. I hope to show how the heritage of this architecture of resistance is being used to cultivate a 'cosmopolitan aesthetic' linked to specific notions of good taste and locality, which relegates large chunks of Warsaw's post-war built environment to the status of historical aberrations.

For many contemporary observers, the continuity of Warsaw's historical development was stymied by enforced homogenisation and isolation during the half-century between the beginning of the Second World War in 1939 and the fall of the People's Republic (PRL – *Polska Rzeczpospolita Ludowa* in Polish) in 1989. With the possible exception of the German occupation (1939–1945), the events of the years between 1949 and 1956 – the high point of Stalinism in post-war Poland – are considered to have done the most to divert Warsaw from its 'natural' historical trajectory. In Poland, as in other countries of the Soviet bloc, Stalinism found its aesthetic expression in socialist realism, established in the Soviet Union as the 'official' method in the arts during the 1930s, and exported to Eastern Europe after 1945. In urban architecture, this entailed an emphasis on monumental forms intended to transform the appearance and existing fabric of pre-socialist cities. This future-oriented, transformative social mission was something that Stalinist architecture had in common with politically radical manifestations of the stylistically abstract and anti-ornamental modernism popular in the Soviet Union and elsewhere in Europe and beyond since the 1920s.[2] In opposition to the modernists, however, socialist realist architects borrowed heavily from historical styles, while simultaneously claiming to anchor their designs in locally-specific traditions. In the language of its ideologues, the task of socialist realist architecture was to create a built environment that was to be 'socialist in content' but 'national in form'. As modernism in architecture was associated with self-conscious internationalism and hostility to tradition, architects adhering to modernist principles were routinely condemned for their 'rootlessness' and so-called 'cosmopolitan deviations' from the Stalinist incarnation of the socialist project.

In post-socialist Warsaw, and especially during the last several years, the buildings which the Stalinists condemned as cosmopolitan deviations have become the focus of increasingly widespread interest. Warsaw's 1950s modernist architecture is celebrated for having resisted the dictates of socialist realism, and is lauded as evidence of Polish architecture's natural embeddedness in international (or Western) architectural trends, unshaken even in the face of imposed 'totalitarian' (or Eastern),[3] aesthetic-political doctrines. Further, these architectural bastions of modernity and worldliness are being enlisted in attempts to construct a heritage for the new, cosmopolitan Warsaw, to prove that this is the kind of city it always was at the core.

In fact, today's popularisers of Warsaw's cosmopolitan aesthetic sometimes betray a striking tendency to replicate the language of their historical villains, the socialist realist theoreticians who persecuted Stalin-era modernist 'rebels'. In his account of the symmetry between1950s aesthetic debates in the two Germanys, Greg Castillo shows how the propagandists of Soviet socialist realism in the East, and of Marshall Plan modernism in the West, relied on 'looking glass inversions' (Castillo 2008: 758) of each others' arguments. In both instances, fear of 'barbarian invasion' and calls to 'cultural resistance' were deployed as weapons in an ideological conflict to determine which side would emerge as the true guardian of Europe's cultural heritage. Despite no longer having the geopolitics of the Cold War to sustain it, this kind of belligerent heritage-making seems to be alive and well in post-socialist Warsaw. As a student of the history of architecture told me on hearing the phrase 'cosmopolitan deviation', 'it was not cosmopolitanism which was the deviation, it was socialist realism', further referring to socialist realism as 'obscene' and 'aberrant'.

Consequently, I argue that this 'cosmopolitan' modernist material heritage, formerly condemned as deviant, is today a key component in a strategy of 'normalisation',[4] which pathologises in turn the core material legacy of the PRL, most vividly identified with the 'repressive' socialist realism of the 1950s. However, Warsaw's architectural antibodies are also being mobilised to resist the aesthetic threat associated with the rampant expansion of the market economy. The city's giant new office towers and gleaming shopping centres, as well as the tumbledown capitalism of its kiosks and bazaars, function as markers of Warsaw's potential descent into a new form of 'provincial' marginality – this time as an undistinguished, generic facsimile of the globalised city, laid out as a chaotic battleground for the indulgence and cowboy profiteering of the world's capitalists. In the face of this threat, many in Warsaw are keen to stress that the city should embrace a cosmopolitanism which is not merely derivative of global trends, but which emerges from within a vernacular idiom. I want to show that the cosmopolitan Warsaw under construction sees its cosmopolitanism not as abstract and rootless but as 'indigenous', as emerging from within its own, historically specific contributions to the canon of world architecture.

Lastly, I hope to demonstrate that the modernist architecture of the 1950s is benefiting from its central place within an emerging order of 'distinction'. Following Pierre Bourdieu's (1984) insights on the capacity of aesthetic categories to legitimate and reinforce social hierarchies, I outline how the normalising ideology of Warsaw's cosmopolitanisation also has a tendency to identify those past and present social entities it pathologises (whether human, material or abstract) with a lower station in the hierarchy of aesthetic judgement. In short, Warsaw provides a case study in the contingency and interrelatedness of two related Kantian transcendentalisms: cosmopolitanism and aesthetics. Warsaw's architectural 'cosmopolitan aesthetic' is not rootless and disinterested, but grounded in locality, and inseparable from the social, economic and ideological conditions which engender it.

In addition to ethnographic material derived from conversations with my informants, I also rely on both historical and contemporary citations from Polish journalistic and scholarly sources. Although I make reference to Warsaw's history throughout the text, my intention is not to express my own take on the past but to produce an account of the historical narrative which tends to accompany an identification with the 'cosmopolitan' element of Warsaw's material heritage. Where I cite sources from the 1950s and 1960s, this is usually because they have influenced (positively or negatively) the work of present-day figures I associate with the cosmopolitan aesthetic.

Anti-cosmopolitanism and Stalinist socialist realism

The years after the Second World War saw the gradual consolidation of the Soviet Union's influence over Poland, culminating with the formal foundation of the Polish People's Republic in July 1952. Correspondingly, it took some time before the manner of the nascent regime's interest in the arts aligned itself consistently with the Soviet example. Between 1945 and 1951, for example, Helena and Szymon Syrkus, leading 'avant-garde' modernists during the interwar period, were able to design and build two housing estates (Praga I and Koło II, see Fig. 5.1a) which the contemporary architectural historian Marta Leśniakowska praises as being one of only a few examples of 'pure' international-style modernism in post-war Warsaw (Leśniakowska 2003: 146).

Figure 5.1a. From modernism to socialist realism. Koło II housing estate. Architects Helena and Szymon Syrkus, 1947–1951. Photo by the author.

Figure 5.1b. From modernism to socialist realism. Palace of Culture and Science, Architect Lev Rudnev and others, 1952–1955. Photo by the author.

However, as Poland became increasingly reliant on the stewardship of the Soviet Union, the situation in the arts came to mirror politics. At a congress of Party-affiliated architects in Warsaw on 20 and 21 June 1949, the architect Edmund Goldzamt declared socialist realism, 'national in form, socialist in content', but 'drawing from the treasury of Soviet architecture', to be the 'mandatory creative method' (cited in Baraniewski 2004: 104). Reciting the mantra repeated programmatically in the Soviet Union after 1946 by Stalin's culture commissar, Andrei Zhdanov, the resolutions adopted by the congress condemned 'formalism and cosmopolitanism in architecture' and represented Polish architecture as a front in the struggle between two opposing camps: 'On the one hand, the camp of democracy, socialism and peace – with the Soviet Union as its main bastion – and on the other, the camp of imperialism, economic crisis and warmongering' (cited in Aman 1992: 59). The premises behind the new 'method' were given particularly clear expression in a 1950 text by Jan Minorski, a Moscow-trained Polish architect. According to Minorski:

> The political foundation of valueless and formalist-constructivist architecture is a capitalist foundation. The intermediary here is cosmopolitanism. The so-called 'value' at the source of the penetration into our architecture of the assorted debris of bourgeois art's downfall ... is the ideology of cosmopolitanism. Theories serving the interests of capitalism ... derive from this ideology of cosmopolitanism. ... Cosmopolitanism in art takes the form of attempts to snatch away national foundations, national pride, because people with trimmed roots are easier to push out of place and trade to the slavery of American imperialism. (Minorski 1950: 222)

The delimiting of a local aesthetic repository from which to assemble a rooted, popularly comprehensible counterpart to cosmopolitanism would therefore be a crucial aspect of the arduous path towards establishing socialist realism as the canonical style in each of the people's democracies. Broadly speaking, for roughly six to seven years after 1949, renaissance and classical architecture came to form the bedrock of the Polish 'national form' and the word 'cosmopolitanism' remained the strongest invective in the critical vocabulary of socialist realism.[5]

For today's partisans of the anti-Stalinist architectural 'resistance movement', the very antithesis of modernist cosmopolitanism and the crowning achievement of socialist realism in its Polish edition is the Palace of Culture and Science (see Fig. 5.1b), a gargantuan 231-metre high 'gift' from Stalin, built between 1952 and 1955 according to a design by the Soviet architect Lev Rudnev and his team of assistants. Together with a group of Polish architects, Rudnev embarked on a widely publicised two-week tour of Poland, driving from one historical location to another, in order to determine which aspects of the Polish architectural heritage could most appropriately be integrated into the design for the Palace. Most notably, Rudnev and his colleagues were inspired to lavish the roofs of almost every tower, tier and wing of the Palace of Culture with elaborate versions of the rooftop crenellations ('attics') characteristic of the late Polish renaissance. A journalist writing in a 1953 edition of *Stolica* expressed his 'admiration' for the Palace, a 'monumental work' which 'represents the new architectural tendencies of socialist architecture, and, at the same time, forms an excellent connection to the best national traditions of Polish architecture' (cited in Crowley 2003: 40).

'Here Comes the Youth!' The Trojan horse of modernism

Following Stalin's death in March 1953, the vigour with which the Stalinist approach to the arts was implemented had begun, cautiously, to slacken. For today's cosmopolitan aesthetes, perhaps the most frequently cited indicator of this first stage of de-Stalinisation is the opening in July 1955 of the Stadion Dziesięciolecia, the Tenth Anniversary Stadium (see Fig. 5.2a), whose name celebrates the closing of the first decade of socialist rule in Poland. The initial competition for the stadium's design was carried out in 1953. In an article on the stadium's architecture, the critic Grzegorz Piątek refers to the results of the competition as a pleasant surprise – despite the dominance of socialist realism at that time, 'all eight of the invited teams presented proposals stripped of the neo-classical pomp and overblown iconography of propaganda' (Piątek 2008: 21). The final design for the stadium produced an oval crater, sunk into the ground near the right-bank of the Vistula river, largely free of what Piątek refers to as 'socialist realist sugar coating' (2008: 22).

The building of the stadium was hastened to coincide with the opening on 31 July 1955 of the 5th World Festival of Youth and Students, a travelling culture and sports propaganda jamboree. Alongside Polish festival participants from the Union of Polish Youth (ZMP – *Związek Młodzieży Polskiej*) were 25,000 foreign visitors (Osęka 2007), many of them delegations of 'progressive youth' from 'the west', as well as representatives from the decolonising nations of Asia and Africa. According to Piątek, these foreigners were 'dressed in imaginative clothes, listened to forbidden music, and discussed degenerate art' (Piątek 2008: 23). In his account, the 'socialist games' turned out to have the effect of an 'injection of cosmopolitanism and free thinking' and became a 'beachhead for Western pop culture and arts' (Piątek 2008: 23). *To Idzie Młodość!* (Here Comes the Youth!, see Fig. 5.2b),

Figure 5.2a. The Trojan horse of modernism. The Tenth Anniversary Stadium. Architects Jerzy Hryniewiecki, Marek Leykam and Czesław Rajewski, 1953–1955 (photograph from Ciborowski and Jankowski 1971, photographer E. Kupiecki).

Figure 5.2b. The Trojan horse of modernism. A scene from the musical *Here Comes the Youth!* depicts previously stiff and repressed ZMP members 'injected with freedom' during the 5th World Festival of Youth and Students (photograph by Michał Englert, courtesy of Warsaw's Teatr Współczesny).

a musical which has been receiving standing ovations in Warsaw since November 2008, depicts the oppressive boredom of young men and women living in puritan ZMP hostels in the months leading up to the festival. They seek an outlet for their repressed rebellion and eroticism by wistfully listening to *Summertime* or *Rum & Coca Cola* on Voice of America radio, or by covertly fraternising with local *bikiniarze*, the bohemian dropouts of the Stalinist 1950s. The musical portrays the stifling of these 'natural' tendencies by tyrannical political commissars and by the obligatory *kapuś* (collaborator), a fellow member of the ZMP exceptionally devoted to pursuing the Party's dictates – depicted as short, spotty, pathologically enamoured by authority and alien to the lifestyle and longings of his 'normal' peers.

As the festival gets underway, however, the *Summertime*, which had previously been the subject of tense dreams fed by banned airwaves, explodes into the reality of a hot August in Warsaw. As ZMP members, *bikiniarze* and foreigners engage in fleeting romances and dance wildly in the streets to the *Banana Song* and *Rock Around the Clock*, even the dastardly *kapuś* sheds his red tie and succumbs to the uncontrollable forces of change sweeping the city. According to Piątek, it is no accident that the Stadion Dziesięciolecia was the primary setting from which this 'wave of freedom' was launched. The geometry of the stadium, the 'complex play of the formal ellipse within a circle' was firmly inscribed into the legacy of 'worldwide modernism' (Piątek 2008: 23). The Palace of Culture had been opened several days before the beginning of the Festival, on 22 July 1955. 'In the span of a week or so it transpired that the regime also had another face, a face beyond the Party, that of a cosmopolitan intellectual' (2008: 23). Whereas for David Crowley, the Palace of Culture had been the 'Trojan horse' of socialist realism in Warsaw (Crowley 2003), Piątek refers to the stadium as the 'Trojan horse' of modernism (2008: 23).

The stadium's architects received the highest state prizes for architecture in 1955. In tandem, de-Stalinisation gathered pace. Beginning in April 1955, the architectural press published a number of articles systematically decrying the Stalinist legacy and attempting to determine a new direction for Polish architecture. One author coined a phrase that would ensure a second life for his text more than four decades after its publication. According to Strachocki, the integrity of Polish architecture during the postwar decade was only maintained thanks to the activities of an anti-Stalinist 'architectural resistance movement'. The insubordinate members of this movement were instrumental in keeping alive a 'thread of continuity', both with 'recent achievements in western architecture' as well as with the 'indigenous needs and possibilities' which socialist realism is said to have ignored, despite its rhetoric of 'rootedness' and 'national form' (Strachocki 1957: 8–10).

From obsequiousness to rebellion: a typology of resistance

The term 'resistance movement' is today frequently used to refer to those 'avant-garde' modernist projects which 'held their own' during the darkest years of socialist realism. The narrative surrounding the 'resistance movement' suggests three distinct modes according to which Polish architects responded to the imposition of socialist realism, varying along a complex, non-linear spectrum including positions of submissive accommodation and active rebellion. Architects who might have been expected to 'resist', but did not, tend to be presented as 'obsequious' individuals of 'feeble' character, whereas modernist architecture which carries an obvious trace of socialist realist intervention is often characterised as absurd and farcical. On the other hand, a number of 'strategies of resistance' are delimited, varying from the intermediary 'meandering' or 'procrastination', to 'active rebellion', which could take the form of a canny ability to realise modernist designs 'despite' overriding dogma, a refusal to work, or a 'mocking' stylistic over-identification with socialist realism. These categories, of course, are not mutually exclusive. The division between procrastination and rebellion is shifting and unclear, and 'mocking' could easily be confused with 'obsequiousness'.

'Obsequiousness'

Helena and Szymon Syrkus, mentioned above as designers of the functionalist Koło II and Praga I housing estates in the years of 'ideological camouflage' (Majewski 2003) between 1945 and 1949, had been among the most vigorous and well-known promoters of radical, avant-garde modernism in Eastern Europe before 1939. Both had long been declared communists, but the eagerness with which they embraced the new political and aesthetic regime after 1949 came as a surprise to many. The pages of the architectural press and the minutes of architects' meetings from the Stalinist period are replete with condemnations of 'cosmopolitanism' and 'western influences' from both Helena and Szymon. I have often heard Warsaw architects and scholars express the feeling that the post-war Szymon and Helena Syrkus had turned into rather dismal individuals, broken and psychologically scarred by their wartime experiences (Szymon survived Auschwitz) and unable to summon the strength to engage in the 'resistance' which otherwise would have been expected of them.

The Muranów housing estate (see Fig. 5.3), built on the ruins of a section of the wartime Jewish ghetto, was designed by Bohdan Lachert, another leading representative of Warsaw's radically left-wing, avant-garde modernists in the interwar years. The diarist Leopold Tyrmand judged

Lachert to be 'known for his obsequiousness' (Tyrmand 1995 [1954]: 203, Piątek's translation). Lachert's architecture is said to carry a much more tangible testimony to this 'obsequiousness', however, than the verbal and textual declarations of the Syrkuses. Lachert agreed to change his original design for Muranów after 1949, but the alterations were introduced late, and could only be applied to the exterior facades of some of the buildings. This resulted in the earliest completed blocks in the complex, from 1950, featuring historicising detailing, bas-reliefs and neo-classical porticoes on one side, and taking the form of functionalist blocks with long access balconies on the other. Today, the architecture critic Jarosław Trybuś dismisses the estate's architecture as 'functionalism at a fancy-dress party' after Tyrmand, who mocked it in his 1954 diaries as 'reminiscent of a costume ball of schizophrenics posing as Napoleon, Julius Caesar and Nebuchadnezzar, with glued-on beards, eyebrows and moustaches, just like a small-town theatre' (Tyrmand 1995: 103).

Figure 5.3a. The Muranów Estate. 'Functionalism at a fancy dress party'. Architect Bochdan Lachert, 1948–1956. Modernist access balconies at the rear of one of the blocks. Photo by the author.

Figure 5.3b. The Muranów Estate. 'Functionalism at a fancy dress party.' Architect Bochdan Lachert, 1948–1956. A grand entrance portico at the front. Photo by the author.

'Meanderers/Procrastinators'

The next category of architects are said to be those, who, in Piątek's description, succeeded in 'intelligently meandering between socialist realism and modernism'. Tyrmand praised 'a few clever procrastinators who rebel carefully and effectively, all the more so because their knowledge and talent make them strong' (Tyrmand 1995: 201, Piątek's translation). The project for the Tenth Anniversary stadium (co-authored by Leykam) is frequently cited as the clearest instance of this kind of cautious rebellion. It is sometimes suggested that whereas architects like Lachert submissively 'lacquered' their modernist designs with elaborate decorative features, Leykam's 'resistance' manifested itself most clearly through a 'mocking' or 'playful' distortion of or over-identification with canonical, socialist realist forms. For example, he re-conceived one previously criticised design as a monumental five-storey rectangle, clad in bold, rusticated masonry, containing an elaborate arcaded courtyard topped by a strikingly modern concrete dome cut through with circular skylights, completed in 1952 and assigned to house the office of the Government Presidium. A PhD thesis currently being completed by one Warsaw architect argues that Leykam's frustration at the pedantic rejections he suffered led him to 'mock' socialist realist dogma by designing a Party office in a style at once inflected with elements of modernist design and subversive in its quasi-historicist invocation of the early renaissance Palazzo Strozzi in Florence, identified as a material embodiment of 'proto-capitalism'. In a similar vein, a 2006 Warsaw travel guide refers to the building as a 'veiled parody of socialist realist principles', whose facades are simultaneously modern and 'variations on the theme of a 15th century Florentine banker's palace' (Omilanowska and Majewski 2006: 133).

'Rebels'

The next category consists of those architects whom the diarist Tyrmand referred to as 'clearly identifiable rebels' (Tyrmand 1995: 201). In Tyrmand's description, 'they do not build; they are frowned upon and vegetate in teaching jobs' (1995: 201). Some of the designs produced by this group of architects eventually saw fruition during the period of the most intensive de-Stalinisation; these include the four 'radically modern' (Leśniakowska 2003: 205) cross-city stations of Warsaw's suburban railway: Ochota, Śródmieście, Powiśle and Stadion, designed by Arseneusz Romanowicz and Piotr Szymaniak in the mid- to late 1950s, and built between 1956 and 1965, featuring expansive curtain walls as well as dramatically curved and pointed roofs and pavilions. Contemporary commentators are often keen to emphasise the determination of architects who produced avant-garde designs despite official condemnation and a lack of up-to-date access to international journals and publications, especially during Stalinism but also after the thaw. The critic Marta Leśniakowska points out that Polish publications were diligently censored throughout the PRL era, and only after the mid-1950s did very few carefully selected foreign publications become available, placed in single copies in several libraries. In Piątek's words, 'It is comforting for me, as a Pole, that despite these wild barriers, during a time when one copy of some journal or other would reach the Association of Polish Architects, from which it would be passed hand-to-hand among the whole community of architects, designs like Romanowicz's cross-city railway stations were created and realised'.[6]

'The most cosmopolitan building in Poland': the Central Department Store

Figure 5.4a. The Central Department Store (CDT), Zbigniew Ihnatowicz and Jerzy Romański, 1948–1951. The CDT in 2009.

In order to shed some light on the complex medley of associations and connotations attached to the architectural 'resistance movement' in Warsaw, I want to look in more detail at a building which is frequently pinpointed as Warsaw's foremost piece of 'actively rebellious' architecture, the city's first post-war Central Department Store (see Fig. 5.4a). Designed by Zbigniew Ihnatowicz and Jerzy Romański, the CDT (*Centralny Dom Towarowy*) was the winning entry in a contest organised by the Association of Polish Architects (SARP) in 1948, just before the introduction of socialist realism as the mandatory creative doctrine.

The building and its designers were subjected to intense criticism at meetings and in the architectural press after 1949. In the course of a discussion about the CDT organised by the Association of Polish Architects in November 1951 (documented in the journal *Architektura*), the CDT

Figure 5.4b. The Central Department Store, Zbigniew Ihnatowicz and Jerzy Romański, 1948–1951. The CDT tomorrow; a visualisation of the refurbished CDT (courtesy of the investor).

was showered with damning statements: 'There is no doubt', according to one architect participating in the discussion, that the CDT's architecture 'is clear formalism and cosmopolitanism of the purest kind' (SARP 1952: 100). In a statement that has been gleefully appropriated by the CDT's admirers today, another architect declares, 'There could hardly be any more drums and cymbals amidst this jazzy clamour' (1952: 100). Despite these routine condemnations, the CDT was doggedly completed at the end of 1951, without any substantial changes being made to the original design (Leśniakowska 2003: 34).

The CDT did not have to wait long for its rehabilitation. According to a 1958 article in *Architektura*, 'the CDT is soaked in modernity' (Strachocki 1958: 214). The author compared the 'anachronistic' image of a horse-drawn cart in front of the department store, with the 'fitting sight' of a modern motorcar against the same background, adding 'how painlessly the main façade lends itself to the serpentine form of the neon advertisement on its front' (Strachocki 1958: 214).

In September 1975, however, the building was partially destroyed by fire. Although it was subsequently reconstructed, many of today's commentators consider Polish modernism in the 1970s to have turned very dull and formulaic in comparison to the innovative, radical design characteristic of the 1950s and early 1960s. The architect Andrzej Chołdzyński describes the post-1975 CDT as a 'banal and flat ... caricature of the protoplast from the 1950s' (cited in Bartoszewicz 2008 in *Gazeta Stoleczna*), whereas a recent newspaper article compares the 'refined partitions between the window panels' before the fire with the 'homogenous, brown glass shell' that replaced it (Zieliński 2009 in *Dziennik*).

At a lively press conference in November 2008, the building's owners declared their intention to refurbish CDT, recreating the 'avant-garde' glamour of the store's first incarnation. According to the developer's plans, the building's exterior will be restored to its original condition, the giant spiral neon arrow on its side will be returned to the façade, and the octogenarian avant-garde artist Wojciech Fangor, commissioned in 1955 to design uncompleted mosaics for the building's interiors, has been engaged to finish his work. The investor's marketing campaign placed tremendous emphasis on the historical significance of the department store, and this strategy was rewarded by the extensive attention the project received in the press as well as on internet forums and blogs. One journalist heaped praise on the proposal to restore the 'metropolitan chic' of the CDT, which 'during the previous regime was considered the most cosmopolitan building in Poland' (Jóźwicki 2008 in *Gazeta Wyborcza*), while another referred to the store as the most vivid example of the tendency in the first years after the war to continue 'the most fashionable stylistic trends of pre-1939 Poland ... created with such flair and fantasy as if the city's death had never taken place' (Zieliński 2009 in *Dziennik*).

According to a citation from the architect's son in the developer's pamphlet, the CDT 'materialised dreams of a new, better world and a modern Warsaw. Its glass, avant-garde façade was to be, as my father put it, "a giant lantern shining from afar", as if cutting across the greyness of its surroundings at the time' (Centrum Development Investments 2008: 17). The architect Andrzej Chołdzyński, commissioned to oversee the building's restoration, describes the CDT's design as 'a dream in ruined Warsaw of the elegant, modernist, plentiful world of the West'. For Chołdzyński, whereas the architects 'took inspiration' from the arch-modernist Le Corbusier and the German expressionist architect Erich Mendelsohn, they also intended the CDT to be a 'distinctively Varsovian building' rooted in the rich heritage of Warsaw's interwar modernist architecture, the embodiment of a period, during which, in Chołdzyński's characterisation, 'Poland steamed forward like a transatlantic ocean liner'. Chołdzyński is very keen to emphasise the significance of the building's role during the 1950s and 1960s, as a result of which it 'has written itself into the history and material culture of this place', a 'beacon' testifying to the continuity of Polish culture with its own past and with the international heritage to which it belongs. According to Chołdzyński, in the CDT's heyday there 'reigned a chic which was Polish, native, but simultaneously European and worldly' (Bartoszewicz 2008 in *Gazeta Wyborcza*).

From the 'period of devastation' to the rise of the cosmopolitan aesthetic

The developer behind CDT's 'revitalisation', Centrum Development Investments (CDI), is the privatised successor to Poland's former state department store company. The firm is currently undertaking similar projects at several of its properties, with those considered to be examples of 'exceptional' architecture from the PRL period receiving the most attention. The timing of CDI's interest in 'revamping the splendour' of the 'forgotten pearls' of Polish modernist architecture in its portfolio has coincided with the initiation of a number of other, comparable redevelopment projects in Warsaw, including several relating to buildings discussed earlier in this text.[7]

The Government Presidium Office – Marek Leykam's 'Florentine palazzo' – is currently owned by one of Poland's wealthiest businessmen, whose investment firm plans to transform the building from a 'pride of socialism' into a 'luxury office centre', while staying true to its past by carefully 'underlining all of the building's positive features' and installing a memorial plaque to Leykam (Wojtczuk 2006 in *Gazeta Wyborcza*). Further, a modernisation project underway at Ochota and Powiśle cross-city railway stations since early 2008 is intended to allow Arseneusz Romanowicz's mid-1950s, neglected 'wilting flowers' to 'blossom' once more (Bartoszewicz 2007 in *Gazeta Wyborcza*). A recent newspaper article reports the hope of the railway authorities that the revitalised stations, referred to as 'pearls of the avant-garde', whose architecture is 'modest, but on a world level' (Bartoszewicz 2007 in *Gazeta Wyborcza*), will impress crowds of fans from all over the world travelling to Warsaw for the European Football Championships in 2012.

The revitalisation programme at the cross-city stations, however, encopassed only the most visible parts of the buildings. A distinctive, mushroom-shaped ticket hall at the lower end of the Powiśle station, bypassed in the railway authorities' project, was taken over in the spring of 2009 by a group of young 'cultural entrepreneurs', intent on creating a culture and entertainment venue in a setting which does justice to the dynamic, quirky atmosphere generated by the architecture of the pavilion. Since opening, the Powiśle café has held several meetings and lectures concerned with Warsaw's built environment, including a packed discussion marking the publication of a special issue of the *Architektura* monthly, devoted to promoting the conservation of Poland's post-war modernist architectural heritage (see Fig. 5.5b). And the Warsaw architectural community's favourite society event, the 2009 *Architektura* ball, devoted the proceeds from ticket sales to financing the restoration of the old neon sign gracing the Powiśle pavilion.[8]

The fate of Supersam, a supermarket designed as early as 1953 but only built between 1959 and 1962, sheds light on some of the circumstances leading to the development of this trend. Despite two years of intensifying dissent, Supersam was eventually demolished in December 2006 to make way for a large commercial and residential development. Supersam's passing was followed by a number of 'memorial' events, including a 'posthumous homage' in the form of an exhibition at the prestigious Kordegarda gallery (Kowalska 2007 in *Gazeta Wyborcza*), and the act of its destruction is still regularly invoked with revulsion by the ever-more numerous defenders of PRL-era modernism. Piątek told me he considers the public outcry which followed Supersam's demise to have been a 'pivotal moment', which resulted in an increased public awareness of the significance of Warsaw's modernist buildings in its architectural heritage.

Figure 5.5a. Trendy modernism. A public meeting devoted to Warsaw modernist architecture at the Warszawa Powiśle station café (photograph courtesy of Monika Zając).

Figure 5.5b. Trendy modernism. An after-party at the station café (photograph courtesy of Monika Zając).

The January 2008 demolition of the derelict Skarpa Cinema (built between 1956 and 1960) was similarly widely mourned. The elaborate mosaics from the interior of the cinema have been salvaged by a Warsaw hospice (Majewski 2009 in *Gazeta Wyborcza*), and the giant neon sign that used to decorate the front of the cinema has found its way into the collection being assembled by Warsaw's Museum of Modern Art (see Fig. 5.6a). The first exhibition of the nascent collection organised at the museum's temporary home referred to the Skarpa neon sign as 'a testimony to the changes as a result of which many valuable examples of historical architecture and design are being destroyed as private investment aggressively pushes into public space' (Sztuka Cenniejsza Niż Złoto 2008). Both Supersam and the Skarpa cinema are now immortalised in an avowedly sentimental collection of six miniature ceramic replicas of PRL-era modernist buildings. The young designer behind the creation and marketing of the figures claims to have done so with the intention of making Varsovians 'reflect on the fact that these symbols of the city landscape may disappear irretrievably' (see Fig. 5.6a).

Piątek points out that the demolition of several important modernist buildings in the 1990s passed by unnoticed, with almost no significant discussions or protests in the everyday press, whereas the architect Andrzej Chołdzyński recalled that CDI's first question to him ('several years ago') regarding the CDT department store was concerned with how it could be most effectively torn down. In 2004 and 2006, however, the firm willingly participated in the process of placing CDT (as well as several of its other Polish properties) under the protection of the register of historical monuments. According to one journalist, things have changed since the 'period of devastation' during the 1990s and early 2000s. Debates in architecture are ahead of those between politicians, and 'the climate of reckoning' has given way to a more 'tolerant, relativistic' atmosphere (Jarecka 2007 in *Gazeta Wyborcza*). This trend towards a more careful, allegedly 'mature' attitude to the past is developing despite the fact that, as one critic pointed out, brute market logic should dictate that twentieth-century architecture is more at risk in Warsaw than anywhere else in Poland, and more in the last few years than ever before (Majewski 2006 in *Gazeta Wyborcza*). Since Poland's entry into the European Union, ground rents have been rising at

Figure 5.6a. Mourning modernism after the 'period of devastation'. The neon sign from the Skarpa cinema (architect Zygmunt Stępiński, designed in 1953, built 1956–1960, demolished in 2008) at the Museum of Modern Art, December 2008. Photo by the author.

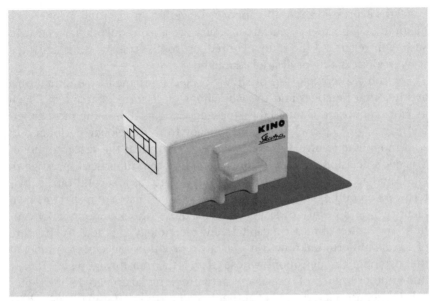

Figure 5.6b. Mourning modernism after the 'period of devastation'. A miniature ceramic replica of Kino Skarpa, designed by Magdalena Łapińska, 2009 (photographer Jan Kriwol).

the fastest level since 1989, and the potential for profit has increased with an exponential growth in consumption. How, then, is the recent popularity of PRL-era modernist architecture to be explained?

'There is no distinction without locality': good taste and the vernacular universal versus pseudo-cosmopolitanism

In an article evaluating the condition of Polish architecture since 1989, the critic Piątek gives clear expression to a widespread attitude which identifies the development of an authentic, developed 'normality' with sophistication, maturity and moderation, as opposed to a reckless, post-traumatic gigantomania. Although he believes that Poland recovered a sense of 'normalcy' after 1989, the recovery was followed by a regression into a new kind of fragmentation and disarray, dictated primarily by the whims of the market and a naïve embrace of the possibilities of unhampered creativity and free enterprise. Emphasising the value of restraint, he questions whether Poland's 'recovered normalcy' needs to seek affirmation in ever more dramatic architectural 'icons' and 'monuments' (Piątek 2006: 98). The concerns expressed about the 'abnormal', overblown scale and incoherence of some of Warsaw's recent architecture are also frequently layered with suspicion regarding their 'unanchored' or 'rootless' abstraction, unsuited to Warsaw's existing or desired character.

For some, the explosion of showy projects designed by multinational architectural practices and the workshops of celebrity 'starchitects' such as Norman Foster, Daniel Libeskind and Zaha Hadid, is the most tangible marker of Warsaw's perceived journey from the global 'periphery' to a cosmopolitan 'centre'. Others, however, believe that the susceptibility of Warsaw's decision-makers to be charmed by the 'superficial' prestige of big-brand architecture testifies to the city's status as a 'second-rate', subaltern version of the global city, unfamiliar with or unable to respect its own identity. Marta Leśniakowska is amongst those who sound a note of caution. The 'influx of massive capital, new technology and new architecture of a scale hitherto unknown' in Warsaw reproduces the 'current model of the cosmopolitan metropolis', whose effect is the transformation of Warsaw into another branch of the self-perpetuating, fractal archetype of the globalised 'generic city', devoid of authenticity or locality (Leśniakowska 2004 after Koolhaas and Mau 1995).

The text of a lavish promotional volume, published to advertise Libeskind's new 192-metre residential tower, opens by proclaiming: 'Warsaw was always at the heart of Europe, but now its beat is beginning to follow Europe's lively rhythm. New energy is liberated here every day, which allows Warsaw to keep abreast of world trends, *themselves acquiring new values in the Polish capital*' (Orco 2009, emphasis added). As if to avert accusations of rootless abstraction, Libeskind's tower is presented as a manifestation of this symbiosis, 'a very particular building which could only be created here ... Its creator knows this city and its history – he has a feeling for its past' (Orco 2009).

Despite such pre-emptive rhetoric, many in Warsaw pour scorn on attempts by international starchitects to decorate their buildings with a local lustre. Andrzej Chołdzyński, the architect of CDT's revitalisation, describes Libeskind as a 'person from nowhere'. For Chołdzyński, 'Libeskind is neither from Łódź' – the Polish city in which Libeskind was born and spent his childhood – 'nor is he from New York'. Chołdzyński is just as unappreciative of Iraqi-born, British architect Zaha Hadid, whom he accuses of having managed, despite herself, to become another 'person from nowhere'. 'She spent half an hour in Warsaw drinking a cocktail' and now is qualified to design gigantic buildings in the middle of the city. Chołdzyński argued that the 'generic', pseudo-cosmopolitanism of the Libeskind-Hadid mould is shallow and inconsequential, because it negates the imperative to negotiate between the vernacular and the universal. For Chołdzyński, 'it is impossible to be worldly, and to be from nowhere', there is 'no distinction without locality'.

These statements represent a tendency to claim that contemporary Warsaw should build upon its own, pre-existing heritage of cosmopolitanism, which was not merely 'indigenously' formulated, but was so strongly rooted that it was able to survive the retrogressive, totalitarian ravages of socialist realism. In its attempt to straddle the boundary between the vernacular and the universal, the notion of cosmopolitanism with which Warsaw's modernist architecture is identified appears to resemble the 'oxymoronic' reconfigurations of cosmopolitanism, towards the 'rooted' (Appiah 1998, 2005), 'vernacular' (Bhabha 1996) or 'discrepant' (Clifford 1992) expounded by writers seeking to move away from the universal Kantian model of cosmopolitanism as world citizenship. In Pnina Werbner's rendition, for example, 'cosmopolitanism … does not necessarily imply an absence of belonging, but the possibility of belonging to more than one ethnic and cultural localism simultaneously' (Werbner 1999: 34). Warsaw's architectural cosmopolitanism reflects the 'emancipatory' connotations of these oxymoronic cosmopolitanisms in its derivation from a heritage of resistance to 'totalitarianism' and aesthetic 'homogeneity' and in its contemporary opposition to the depredations of 'wild' capitalism.

Simultaneously, however, this does not stop it from being intrinsically tied to notions of class, refinement and distinction. As Piątek recognises, the re-discovery of Poland's modernist architectural heritage is still an 'elite phenomenon', alien to the tastes of many ordinary Poles. At the same time, however, many critics applaud the apparent shift towards an increasingly widespread appreciation of modernist aesthetics. According to the architect Chołdzyński, this developing 'refinement' can be partly explained by increases in disposable income and mobility. As he put it, 'Poles who visit Paris antique shops are becoming accustomed to the notion that a piece of furniture from the 1940s or 1950s can be more expensive than one from the baroque. Poles are wealthier, they travel, and their financial independence is expressed in a greater cultural refinement and understanding of the world'.

At a fashionable café in Saska Kępa, a leafy, riverside district endowed with a high concentration of interwar, functionalist villas and apartment blocks, a well-groomed audience took part in a discussion about local architecture. The Saska Kępa-dwellers shared anecdotes and commented on a collectively compiled slideshow of photographs and drawings depicting the Saska Kępa of the interwar period, a 'multicultural, tolerant, ecumenical' quarter of villas, gardens, sleek motorcars and smart restaurants, which, they largely agreed, was slowly coming back to life. Some old photographs were shown of a thirteen-storey residential tower designed by Marek

Leykam at the edge of the district. When it was completed in 1963, the building featured Warsaw's first all-glass curtain wall, but the glass planes leaked and had to be replaced by prefabricated concrete slabs several years later. Half-jokingly, several residents discounted this 'practical' explanation, and suggested that the real reason lay in the communist attempt to diversify the district's social make-up, traditionally dominated by the intelligentsia and upper-middle classes; someone recounted the anecdote that Leykam was so distressed by the sight of the frilly lace curtains with which the building's new inhabitants disfigured its smooth, transparent façade, that he decided the curtain wall had to be concreted over.

The meeting's attendees were also impressed by 1950s and 1960s photographs of Leykam's co-authored Tenth-Anniversary Stadium, situated just to the north of the quarter's boundary. Remarks were made about the excellent integration of the stadium's design with the 'spirit' of the luxury modernist buildings nearby, regret was voiced at its passing, and uncertainty was expressed as to the consequences of the bombastic new National Stadium currently being built on the site. There was very little mention, however, of the ramshackle cosmopolitanism of the Jarmark Europa, in its 1990s heyday the largest outdoor bazaar in Europe, with most of its traders and much of its clientele hailing from Vietnam, West Africa, India, Uzbekistan or the Ukraine, built on the crown and around the decaying, disused Stadium after 1989.[9]

Conclusion

For John Binnie et al., it is impossible to overlook class when discussing the practices, competencies and preferences attendant to being an 'urban cosmopolite'. City-dwelling practitioners of cosmopolitanism draw symbolic boundaries between 'acceptable' and 'non-acceptable' difference, which often 'translate into a defence of locality' particularly through an imperative to preserve selected elements of the local architectural heritage (Binnie et al. 2006: 16). From this point of view, the recruitment of Warsaw's modernist architectural heritage to bolster the notion of an 'indigenous', Polish cosmopolitanism is simultaneously 'oxymoronic' and restrictive, embedded in processes of resistance as well as processes of domination. As in Hannerz's (1990) characterisation of the 'cosmopolitan ethos', critiqued by Werbner for its transcendent understanding of cosmopolitanism as entailing the 'absence of belonging', Warsaw's architectural cosmopolites cultivate an 'intellectual and aesthetic openness' to disparate, radical or innovative experiences and encounters. However, they are almost all members of an educated, well-off elite; they seek to ingrain an 'cosmopolitan' aesthetic in the quotidian reality of the city, but self-consciously define themselves against those people, buildings and social forces (past and present), whose aesthetic deviates away from 'good' towards 'bad' architecture in the spectrum of distinction – whether these happen to be unwieldy Stalinist columnades, ramshackle pavement bazaars or wacky corporate skyscrapers.

Standing in active opposition to these myriad abnormalities are the 'flowers' and 'pearls of the avant-garde', glamorous 'lanterns shining from afar', 'transatlantic ocean liners' and subversively modern Florentine Palazzos, which are said to have meandered, procrastinated and rebelled against attempts to drag the city onto a course aberrant to its (allegedly) natural trajectory during the years of the Polish People's Republic.[10] Furthermore, in the imagination of the cosmopolitan aesthetic, these select elements of Warsaw's built environment have not outlived their usefulness. Today, they are hailed as the raw materials, which, if properly harvested, are to allow an authentically cosmopolitan but doggedly indigenous Warsaw of the twenty-first century to come into being.

Notes

For their assistance and feedback, I am especially grateful to Józef Zabrocki, Grzegorz Piątek, Jarosław Trybuś, Marta Leśniakowska, Andrzej Chołdzyński, Dorota Wojciechowska, Paweł Gawłowski and Agnieszka Rokicka. I would like to thank Caroline Humphrey as well as Charlotte Bruckermann, Katarzyna Murawska-Muthesius and Stefan Muthesius for poring over successive versions of the text. I am grateful to Magda Łapińska, Monika Zając and the staff of the Teatr Współczesny for providing me with photographs.

1. As the narrator in Leopold Tyrmand's novel *Zły* remarks after surveying Warsaw's rooftops, 'In the fifties everybody in Warsaw knew at least a little about architecture, in the same way that everyone knew about gold hunting once upon a time in Alaska. Architecture was the main interest of nearly everybody in this city' (Tyrmand 1990 [1955]: 51). Many in Warsaw agree that, to an extent, this observation still applies today. Warsaw's built environment is particularly productive ground on which to observe whether or not buildings are capable of functioning as agentic entities in their own right, 'full blown actors' (Latour 2005: 70) exerting a (more or less) autonomous impact on social relations. See also my presentation of this issue in relation to Warsaw's rebuilt Old Town (Murawski 2009).

2. A seminal text by Boris Groys (1992) challenged the established view among Western art historians (Greenberg 1986; Gray 1962) that Stalinist socialist realism constituted a radical departure from the avant-garde of the 1920s, pointing out the totalising politico-aesthetic dynamic that both projects shared. Castillo (1995) has applied Groys' argument to architecture. Significantly, although Groys' book has gained widespread currency in Western Europe and

the US since its publication, most of the Polish art and architecture critics I spoke with about his work seemed reluctant to accept such a radical continuity between modernism and socialist realism.

3. If the attitudes of Warsaw's 'cosmopolitan aesthetes' towards socialist realism are orientalist, Castillo (1997) shows that socialist realist attitudes towards the eastern realms of the Soviet Union were no less so. Any notion of the eastwards movement of cultural essentialisms is disrupted, however, by the extent to which socialist realists' attitudes towards Inner Asian vernacular traditions paralleled their approach to the Polish 'national style'.

4. I refer here to the notion of the 'normal' and 'pathological' developed by Georges Canguillhem (1989) in reference to medicine and biology. In his work on the Panopticon, Canguilhem's pupil Foucault (1979) was the first to suggest a link between procedures of normalisation and architecture. It is interesting to observe that the connotations attached to the post-1989 'return to normality' in Poland are paralleled remarkably closely throughout many of the eastern European countries struggling to define their attachments to a politically and economically shifting European continent over the last two decades. See Fehérváry (2002); Rausing (2002); Kiossev (2008).

5. For a parallel description of the consolidation of socialist realism in the German Democratic Republic, see Castillo (2008).

6. This example in particular brings to mind Bruce Robbins' (1998) notion of 'actually-existing cosmopolitanism'. See Humphrey (2004) for a description of a 'make-do', actually-existing cosmopolitan practice in Soviet Russia, as distinguished from the officially-condemned notion of *kosmopolitizm*, the former flourishing despite the enveloping crackdown on the latter.

7. It is important to point out that the rapid growth in conservationist attitudes towards post-war architecture has not been limited to modernism. The Palace of Culture (in 2007) and several other socialist realist buildings have recently been written into the register of historical monuments. Advocates of protecting the Palace tended to point out how much high-quality Polish craftsmanship found its way into the interiors 'despite' socialist realist strictures (see also n.9) or to carefully adopt 'apolitical' postures, arguing that the Palace is a 'unique', fascinating oddity, academically significant, or too expensive to destroy.

8. A recent text about the Powiśle station building and Warsaw's PRL-era modernist architecture in *Blueprint* magazine neatly reproduces many elements of the discourse surrounding Warsaw's cosmopolitan aesthetic in English. See Kelly (2009).

9. On the other hand, there have also been notable attempts to integrate the stadium's past and present, and to an extent even the bazaar itself, into a consciously wide-ranging vision of cosmopolitan Warsaw. See Warsza(2009). The bazaar debate intensified at a new site in 2009 during the ongoing and sometimes violent process of closing and dismantling two large, corrugated trade halls that have stood on the Parade Square in front of the Palace of Culture since the 1990s. Humphrey and Skvirskaja (2009) examine similar issues in relation to a container market outside Odessa, Ukraine.

10. It is useful to point out that some architects and critics in Warsaw have a tendency to claim that there is not really any 'pure' socialist realism in Warsaw (of the sort said to be seen, for example, in Moscow), since all Polish architects were culturally hard-wired to undermine it. It is frequently claimed that the only 'really' Stalinist building in Warsaw is the Palace of Culture, designed by a Soviet architect. However, even this is sometimes called into question. Leśniakowska and several others have repeated to me the suggestion that perhaps the Palace's 'svelte' proportions (relative to the alleged 'Byzantine' dumpiness of Stalin's Moscow skyscrapers) suggest that its architects must have been influenced by the more 'European' visual language which they witnessed and to some extent absorbed when working on the project in Poland.

REFERENCES

Aman, A. 1992. *Architecture and Ideology in Eastern Europe During the Stalin Era*. Cambridge, MA.

Appiah, K.A. 1998. 'Cosmopolitan Patriots', in P. Cheah and B. Robbins (eds), *Cosmopolitics: Thinking and Feeling Beyond the Nation*. Minneapolis.

———. 2005. *The Ethics of Identity*. Princeton and Oxford.

Baraniewski, W. 2004. 'Między Opresją a Obojętnością: Architektura w Polsko--Rosyjskich Relacjach w XX wieku', in *Warszawa-Moskwa/Moskwa-Warszawa 1900-2000*. Warsaw: Zachęta National Gallery of Art.

Bartoszewicz, D. 2007. 'Rozkwitną Warszawskie Dworce PKP', *Gazeta Wyborcza*, 10 October.

———. 2008. 'Dom towarowy Smyk urośnie dwa razy', *Gazeta Wyborcza*, 13 November.

Bhabha, H. 1996. 'Unsatisfied: Notes on Vernacular Cosmopolitanism', in L. Garcia-Moreno and P.C. Pfeiffer (eds), *Text and Nation: Cross-Disciplinary Essays on Cultural and National Identities*. Columbia.

Binnie, J. et al. 2006. 'Introduction: Grounding Cosmopolitan Urbanism. Approaches, Practices and Policies', in J. Binnie et al. (eds), *Cosmopolitan Urbanism*. Abingdon and New York.

Bourdieu, P. 1984. *Distinction: A Social Critique of the Judgment of Taste*. Cambridge, MA.

Canguilhem, G. 1989. *The Normal and the Pathological*. New York.

Castillo, G. 1995. 'Classicism for the Masses: Books on Stalinist Architecture', *Design Book Review* 34/35: 78–88.

———. 1997. 'Soviet Orientalism: Socialist Realism and Built Tradition', *Traditional Dwellings and Settlements Review* 8(2): 32–47.

———. 2008. 'East as True West: Redeeming Bourgeois Culture, from Socialist Realism to Ostalgie', *Kritika* 9(4): 747–68.

Centrum Development Investments. 2008. *Cedet*. Warsaw.

Ciborowski, A. and Janowski, S. 1971. *Warszawa 1945, dziś, jutro*. Warsaw.

Clifford, J. 1992. 'Travelling Cultures', in L. Grossberg, C. Nelson and P.A. Treichler (eds), *Cultural Studies*. London.

Crowley, D. 2003. *Warsaw*. London.

Fehérváry, K. 2002. 'American Kitchens, Luxury Bathrooms, and the Search for a "Normal" Life in Postsocialist Hungary', *Ethnos* 67(3): 369–400.

Foucault, M. 1979. *Discipline and Punish: The Birth of the Prison*. New York.

Gray, C. 1962. *The Russian Experiment in Art*. London: Thames and Hudson.

Greenberg, C. 1986. *Collected Essays and Criticism*, vol. 1. Chicago: University of Chicago Press.

Groys, B. 1992. *The Total Art of Stalinism: Avant-Garde, Aesthetic Dictatorship and Beyond*. Princeton, NJ: Princeton University Press.

Hann, C. 1996. 'Ethnic Cleansing in Eastern Europe: Poles and Ukrainians beside the Curzon Line', *Nations and Nationalism* 2(3): 389–406.

Hannerz, U. 1990. 'Cosmopolitans and Locals in World Culture', in M. Featherstone (ed.), *Global Culture. Nationalism, Globalization and Modernity*. London.

Humphrey, C. 2004. 'Cosmopolitanism and Kosmopolitizm in the Political Life of Soviet Citizens', *Focaal: European Journal of Anthropology* 44: 138–54.

Humphrey, C. and V. Skvirskaja. 2009. 'Trading Places: Post-socialist Container Markets and the City', *Focaal: European Journal of Anthropology 55: 61–73*.

Jarecka, D. 2007. 'Nie burzyć, uczłowieczać', *Gazeta Wyborcza*, 14 January.

Jóźwicki, J. 2008. 'Wielkomiejski szyk Smyka', *Gazeta Wyborcza*, 13 November.

Kelly, P. 2009. 'New Polish Architecture', *Blueprint Magazine* 274, October.

Kiossev, A. 2008. 'The Oxymoron of Normality', *Eurozine*, 1 April (accessed at www.eurozine.com).Koolhaas, R. and B. Mau. 1995. *S,M,L,XL*. New York.

Kowalska, A. 2007. 'Pośmiertny Hołd dla Supersamu', *Gazeta Wyborcza*, 12 January.

Latour, B. 2005. *Reassembling the Social: An Introduction to Actor-Network Theory*. Oxford.

Leśniakowska, M. 2003. *Architektura w Warszawie. Lata 1945–1965*. Warsaw.

———. 2004. 'Warszawa XX Wieku: Strategie Niepamięci', in *Rocznik Warszawski XXXIII*. Warsaw.

Majewski, J. 2006. 'Znikające perły architektury PRL', *Gazeta Wyborcza*, 30 March.

———. 2009. 'Mozaiki ze zburzonego kina Skarpa w hospicjum', *Gazeta Wyborcza*, 31 March.

Majewski, P. 2003. 'Jak Zbudować "Zamek Socjalistyczny"? Polityczne Konteksty Odbudowy Zamku Królewskiego w Warszawie w Latach 1944–56', in J. Kochanowski et al. (eds), *Zbudować Warszawę Piękną: O Nowy Krajobraz Stolicy (1944–1956)*. Warsaw.

Minorski, J. 1950. 'Analiza obecnego etapu rozwoju twórczości architektów Warszawy na tle współczesnych zadań architektury', *Architektura* 7/8: 216–32.

Murawski, G.M. 2009. '(A)Political Buildings: Ideology, Memory and Warsaw's Old Town', presented at *Mirror of Modernity: The Postwar Revolution in Urban Conservation*, annual meeting of the Architectural Heritage Society of Scotland, Edinburgh College of Art, 1–2 May 2009.Omilanowska, M. and J. Majewski. 2006. *Warsaw: Eyewitness Travel Guide*. London.

Orco Property Group. 2009.*Złota 44*. Warsaw.

Osęka, P. 2007. *Rytuały Stalinizmu: Oficjalne Święta i Uroczystości Rocznicowe w Polsce 1944–1956*. Warsaw.

Piątek, G. 2006. 'Architecture of Recovered Normalcy 1989-2006', *Architektura-Murator* 5(140): 92–99.

———. 2008. 'A Palimpset Inscribed on an Ellipse: On the Stadium's Architecture', in J. Warsza (ed.), *Stadium X: A Place that Never Was. A Reader*. Warsaw and Cracow.

Rausing, S. 2002. 'Re-constructing the Normal: Identity and the Consumption of Western Goods in Estonia', in R. Mandel and C. Humphrey (eds), *Markets and Moralities: Ethnographies of Postsocialism*. New York.

Robbins, B. 1998. 'Introduction Part 1: Actually Existing Cosmopolitanism', in P. Cheah and B. Robbins (eds), *Cosmopolitics: Thinking and Feeling Beyond the Nation*. Minneapolis.

SARP. 1952. 'Dyskusja na temat Centralnego Domu Towarowego w Warszawie', *Architekura* 4: 96–100.

Strachocki, J. 1957. 'O Architekturze Dzisięciolecia na Nowo', *Architektura* 1: 8–22.

———. 1958. 'Domy Towarowe w Warszawie', *Architektura* 6: 214–28.

Tyrmand, L. 1990 (1955). *Zły*. Warsaw: Czytelnik.

———. 1995 (1954). *Dziennik 1954. Wersja oryginalna*. Warsaw: Wydawnictwo Tenten.

Warsza, J. (ed.) 2008, *Stadium X: A Place that Never Was. A Reader*. Warsaw and Cracow.

Werbner, P. 1999. 'Global Pathways. Working Class Cosmopolitans and the Creation of Transnational Ethnic Worlds', *Social Anthropology* 7(1): 17–35.

Wojtczuk, M. 2006. 'Chluba socjalizmu luksusowym biurowcem', *Gazeta Wyborcza*, 24 August.

Zalewska, G. 1996. *Ludność Żydowska w Warszawie w Okresie Międzywojennym*. Warsaw: PWN.

Zieliński, J. 2009. 'Gmach CDT, czyli transatlantyk w centrum miasta', *Dziennik*, 1 January.

EXHIBITION

Sztuka Cenniejsza niż Złoto, held at the Museum of Modern Art in Warsaw (6 December 2008–24 January 2009).

between different cultures (Braudel 1975). But perhaps the most significant factor of all is that the Venetians never were a single indigenous people. The city was born as a community of exiles. It was founded in 421 by a group of refugees fleeing Longobard and Hun tribes and seeking safety on the islands of the Adriatic lagoon (Carile 1978). The settlement first looked toward Byzantium for its trade, security and identity. As the Byzantine domination of the Mediterranean weakened, in 726, Venetians declared an independent city-state and developed stronger links with the Levant. They dominated the eastern Adriatic region and controlled a number of colonies in the Aegean and Ionian Sea. The Venetians finally proclaimed their dominance by sacking Constantinople in 1204 and adorning their city with the Byzantine spoils. For the following four centuries, they ruled a vast trading empire stretching from the Mediterranean to the Levant and Northern Europe.

As a major port and a flourishing trade centre, Venice attracted a diverse population of merchants. The Jewish Levantine and Christian Ottoman merchants had been living there for many generations. The Armenians established trading colonies in Venice in the twelfth and thirteenth centuries. In the fifteenth century, German, Dutch and English merchants settled in Venice and opened their warehouses. The city became a safe haven for various adventurers, vagabonds and fortune seekers from the West as well as the East, and not just merchants but also religious minorities, war refugees, redeemed slaves, and colonial émigrés from Eastern Mediterranean and Adriatic regions: Cypriots, Slavs, Moors, Albanians, Ottoman and Safavid subjects, and other sojourners from the Venetian-Ottoman frontier. Such a significant ethnic and religious diversity ensured that Venice was a place of cross-cultural encounters and mediation.

Citizenship and coexistence in early modern Venice

Due to this large presence of foreign communities, Venice has often been portrayed as the first genuinely cosmopolitan city where 'diverse ethnic subcultures of Greeks, Germans, Jews, Turks, and Armenians lived in relative harmony' (Martin and Romano 2000: 8). Despite this image of harmonious coexistence, however, the population movements and the consequent necessary cohabitation of different minorities in the city often provoked conflicts and tensions. Not only did the Shiite Persians clash with the Sunnite Turks but the Orthodox Greeks did not always get along well with Muslim Balkan Slavs, while the Jewish and Muslim populations had been kept under strict control by the Venetian authorities. On the institutional level, there was a sharp distinction between those who enjoyed the status of the citizen and 'foreigners'. Rather than endorse uncritically the ahistorical image of cosmopolitan Venice, therefore, it is important to understand how the difference between a local and a foreigner was perceived and practised in early modern Venice.

The notion of citizenship in Venice was linked to the question of origins – citizenship by birth (*cittadini originari*). It was not restricted to one social group but incorporated patricians and commoners (Cochrane and Kirshner 1975: 328), and was defined in opposition to those who were perceived as aliens, strangers (*stranieri, oltramontani*). Venetian ancestry qualified members of non-noble classes to certain positions in the Republic's civil service (though they had no legislative or electoral power) and granted them commercial and fiscal privileges that could not be obtained by foreigners. Thus the distinction between a citizen and foreigner was not just a social 'fact' but an exclusive legal category clearly defined by Venetian law, privileges and political institutions (Kirshner 1973; Herzog 2003). Nevertheless, it was also a constantly negotiated and contested category, as the continuous coming and going of traders kept the city's citizenship fluid and transient.

Immigrants could claim membership in Venetian society not only through the legal act of naturalisation (citizens *de intus et extra*) but also through trans-imperial business networks, commercial partnerships, apprenticeship contracts, marriage, adoption and religious conversion. These various modes of interaction between locals and foreign sojourners in the city challenged the legal boundaries of citizenship and subverted institutional efforts of differentiation and segregation. In general, early modern Venice was not characterised by a high degree of zoning and spatial segregation. Still, the members of the various foreign communities tended to live in the same neighbourhood near their national church, like the Greek enclave near San Giorgio dei Greci in Castello district, or the Armenian community near Santa Croce degli Armeni in San Marco (Pullan 1983; Thiriet 1977).

The only group that was segregated was the large Jewish community. In 1516, in response to an exceptionally large wave of Jewish immigrants fleeing the warring territories on the Venetian mainland, the Venetian state created a designated Jewish quarter in the old foundry area (*getto*), which for security reasons was walled in and isolated from the neighbouring islets.[1] Because of its unique clear topographical structure the area became synonymous with ethnic segregation and its name spread across Italy and Europe. The Venetian authorities required their Jewish subjects to live and earn their living (mainly as money-lenders) within the confines of the ghetto where Christians could no longer reside. But the urban experience of Venetian Jews was not so radically different from that of the other minorities. The ghetto had its own distinct urban and cultural dynamic that sometimes defied the original aim of segregation and control. To a large extent, it functioned as a semi-autonomous city quarter and a point of identification and preservation of a distinct heritage (Pullan 1983: 151).

The Jews were not isolated from the city's commercial and cultural life and their kinship, social and commercial ties extended far beyond the ghetto. Although they were denied full citizenship for religious reasons and suffered economic restrictions, especially an excessively high tax rate, they were an important economic force in Venice and thus were able to negotiate and re-negotiate their position on the basis of their loyalty and service to the state. Many unlicensed Jewish brokers were able to operate outside the ghetto through bilateral partnerships with Venetian merchants and they also engaged in a variety of contractual agreements with non-Jew artisans to bypass Venetian legislation. The Jews felt themselves to be an integral part of the Venetian urban milieu. Many of the Levantine and Sephardic Jews were transients (*viandanti*) with no permanent roots in the city, but resident Jews, especially of western and Germanic origins, gradually merged into one single group and came to regard themselves as more Italianate than foreign, and proudly called themselves 'we, the Venetian Jews' (Pullan 1983: 149). This sense of belonging and identification with the city was also expressed through their idiosyncratic way of speaking – a Judeo-Venetian jargon, which was made up of the local language enriched with Hebrew terms (Fortis and Zolli 1979).

Other ethnic quarters and concentrations of foreign traders gravitated around *fondachi*. The term *fondaco* comes from the Arab word *fundouk*, exchange-house or hotel, where people and merchandise in transit could be housed (Concina 1997). These structures provided storage for goods and the living quarters for their importers who engaged in banking. The Venetian *fondachi* imitated this model and were not dissimilar from the exchange houses that the Venetian merchants travelling through Byzantium, Alexandria and the Islamic cities would have encountered long time ago. Like these older institutions, the Venetian *fondachi* offered commercial advantages and 'residence' to Germans, Turks, Persians, Arabs, Greeks, Armenians and other foreign communities trading with the Republic. Rather than imposing residential segregation the *fondachi* were specialised zones of hospitality and natural foci for foreign communities sharing the same language, faith or kinship ties. They allowed the enclaved minorities of Orthodox Greeks, Muslim Albanians and Armenians or German and Dutch Protestants to maintain a degree of self-autonomy and practice their ceremonies and rites freely. Like the ghetto, they established a community that, while sometimes closed within itself, was often open to the surrounding city. Indeed, when Turkish merchants petitioned in 1573 for the establishment of their own warehouse, they wanted 'a place of their own, as the Jews have their ghetto, to accommodate their merchandise' (Pullan 1983: 54). When such a place (*Fondaco dei turchi*) was finally established in 1621, it featured not only a Turkish *hammam* but also a mosque, probably the only one in Western Europe at the time. The compound housed Turkish, Anatolian, Persian as well as Balkan 'Turks', that is Slavs of Muslim religion (*schiavoni*), Bosnians and Albanians (*scutarini, dulcignotti*), all of whom were identified by the generic term 'Turk' (*turco*) (Kafadar 1986; Goffman 2002). Since not all of these different ethnic and religious groups easily accepted living under the same roof, the Arabic and Asiatic element of the people of Constantinople were designated a separate living space from the Bosnian and Albanian subjects of the Ottoman Empire. The Venetian authorities also hired a guardian, someone who had proved to be 'very Christian' and could protect the Venetians by forbidding women, stragglers or Christians from entering the quarters (Sagredo and Berchet 1860).

Although the Venetian state made some efforts to keep various religious and ethnic groups under surveillance, living 'together' as opposed to 'dispersed' throughout the city was considered a privilege and a guarantee of certain limited religious freedoms. The Venetians were more interested in commerce and coexistence than in religious and cultural divisions. Their refusals to join western Crusades against the Ottoman Porte and their relative tolerance towards their Jewish, Muslim and Protestant commercial partners regularly annoyed the popes in Rome. This pragmatic approach allowed for a variety of interactions and exchanges across social, ethnolinguistic and religious divides.

Domestic space was central to the contestation and crossing of these various divides. The numerous examples of Muslim lodgers living in Christian houses, or Venetian citizens eating Jewish food and socialising with the Jews in the ghetto, reveal several transgressive intimacies across religious, linguistic, social and political boundaries. The sixteenth-century household of the Greek commercial broker and naturalised citizen Francesco de Demetri Lettino and his wife Giulia Moier (probably of German Protestant origins), who rented rooms to the Ottoman-Turkish Muslim merchants with whom they socialised and shared Turkish food, is a case in point (Rothman 2006: 47). Concubinage between Venetian masters and Muslim women employed as domestic slaves and servants in their houses was another way of crossing cultural, political and religious boundaries.

Cross-cultural socialising took place not only within people's homes, their attics and kitchens, but also in the city's squares, markets, coffee shops, gambling houses and brothels. The Turkish patisserie-cafés frequented by local intelligentsia, foreign merchants and the cosmopolitan bourgeoisie of the city are one example of such a cross-cultural space. There were thirty-four such shops in St Mark's Square alone in the eighteenth century. Visiting in 1782, the English author William Beckford had written: 'the variety of exotic merchandise, the perfume of coffee, the shade of awnings, and the sight of Greeks and Asiatics sitting cross-legged under them, make me think myself in the bazaars of Constantinople' (1783: 87).

The impact of these various contacts and exchange of peoples, goods and ideas shaped Venetian society in fundamental ways and left a lasting mark not only on its palaces and churches but also on its traditions, lifestyle, and value system. Thus although the 'Turks' were often feared as the enemies of the state and religion, the frequency and intensity of trading relations made both Turkish and the Venetian subjects develop a curiosity about each other's way of life. Not only were Turks said to dress in Italian fashion (*all'italiana*) but Venetians were caught wearing 'oriental clothes and shoes', such as Turkish *caftan* or *zamberluco* (long coat) or growing a 'huge moustache which makes them look like a Turk' (Preto 1975: 316, 319). The impact of these relations could also be felt on the Venetian language and popular culture. Numerous Arab words were adopted by the Venetians, including *sikka* (mint), *tariff* (duty), *arsenale, founduk* (warehouse), *doana* (customs) in the sphere of politics, war and commerce; while terms such as *sofa, divan* and *damasco* were borrowed to name luxury goods. By the end of the sixteenth century, ordinary Venetians could understand jokes based on Italianised Slavic language and by the end of the eighteenth century they were able to understand the some 278 Greek words that had been introduced into their dialect (Cortelazzo 1970). The case of a sixteenth-century redeemed slave, Giulio Torquato, who had served as a slave in Istanbul for twelve years and not only spoke Italian but also knew 'Greek, Turkish, Slavic, and other languages very well, so that he could be of universal use', hints at the extraordinary heterogeneous identity of the citizenry (Rothman 2006: 75). Extensive links to merchants of all nations and speaking various languages fostered intellectual ties too. Venice became the world centre for publishing in Hebrew, Greek and Armenian and a conduit for the aesthetic and intellectual traditions of Byzantium, the Hellenic world and Medieval Islam.

These multifaceted cultural exchanges and urban interactions suggest that early modern Venice could be characterised in terms of a cosmopolitan city. However, this 'cosmopolitanism' applies to the more restricted usage of the term, which draws attention to the existence of positive forms of intercultural encounters despite underlying divisions and conflicts. The city welcomed many foreign merchants and prided itself on offering protection to various religious and political refugees, but the attitudes of the Venetian state were often contradictory. Differences were perceived and practised and economic discrimination against non-citizens enforced, even though everyday business and personal relations were marked by courtesy, openness and curiosity about each other's customs, habits and food.

Venice's cosmopolitan paradigm did not last forever. If the city had grown into a cosmopolitan metropolis by looking away from Europe towards the East, its shrinking maritime empire, invasions and conflicts, and the city's economic, social and political decline damaged the multicultural tissue of the city; many members of the foreign merchant community began to leave Venice to seek their fortune elsewhere. With the long and costly campaigns against the Ottoman Empire from 1684 onwards, the diversity and size of the Ottoman population rapidly declined. The last remaining resident of the Turkish warehouse left in 1838 (Preto 1975: 140–41). The Persian warehouse was demolished in 1908. Earlier, Ottoman and Levantine Jewish traders had left as Portuguese, Spanish and English explorers opened new merchant routes to the East through the Indian and Atlantic Oceans. The communities of colonial émigrés from the Eastern Mediterranean and Adriatic also suffered as Venice lost its dominance in this region.[2]

These centrifugal tendencies continued in the next centuries. After Napoleon abolished the Republic in 1797, and ceded the city to the Austrians in 1798, Venice slipped quietly into post-imperial marginalisation, as a peripheral port and a provincial town stifled by bungling Hapsburg bureaucracy. The economic depression continued after the annexation of Venice to Italy in 1866 and caused mass migration to South America and Mexico between 1870 and 1905, and to the USA, Canada and Australia between 1945 and 1960.[3] Those who remained of the former foreign minorities integrated into a Venetian society as a result of the processes of Italianisation (nationalisation) imposed by the central government and later Italian Fascist regime (1922–1935), comparable to the case in Greece discussed in chapter 7. The only former minority that remained somewhat distinct was the Jewish community.

Demise of the Jewish community and the new 'cultural' reclaiming of the ghetto

The fortunes of the Jewish ghetto intermeshed with the destiny of the city. When Napoleon took control of Venice, the wooden gates of the ghetto were publicly burned, taxes were lifted and Jews were free to reside where they wished. But full civil rights were granted only in 1818 and Jews were subjected to several restrictions under the Austrian regime. In the seventeenth century, the ghetto had accommodated around 5,000 inhabitants (in a Venetian population totalling about 150,000). By 1869, the number of Venetian Jews was estimated at 2,415 (Calimani 1988: 263). By this time, significant social and economic differences developed between poor 'lower' (*zo*) Jews (sixty-four per cent), who had remained in the ghetto, and the wealthier 'upper' (*so*) Jews who lived in the city centre and had entirely assimilated into Venetian society. However, any sense of integration that developed was shattered in 1938, when Mussolini issued racial laws which expelled Jews from schools, universities, civil service and professional associations, creating a new social ghettoisation. Discriminations by the Fascist regime brought the Jewish population down to 1,200 on the eve of the Second World War. Between 1943 and 1945, 246 members of the old Jewish families that lived in the ghetto were deported to Germany and killed.

Today, the ghetto has become a tourist landmark rather than a living community. Only two old Jewish families still live there (although the city still harbours a small Jewish community of approximately 250 people). But the deserted space has been taken up by a new kind of newcomer, people who are reclaiming the ghetto as a historical site and a pilgrimage destination. Among these newcomers are members of various international organisations and orthodox Jewish families from Israel and the USA, including the Hassidic Jewish-American Lubavitch movement. Having settled in Venice in the late 1980s, these well-travelled international families have been very successful in capitalising on the historical fame of the ghetto, opening the first Kosher restaurant, celebrating Jewish holidays in public, and staging other cultural events, which have all become major tourist attractions.

This new cultural reclaiming of the ghetto has made it once again a sensitive spot in Venice and a place apart from the rest of the city. The outward manifestations of orthodox Judaism by the Lubavitchers not only provoke occasional anti-Jewish graffiti and right-wing extremist demonstrations but also antagonise the few Jews remaining of the old reformed Jewish community who feel more discrete and protective of their identity. They feel that their heritage has been kidnapped and trivialised by the ultra-orthodox Lubavitchers, who now often take credit for being the 'most authentic' Jews in the ghetto (see chapter 3 for a comparable process in contemporary Odessa). An observant visitor will notice that the sudden appearance of distinctively dressed Hassidic Jews selling traditional Jewish crafts and promoting the 'authentic' culture of the ghetto has a distinct hint of a commercial operation, a renewed ethnicity with an eye to tourism's lust for the folkloric.

The lucrative businesses and cultural interventions of the Lubavitchers not only sharpened differences amongst the Jews but also posed an economic threat to local entrepreneurs and exposed some deeply rooted contradictions of the Venetian attitudes to the Jews. Traditionally, Jews were accepted as an integral part of Venetian society as long as they remained manifestly segregated in such a way that they did not jeopardise Venetian businesses or 'pollute' Venetian (Christian) culture. This 'inclusive exclusion' stabilised the state of acceptance in the past but also in the present (Zanini 1997: 96). Today, however, although the public manifestations of Jewishness still elicit fear of 'contamination', the main concerns circulate around the issue of economic competition, which jeopardises the local tourist business. 'Why do the Jews display the Hanukkah lights outside the boundaries of the ghetto?' 'Have they paid taxes for the Sukkah shelters which sell Jewish food on the fondamenta di Cannareggio?' Such local reactions are rare, but they show that the ghetto, albeit now largely non-Jewish and an open space, still remains a symbol of Jewish separateness.

Modern Venice: tourism and social transformation of the city

The fortunes of the ghetto, its tourist success, its demographic decline and erosion of its formerly diverse Jewish identity, epitomise the struggles and contradictions of the city as a whole. Venice's former multiethnic communities have disappeared, but today the city has become host to new kinds of visitors and sojourners. Each day Venice is visited by thousands of tourists from all over the world while tourism-focused enterprises bring an increasing number of immigrant workers from China, Africa, Pakistan, Bangladesh and Eastern Europe. While these new groups of global migrants introduce new forms of intercultural encounters in Venice, they also generate new divisions and conflicts.

Tourism development has in general negative effects on the formation of cosmopolitan attitudes in Venice. Several factors are responsible for this. Firstly, the rapid and intense development of the tourism industry in Venice poses a threat not only to the city's environment but also to its social fabric. While the numbers of tourists are increasing, the city struggles to retain urban life with its rapidly shrinking population, which has fallen from about 200,000 residents at the end of the Second World War to fewer than 61,000 today. The main causes of this continued exodus of the inhabitants are the high cost of living, the exorbitant property prices and a lack of work. There is virtually no employment base besides tourism. A few minor manufacturing workshops of the older generation of craftsmen – glassblowers, goldsmiths, boat makers and textile artists – continue to ply their trades for a clientele that appreciates (and can afford) traditional quality, but their offspring leave the city in droves as poorly paid and part-time jobs in the service and tourism sectors appeal less and less to them. Mario Zago, a gondola maker, still forges and burnishes gondola bow flags in his workshop at Santa Croce in Calle del Tentor. His family has been passing the secrets of his craft from generation to generation and they originally had a workshop in the Cannareggio district, where the Sotoportego dei lustraferi, literally the 'Passageway of the bowflag burnishers', can still be found today. But Mario's son, Luca, is not interested in preserving family tradition and has left the city to study law at Bologna University. Lack of educational opportunities in Venice, where 'one can be either a street cleaner or a billionaire', as unemployed Beppe bitterly points out, is another factor which forces young Venetians out of the city. Meanwhile, house prices have soared beyond the reach of all but the richest Venetians. There is generally little and poor quality housing, which requires constant renovation and investment due to the humidity and floods. So, many prefer to move to the modern and cheaper apartments in Mestre and Marghera. 'I would never consider leaving the lagoon', confesses a young entrepreneur who owns a small software company, 'I was born here, I have never left and I would never consider living anywhere else. But people are leaving and they will continue to do so if the city administration does not improve people's lives. The city loses around 2,000 inhabitants per year and if it continues to lose its full-time citizens at the same rate it will become soon dead.'

The rapid development of tourism contributes to unfavourable changes not only in demographics but also in the quality of life, social structure and spatial re-organisation of the local population. In the past it was the Jews who were safely kept at the periphery of the city, but today the Venetians themselves are pushed out of the city centre while wealthy hoteliers and foreign investors are taking over their empty apartments and buildings. Half of the six districts that make up the city have already become the international enclaves of hotels, overpriced restaurants, fashion boutiques and art galleries. The recent sale of the Palazzo Grassi, an eighteenth-century palace on the Grand Canal, to French billionaire François Pinault, who transformed the building into a museum of postmodern art, highlights this trend. While foreigners move in, it is the Venetian citizen who is coming to feel more or less like a 'foreigner' – marginalised and excluded, whose only privilege is the minority status of the citizen of a most beautiful ghetto, surrounded by the walls of international houses and closed off by the waters of the lagoon.

This increasing ghettoisation of the local population has made Venice once again a polarised and contested space. It has created new tensions and new territories of cultural encounters with foreigners who are conquering the cityscape. With its dense network of canals, narrow alleyways leading to squares, markets and courtyards, Venice has always been a place of chance encounters and unexpected minglings. Yet today these encounters lack the former openness and civility. The role of tourism in fostering intercultural encounters between foreign visitors and their hosts has been controversial, as modern-day mass tourism often condenses the traditional spontaneous hospitality into commercial activity (Nettekoven 1979; Boissevain 1977). Such interactions do not eliminate prejudices but rather rein-force them. In Venice, the obvious relative wealth of the tourists often leads to exploitative behaviour on the side of the hosts – prices for tourists often double and triple compared to what the locals are charged for the same products and services.

This also means that the locals and tourists rarely mix in the same places for food and entertainment. The tourist establishments are simply too ex-pensive for the locals or serve bad-quality food for undemanding tourists, while the local youth tend to go to the mainland Mestre where they can drive cars and visit shopping centres and night clubs for entertainment. Otherwise, they gather in a 'bacaro', a typical Venetian bar, for an aperitif ('spritz') and home-made snacks ('cichetti'). Some of these local places have adapted to the demands of tourist economy, like the *Trattoria Storica* at the Calle dei Volti in Cannareggio, which offers inexpensive lunch-time dishes for the local workers, whilst in the evening replaces them with an expensive tourist menu. Similarly, the ancient cafés that spread across St Mark and used to be the heart and soul of Venice's cosmopolitan life, like Café Florian or Café Quadri have now been deserted by the local clientele. They have now become places of exclusion as very few Venetians can afford to pay the exorbitant prices for food that the affluent tourists are paying there. 'No one ever has coffee here anymore, so let's go to the Mondatori bar instead', my Venetian friend Matteo suggests when I invite him to Flo-rian's, 'all my friends will be there'. Indeed, this fashionable bar hiding in the Mondatori bookshop, just behind St Mark Square, has become a popu-lar meeting place for local Venetians – a space for political debates, social events or dating.

Venetians no longer find their sense of community and belonging in St Mark Square, once the city's civic and cultural centre and now flooded with *acqua alta* (high waters) and tourists, but in the bars, shops, courtyards, or neighbourhood squares that lie hidden away from the main tourist routes in every Venetian *sestiere*. The entire city has become an awkward pola-rised space divided into tourist and non-tourist zones. There is the city of mass tourism – exotic, commercial and transient – the city of luxury hotels, souvenir shops, restaurants or fast food chains, stretching along the well-known routes (il Canal Grande-Piazza San Marco, and Strada Nuova-Rialto-Frezzerie). This obligatory itinerary defines and segregates the other parallel universe of ordinary residents – less glamorous and increasingly indiscernible. Walking around the city, one can easily see where the ordi-nary life of little grocery stores, bakeries and wine shops ends and the tour-ist territory begins. These two distinct socio-geographical realities co-exist tensely and edgidly. 'Everybody is complaining about the Venetians aban-doning the city centre to live in the peripheries but no one asks why it is so difficult to live in the centre when you have to cohabit with the tourists,' says Marco who lives on Campo Santo Stefano, very popular with the tourists, and who is thinking of relocating to the periphery or maybe Mestre on the mainland. 'I don't know for how long I will be able to endure those street musicians who busk below my windows until 11pm. There should be some sort of local law forbidding these performances which have no consideration for those who have small children, those who have to wake up early to go to work, or those who simply try to *live* in Venice!'

In addition to spatial segregation, there are other cultural threats that undermine the possibility of intercultural understanding. If the exodus of the inhabitants depopulates and ages the society (today, twenty-five per cent of the population is over the age of sixty-four), then tourists and tourism-focused enterprises commodify Venice's culture and dissipate its identity. Cultural exchange cannot occur in a city whose citizens have to be on constant guard to defend their territories, their livelihoods and their 'way of life'. 'The only manifestation of multiculturalism in Venice today,' I was told by a professor of Venetian history at the local university Cà Foscari, 'is the sound of diverse languages one can hear in public spaces; but tourism cannot be reconciled with inter-culturalism because it trivialises and obliterates local culture itself.' This trivialisation comes in the vulgar form of t-shirt stalls along the Strade-Nuove featuring underwear painted with the genitals of Michaelangelo's David, or fake carnival masks from Taiwan, 'Burano lace' from China and 'Murano glass' made by 'Rumanians and other sellers of plastic trash', as the citizens complain. 'This is offensive not just to us but also to tourists who return to their homes with memories of an entertainment park like Disneyland or Gardaland rather than a real city of culture.'

Global and local sensitivities

Commercial exploitation of Venetian heritage creates tensions not only between locals and tourists but also between ordinary citizens and the city political and economic elites. In a conscious effort to attract international investment and tourism, the Venetian municipality has been promoting the development of arts in the city, staging urban festivals, concerts and other tourist attractions all year round, including the Venetian Carnival, the Historical Regatta and the Biennale. However, these events do not embody the rituals and culture of the local people but have become increasingly politicised 'pseudo-events' that threaten the very authenticity and integrity of that culture (MacCannell 1973; Boorstin 1961). They are 'grand spectacles staged for the tourists that actually offend our local sensitivities', as one city-dweller put it. To ordinary Venetians, the public authorities appear to be like the 'Lubavitchers' of the ghetto – the outsiders and impostors who are selling out the city's heritage in pursuit of their own political agenda.

The city's cultural initiatives have increasingly become associated with big money and international media and serve as a political pulpit for the Venetian municipality to attract art patrons and rich donors and raise funds for the maintenance of the city. This cultural agenda dates back to the nineteenth century when tourism began to be consciously promoted as part of the economic regeneration and nation-building ambitions of Italy's ruling elites. The central tenets of this policy were to develop tourist infrastructure (the first major bathing establishment opened as early as 1833), as well as fostering Italian national prestige abroad through the staging of various exhibitions and cultural events, including the Venice Biennale established in 1895 (Bosworth 1993).

Today, the Venice Biennale remains one of the most high-profile events in the art agenda of the entire world – the 'Mecca of all exhibitions' as the organisers boldly claim. It has become an immense social event with participants including internationally renowned artists, journalists and celebrities, from Damien Hirst, Elton John or Yoko Ono to advertising tycoon Charles Saatchi and his girlfriend, or celebrity chef Nigella Lawson. Similarly during the Venetian Carnival the city is taken over by an elegant international crowd that flocks to attend fashionable parties. These events, attracting people from all over the world, are reminders of the cosmopolitan gaiety for which the city was once famous. Indeed, cosmopolitanism itself has become a fashionable subject on the agenda of various public events, such as the 2009 Biennale 'Making Worlds' which focused on multiculturalism. One of its (inter-)cultural installations was the Floating Mosque, recalling the city's former links with Islam. The ordinary citizens, however, frequently show hostility to the city's cultural politics. Gianluca, a local shopkeeper, compares these highbrow art events to popular feasts organised in other cities: 'In Rome, the citizens get festivals organised for the people but we get this nuisance of art exhibitions. We get Truffaut, the Romans James Bond.' The mobilisation of cosmopolitan discourses in public policy-making does not reflect the lived reality of ordinary Venetians. There is no unselfconscious everyday coexistence behind the political slogans. There is no sense of continuity with the city's cosmopolitan past enacted and re-enacted in these municipal cultural events.

To commemorate ten centuries of Venice's former relations with the Islamic world, the city authorities hosted an exhibition on *Venice and Islam 828–1797* in the Ducal Palace (from July to November 2007). When asked, very few residents would admit that they were interested in visiting it: 'This is just yet another event to attract tourists, including the rich Muslims from the Middle East.' 'We want more residents, more schools, more food stores and artisan shops, and entertainment facilities like clubs, pubs and cinemas,' says Enrico who runs a cocktail bar, Muro Rialto, which is popular with the locals. 'We are fed up with the politicians and their fancy exhibitions.' When I asked him about the city's historical links with oriental culture, he responded, 'Well, even if there were some trading relations in the past, they are completely irrelevant to our present life in the city'.

The presence of Muslim minorities has not just been expelled from the residents' historical imagination, but from the contemporary one too. Immigrant Muslim workers from Bangladesh, the Middle East, Albania, Serbia and African countries play an increasingly important role in many sectors of the Venetian tourist industry. In 2002, there were some five thousand officially registered Muslim residents working in the city. This number could be at least doubled if we take into consideration illegal workers. According to the statistics of the Venetian Commune (Document COSES, n. 441.1/2002), twenty-five per cent of the city's population – both transient (including tourists) and non-transient – is Muslim.[4] In order to accommodate this growing Muslim presence in Venice, there is now an intense public debate going on about the possibility of re-opening the old mosque in the Turkish Warehouse. The city's leadership see the construction of a mosque not only as a chance to promote peaceful cohabitation but also as an opportunity to attract investment from the Arab world. But the residents disagree, remarking that there are not many Muslims living in the city. 'Reopening the mosque would only please the greedy hoteliers who are turning Venice into an entertainment park for tourists, including rich Arabs swarming into the city,' one hostile resident says. Such protests were vividly articulated by anti-mosque graffiti sprayed on the posters advertising the project.

Venice's past identity as a cosmopolitan metropolis had long been eroded. Today it is only the city elites who continue to exploit its historical legacy, historicising their new economic relations with the East and re-branding the city as a cosmopolitan city of art. Their strategies surely insert Venice into the international stream of affairs and arguably contribute to what could be defined as an 'aesthetic' or cultural cosmopolitanism, linked to far-reaching aesthetic tastes developed among tourists and elites – globally mobile international consumers of art and culture (Urry 1995). This form of internationalism could be crudely compared to the former cosmopolitan lifestyles of the Venetian patricians who mingled with foreigners on a daily basis and forged transnational diplomatic, economic and cultural alliances. As in the past, this trend is closely associated with political and economic elites – the public administrators, property owners, highly paid international professionals, local intelligentsia, and artists, and so on. However, these global sensibilities and modes of interactions 'from above'

Figure 6.1a. Anti-Muslim graffiti sprayed on the posters advertising *New Mosque in Venice*. Photo by the author.

Figure 6.1b. Anti-Muslim graffiti sprayed on the posters advertising *New Mosque in Venice*. Photo by the author.

do not foster the kind of dense organic neighbourly relations that Venetian city-dwellers experienced in the past. On the contrary, they alienate a major part of the city's population by their evident association with global organisations and higher socioeconomic groupings.

New encounters and fear of pollution from the 'East'

The intensity of international dealings in public life contrasts starkly with the desolated neighbourhoods, rising xenophobia, local cultural *snobbismo* and many other uneasy facts about contemporary Venice. Today, almost any Venetian will say that nothing that comes from abroad can be compared to their own native culture, to their own *sestiere* (neighbourhood), to their own *campanile* (bell tower). And for 'abroad' they literally mean anything that lies beyond the perimeter of the lagoon, including the mainland suburbs of Mestre and Marghera. Italians, as Luigi Barzini noted (Barzini 1964), do not have a deep concept of national unity, and will profess absolute love and allegiance to their own city and region – a tendency that has been named *campanilismo* (meaning allegiance to one's bell tower). In Venice – a city that remains deeply influenced by its historical legacy and its material environment – this tendency is even more pronounced and can sometimes endorse various conservative ideologies. Not long ago, in 1998, to mark the 200th anniversary of the fall of the Venetian Republic, a group of separatist guerrillas dressed in traditional Venetian costumes, climbed their beloved Campanile, unfurled a banner bearing the symbol of the Lion of St Mark and declared the liberation of the Republic from the foreign yoke. Such sentiments play into the hands of Italy's northern separatist party, the Northern League, which is planning to declare an Independent State of Padania with Venice as its capital (one in three voted for the Lega Nord in the recent elections in Venice) (Tambini 2001). One of the representatives of this small but flamboyant radical movement in Venice is Grandpa Gigio (Nonogigio) – Luigi Gigio Zanon, a descendant of an ancient Venetian family and an amateur historian. He considers Italian unification, which was approved by the Venetians in an overwhelming popular vote in 1866, little different from preceding occupations under Napoleon and the Austrians and he advocates the restoration of the Independent Venetian Republic two centuries after its collapse in 1797. A contributor to *Raixe Venete* (Venetian Roots), issued in the local dialect (*il venexian*), he vehemently opposes the central government's attempts to 'italianise' Venice and insists that the local schools should teach in *venexian* to guard the purity of the native culture from foreign influences. Somehow, he fails to remember that *il venexian* is in fact a mixture of several languages and contains many Slavic, Greek, Arabic and Hebrew words.

Heritage and nostalgia play an important part in the local sensitivities and the city still lives in profound thrall to its past. One peculiar aspect of Venice is the fact that the city has remained intact architecturally for the past five hundred years. Yet despite these pervasive architectural and artistic reminders of Venice's past proximity and openness to different worlds, today the ordinary Venetians rarely remember, or refuse to deal with the city's multiethnic past. These memories are now deeply buried in the recesses of the material structures of the city.

Among those who left traces in the city were the three brothers, Rioba, Afani and Sandi who came to Venice to trade from 'the land of the Moors'. Today, three stone figures of the brothers, all wearing turbans, can be found on the façade of a fourteenth-century house in Campo dei Mori. The house features a small Arab fountain at the base of the façade and is customarily referred to as the 'palace of the camel' because of the stone bas-relief of a camel featured there. Not far away, on the Fondamenta dei Mori, another statue of an oriental merchant stands guard in the niche of the palace where Jacopo Tintoretto lived.

One can only wonder what kind of interactions with the Muslim world Tintoretto had – the son of a silk dyer (*tintore*) and a young artist whose workshop was managed by an Arab spice trader funnelling oriental silks, carpets and spices from India and Central Asia along the Silk Road. One can also wonder whether any traces of these intimacies with the oriental world still survive in the memories of the current residents of the square.

Campo dei Mori lies a short distance from the crowded tourist Strada Nuova but today very few tourists pass through here. Occasionally, one can see a few old folks sitting outside and chattering. It is in such secluded neighbourhoods that one can still catch the glimpse of 'real' Venice where citizens experience their embodied sense of identity and belonging. Yet today this identity is fundamentally different. There are no oriental traders, no bustling commercial and cultural life. Silence, emptiness and decay hang mournfully in the air. When an occasional tourist ventures into this area, they are greeted with suspicion and hostility by the local residents who perceive these incursions as an invasion of their territory and a disruptive intervention on their private life. 'So far, this place has been quiet but I fear not for long as more and more tourists are coming to see the Moors. Some bloody tourist book must have given away this place. I saw some Arabs amongst them the other day. It is no longer safe to let our children play in the campo', a grandmother of three complains to me, while the figures of the three Moors stare blankly at the city that has lost its memory and ability to appreciate diversity.

Due to its proximity and frequent encounters with the Ottoman Empire, Venice was often portrayed as the most 'eastern' city in Europe. But present-day Venetians see themselves and their city as profoundly European, both in the present and in the past. So, when tourists in Venice came mainly from Europe and America, the cultural distance between locals and foreigners was not felt to be large. But in the age of global tourism, with an increasing number of visitors coming from Eastern Europe, South-East Asia, China and the Middle East, the perception of cultural distance is sharpening. Paolo, a young Venetian who works as a tourist guide in the city, explained to me: 'We have to ask a serious question about the decreasing number of European visitors – conscious and knowledgeable [about our culture], as compared with the masses coming from corrupted and underdeveloped countries [of the East] which completely disregard our culture. These cohorts of barbarians fill the pockets of their compatriots who have already settled in the city, running bed rentals, camp sites and refugee camps in Mestre … they enrich the street vendors, sellers of plastic trash made in Thailand … and in this way Venice will be gradually eliminated from the West in the name of those who rent apartments to Cuban prostitutes and consume our historical dignity in the Casino.'

Behind these hostilities and xenophobic sentiments linger fears of foreign 'takeovers' of the city's traditional economic activities. Today, the Venetians not only encounter 'exotic' tourists but also racially and culturally different asylum seekers and immigrant workers: war refugees from Iraq, Somalia and Sudan, Chinese, Moroccan and Senegalese street vendors (derogatively called *vucumprà*), Bangladeshi and Afghani cooks, Iranian businessmen and B&B managers, East European cleaners, domestic assistants, waitresses and prostitutes. According to the figures of the local Foreign Office, there were nine thousand immigrant non-EU workers registered in Venice in 2004, but the figure is underestimated, given the amount of illegal immigration that takes place. The Chinese, Moroccan and Senegalese street vendors selling fake Venetian masks, Gucci bags and Murano glass are perceived as economic competition by the local artisans and shopkeepers who sell authentic Venetian crafts at much higher prices. 'I'm fed up with seeing those new Venetians, those Indians, Chinese, the Arabs and Polynesians ... who come here as immigrants and then claim the place for themselves and push us out of the city,' local shopkeeper M. Bondi said when explaining his fear of being put out of a job. Nevertheless, despite such manifestations of xenophobia, the rapid expansion of the tourist industry in the city has created a situation in which intercultural relations may flourish in some unexpected ways.

Informal economy practices and coexistence

In the changed circumstances of mass tourism and depopulation, certain cross-national social and cultural practices of overseas migrants may actually find a welcoming environment in Venice, especially in the informal economy. Due to the significant economic growth of the region, Veneto has turned into a land of immigration and has been attracting more and more immigrants since the 1990s. In 2008 the Italian national institute of statistics (ISTAT) estimated that 403,985 foreign-born immigrants were living in Veneto, equal to 8.3 per cent of the total regional population. As a port city with plenty of opportunities for seasonal work in the burgeoning tourist industry, the city offers more opportunities for employment for the less skilled and often inadequately educated immigrants than other Italian cities. 'I came to Venice because my cousin was already here and secured me a job washing dishes in a restaurant during the summer. It was badly paid but I didn't speak any Italian then and probably would not have been able to find any other job elsewhere. Besides, one can meet so many foreign friends here that one does not feel so homesick,' says Hassan who came to Venice in 2008 from Morocco.

In a city with such a high percentage of residents over sixty-five, there is a demand for *badanti*, domestic helpers who live with and care for dependent elders. The appearance of *badanti* is a relatively recent Italian phenomenon which became popular with Italian elderly men and women who cannot afford expensive retirement homes and who often receive much better care from Eastern European women who take care of them. Since *badanti* are offered not only money but also accommodation and food, this is an excellent opportunity for both young and old, regular and irregular immigrants to get established in the city. 'If you end up in a good house, you can earn as much as 1000 Euros per month and send it home,' says fifty-year-old Adriana, a Rumanian *badante*. The majority of the *badanti* are from Eastern Europe, and according to several interviewees, they come to Venice because they know there is work here. They typically work for three to five years, send money home to their families, and then return to their home countries.

Immigrants play an increasingly important role in many sectors of the Venetian tourist industry by providing low-wage flexible labour which fills gaps that the Venetians emigrating from the city had long been unable to fill (Quassoli 1999). The impact of this mobile labour force is also evident in Mestre and Marghera ports where the local petrochemical industries rely on low-skilled seasonal overseas labour.

As the region with one of the highest levels of immigrant employment in Italy, Venice is slowly getting used to, and is becoming receptive to, the ways of life and forms of social and cultural capital of migrants from Eastern Europe, Middle East and Africa. This openness might be crudely characterised as cosmopolitan. In Altobello quarter of Mestre, for example, Muslim workers rented a big flat where they meet and pray. The flat is situated right next to the Catholic Church but, according to the parish priest, the relations between Christians and Muslims are peaceful, if not amicable, just as in the past when Muslims and Christians prayed side by side. According to Samir, who is vice-responsible for the mosque in Marghera, most of the Muslims who pray there actually work in the lagoon where they are respected as good and hard workers. 'We live and work with Venetians and nobody has problems.' 'The Venetians socialise with Muslims too.'

Beyond the informal economy there are also other cross-ethnic interactions and intercultural practices such as marriages, sexual and romantic relations and cohabiting. Just as in the old times of the Republic, when Muslim women cohabited with their Venetian masters and Slav girls were married to Muslim men, today Slav female workers cohabit with Muslims while Venetian men visit Cuban prostitutes and date and marry Eastern European girls. Marriage between Venetians and immigrants is still stigmatised but is increasingly frequent as young Venetian males find it difficult to locate a Venetian woman to marry them. While young Venetian women leave for the mainland to look for well-to-do partners, the Venetians find partners among immigrant female workers, especially those from Eastern Europe who have the reputation of making good brides because they do not fear the guaranteed hard labour of being a wife of a waiter or a hotel manager. This is the case of Luigi, a young hotel manager who married a Polish waitress and now she works for him. Her cousin Renata has a child with Ahmed, an illegal worker from Pakistan who lives in Mestre and commutes to Venice for work.

Luigi is also the leader of a local activist group that runs an internet portal *Venessia.com*. This group represents the interests of the 'real Venetians' and has been particularly vocal in voicing protests and drawing public attention to many economic, social and environmental problems of the lagoon. In order to draw attention to Venice's rapidly shrinking population and the sale of city properties to foreign investors, for example, they organised a campaign *Ultimi Veri Venexiani* (The last authentic Venetians), selling their photo in front of St Mark Basilica on ebay. Among these remnants of 'authentic' Venetians, I spotted Luigi's Polish wife. The auction attracted forty buyers and sold for five thousand euros. *Venessia.com* has become an important tool of social and political mobilisation in the city but it also offers new modes of conviviality that are changing the way in which an increasingly displaced Venetian community can experience their urban lives. It brought together a new group of 'web' citizens, including long-time city-dwellers and newcomers as well as those who abandoned the city and can now travel via digital highways to connect with their home.

Negotiating modern Venetian identity

From its very origins, Venice was a place where identity was hybrid and negotiated across different cultural and religious boundaries. Even today, the most common family names in Venice are 'Saraceno', 'Turco', 'Moro', 'Albanese', etc., evidence of close relations with the Ottomans during many centuries. Historically, Venetians are undoubtedly a melting pot of mixed blood – Greek, Albanian, Slavic, Jewish, Turk, Italian and so on. These ancient ethnic and religious differences still hide behind the general label of *il venessian*. Among those who claim ancient historic lineage and who is proud of his family links with the Ottomans, is Count Francesco da Mosto, an architect and amateur historian, who turned his extraordinary ancestral history into a series of films and books on Venice's frequent encounters with the East. In the past, constant migration shifts made it difficult to tell exactly who was *venetus originarius*. Similarly today, fewer and fewer city-dwellers can claim Venetian ancestry as the members of the old families have abandoned the city while new entrepreneurs and workers have moved in. Many of the present city-dwellers are second- or third-generation immigrants from the mainland who moved to the lagoon after the Second World War to work in the tourism sector or the booming petrochemical industry at the port of Marghera. These relatively recent additions to the city are less keen to emphasise Venice's multiethnic past, as they strive to protect their increasingly precarious existence against a variety of threats in the sinking and shrinking city. Not surprisingly, this group of working-class citizens appears most protective of their status as 'real' Venetians, defending their livelihoods and identity from cultural interventions from outside and from above. As they struggle to re-examine their own identity against a variety of threats – demographic, environmental, cultural, economic – the old taxonomy of original or 'real' Venetians is re-emerging as a somewhat oblique yet jealously guarded category. While the broad categories of foreigner (*straniero*) and local outsider 'new Venetians' (*novi venessiani*) are unevenly applied to a wide range of newcomers, a restricted group of permanent citizens claims the minority status of 'native' Venetians. They call themselves 'true indigenous people, like the Indians of America'. They insist on being *venessian* rather than Italian, speak the local dialect which remains incomprehensible to most of the Italians, and feel different not only from tourists and immigrants but also from the 'Venetians' who live in the suburbs of Mestre and Marghera of the *terraferma* (mainland) and commute to Venice for work. These geographical sensitivities are often conflated with economic and social ones, since the majority of immigrant Muslim and Eastern European workers settled in Mestre and Marghera, not being able to afford the high cost of living in the lagoon.

The term 'real Venetians' has therefore become a very exclusive category, applied to a restricted group of citizens on the basis of their language, history, religion, and breeding, but also their physical and emotional attachment to their peculiar residential habitat. When the local citizens refer to a 'real' Venetian, they mean not only someone who was born in the city but someone who can also evoke a recognisable idiom of having an existence predicated on the idea of 'survival' in a special aquatic habitat different from the rest of Italy and the whole world. They emphasise their everyday struggle to survive amidst decay, tourism and floods and speak about themselves as the remnants of an ancient amphibious civilisation ('la vera civiltà anfibia') on the verge of extinction, the Atlantis of the modern age. 'The morning I woke up and saw the population counter at San Bartolomeo Square down to 59,756 citizens,' says local patriot Pierluigi Tamburino, 'I realised that this was the end. We are fewer that the gorillas of the Uganda mountains, a species which has been declared at high risk of extinction. There is no one who will save the last Venetians though.' Such discourses of extinction often lead to xenophobic prejudices against tourists and immigrants, especially those religiously and ethnically different from the citizens. However, these discourses are not mainly premised on religion or ethnicity but on the idea of the survival of the city and its people. As such, they allow possibilities of inclusion as well as exclusion and can be broadly applied to anyone who decides to move here permanently and share in the pains of everyday existence. In fact, the metaphor of survival (from foreign invasions, floods, infidels and disease) has been used for centuries as an organising symbol for social mobilisation and a powerful rhetorical tool to defuse various tensions and conflicts within the city. Today, as the combined trends of global tourism and the informal labour market make the city's citizenship increasingly fluid and transient once again, the old rhetoric and new discourses of belonging are seized upon to renegotiate new solidarities, new boundaries and new identities.

NOTES

1. In 1527 and 1541 the ghetto was enlarged to accommodate the growing Jewish population. On the history of the Venetian ghetto see Davis and Ravid (2001) and Calimani (1988).
2. With the fall of Cyprus (1571), Crete (1669) and the Peloponnesus (1715) to the Turks.
3. The major concentration of Venetians is now in Brazil, where they are known as Veneto-Brazilians.
4. Michele Casari, 'Materiali per un Piano Strategico della Città di Venezia. Popolazione quotidiana e comunità: il caso di Venezia', Documento COSES n. 441.1/2002, Comune di Venezia.

REFERENCES

Barzini, L. 1964. *The Italians: A Full Length Portrait*. New York.

Beck, H.G. et al. 1977. *Venezia, centro di mediazione tra Oriente e Occidente, secoli XV–XVI: Aspetti e problemi*. Florence.

Beckford, W. 1783. *Dreams, Waking Thoughts, and Incidents; In a Series of Letters, From Various Parts of Europe*. London.

Boissevain, J. 1977. *Coping with Tourists: European Reactions to Mass Tourism*. London.

Boorstin, D. 1961. *The Image: A Guide to Pseudo-Events in America*. New York.

Bosworth, R.J. 1993. *Italy and the Wider World 1860-1960*. London.

Braudel, Fernand. 1975. *The Mediterranean and the Mediterranean World in the Age of Philip II*, trans. Siân Reynolds, 2 vols. London.

Calimani, R. 1988. *The Ghetto of Venice*. Milan.

Carile, Antonio. 1978. 'Le origini di Venezia nella tradizione storiografica', in G. Arnaldi and M.P. Stocchi (eds), *Storia delle cultura veneta*. vol. 1: *Dalle origini al Trecento*. Vicenza, pp. 135–66.

Cochrane, E.W. and J. Kirshner, 1975. 'Deconstructing Lane's Venice', *Journal of Modern History* 47(2): 321–34.

Concina, E. *Fondaci: architettura, arte e mercatura tra Levante, Venezia e Alemagna*. Venice, pp. 97, 15–26.

Cortelazzo, M. 1970. *L'inlfusso linguistico Greco a Venezia*. Bologna.

Coryat, T. [1611] 1905. *Crudities*, reprint in 2 vols, vol. 1. Glasgow.

Davis, R. and B. Ravid (eds). 2001. *The Jews of Early Modern Venice*. Baltimore.

Fortis, U. and P. Zolli. 1979. *La parlata giudeo-veneziana*, Assisi.

Goffman, D. 2002. *The Ottoman Empire and Early Modern Europe*. New York.

Greene, M. 2000. *A Shared World: Christians and Muslims in the Early Modern Mediterranean*. Princeton.

Herzog, T. 2003. *Defining Nations: Immigrants and Citizens in Early Modern Spain and Spanish America*. New Haven.

Housley, Norma. 1996. 'Frontier Societies and Crusading in the late Middle Ages', in B. Arbel (ed.), *Intercultural Contacts in the Medieval Mediterranean*. London, pp. 104–19.

Kafadar, Cemal. 1986. 'A Death in Venice (1575): Anatolian Muslim Merchants Trading in the Serenissima', *Journal of Turkish Studies* 10: 191–218.

Kirshner, J. 1973. '*Civitas sibi faciat civem*: Bartolus of Sassoferrato's Doctrine on the Making of a Citizen', *Speculum* 48: 694–713.

MacCannell, Dean. 1973. 'Staged Authenticity: Arrangements of Social Space in Tourist Settings', *American Journal of Sociology* 79(3): pp. 589–603.

Martin, J. and D. Romano (eds). 2000. *Venice Reconsidered: The History and Civilization of an Italian City State, 1297–1797*. Baltimore.

Nettekoven, Lothar. 1979. 'Mechanisms of Intercultural Interactions', in E. de Kadt (ed.), *Tourism: Passport to Development? Perspectives on the Social and Cultural Effects of Tourism in Developing Countries*. Kadt, New York, pp. 135–45.

Nicol, D.M. 1988. *Byzantium and Venice: A Study in Diplomatic and Cultural Relations*. New York.

Petrusi, A. (ed.). 1966. *Venezia e l'Oriente fra tardo Medioevo e Rinascimento*. Florence.

Preto, P. 1975. *Venezia e i turchi*. Florence.

Pullan, B. 1983. *The Jews of Europe and the Inquisition of Venice, 1550–1670*. Oxford.

Quassoli, Fabbio. 1999. 'Migrants in the Italian Underground Economy', *International Journal of Urban and Regional Research* 23(2): 212–31.

Rothman, E.N. 2006. 'Between Venice and Istanbul: Trans-Imperial Subjects and Cultural Mediation in the Early Modern Mediterranean' (Ph.D. diss., University of Michigan).

Sagredo, A. and F. Berchet. 1860. *Il Fondaco dei Turchi in Venezia*. Milan.

Tambini, Damian. 2001. *Nationalism in Italian Politics: The Stories of the Northern League, 1980-2000*. London.

Thiriet, Freddy. 1977. 'Sur les communautés grecque et albanaise à Venise', in H.G. Beck (ed.), *Venezia centro di mediazione tra oriente e occidente, Aspetti e problemi*. 2 vols. Florence, Civiltà veneziana studi, 32, vol. 1, pp. 217–31.

Urry, J. 1995. *Consuming Places*. London.

Zanini, P. 1997. *I significati del confine: I limiti naturali, storici, mentali*. Milan.

⊰ Chapter 7 ⊱

Haunted by the Past and the Ambivalences of the Present: Immigration and Thessalonica's Second Path to Cosmopolitanism

PANOS HATZIPROKOPIOU

In assessing its recent experience of immigration, it is often asserted that Greece has transformed from a migrant-sending to a migrant-receiving country, thus depicting the challenges of 'diversity' as a historical novelty. However tangible this assertion may be, it is negligible of a long history of population movements, 'forced' or 'voluntary', within and beyond the country's shifting borders, and of a legacy of multiethnic coexistence that marked Greece's passage to modernity (Baldwin-Edwards and Apostolatou 2008). Nowhere in the country may this history be more explicitly traceable than in Thessalonica, a major port city at the crossroads between East and West. The dawn of the twentieth century found the Ottoman metropolis being claimed by competing Balkan nationalisms, while hosting a multitude of religions and ethnicities, and a Sephardic Jewish majority. Its painful integration into the Greek nation-state was marked by ruptures that altered its demographics and involved deliberate attempts to redraw the city's 'Greek' identity, condemning its cosmopolitan past into oblivion.

This past is now beginning to re-emerge in the advent of internationalisation and new migrations. The presence of migrants challenges not only the city's demographic and social structures, but also its landscape and its ways of understanding itself. This chapter explores a series of contradictions related to Thessalonica's cosmopolitan history and its present-day migratory reality. It will examine the place of migrants in the city and show how this features in discourses about the city's identity, which are inevitably haunted by the spectres of history. Official narrations of the city's 'Greekness', traced in ancient and Byzantine times, are challenged by an emerging discourse that draws parallels between present-day 'multiculturalism' and past cosmopolitanism. As it will be argued, however, such understandings of the present are anachronistic and do not account for the everyday realities of migrants in the city.

The claims of Thessalonica's historical pluralism echo conventional assumptions about liberal cosmopolitanism in Mediterranean port cities during the late nineteenth and early twentieth centuries (Driessen 2005). The discussion that follows draws on contemporary theoretical accounts of the relationship between the cosmopolitan and the urban (e.g. Sandercock 2003; Binnie et al. 2006; Hemelryk-Donald et al. 2009). In the discourse developing in Thessalonica, as will be shown later on, cosmopolitanism is often conflated with 'multiculturalism', with the two terms being used as synonyms to express ethnic and cultural pluralism in both past and present. A term recently introduced in Greek social science and public discourse, 'multiculturalism' is employed uncritically to account for sociocultural diversity, deprived of any political significance (Agelopoulos 2000; 2008).

The chapter begins with two sections offering an historical account of the city's erstwhile pluralism, and of the processes that conditioned its extinction. It then builds a critical discussion of the emerging cosmopolitan discourse and the ways in which it approaches the present-day reality of migrants. There follows a brief and broad sketch of the city's migratory landscape through ethnographic examples of immigrant experiences in the city. Some general conclusions are finally drawn, arguing that beyond vague conceptions of cosmopolitanism, it is rather the dynamics of class and status that shape the 'post-cosmopolitan' city.

Turn of the century: Thessalonica's cosmopolitan past

The many variants of the city's name – Thessalonica, Salonica, Selanik, Solun – are testimonies of its multiethnic past, and of the fact that it was lived in and claimed by various groups of inhabitants and actual or potential rulers. No period in the city's history is more explicitly linked to this cosmopolitan imagery than the time of its turbulent entrance to European modernity at the dawn of the twentieth century. As in the case of other Mediterranean port cities (Driessen 2005), Thessalonica's 'cosmopolitan urbanism' is traced in accounts of urban life amidst the social and political turmoil of the crumbling Ottoman Empire (Yerolympos and Colonas 1993).

Founded by Cassander, king of Macedonia, in 315 BC, Thessalonica flourished as a Roman port-city on Via Egnatia almost half-way between the Adriatic and the Black Sea. Under Justinian I, it was made capital of the Empire's western provinces and by the eleventh century it had become a regional commercial hub. Its strategic location and growing wealth attracted various invaders over the centuries, until the Ottoman conquest of 1430 AD under Sultan Murad II. Half a century later, the city became home to Sephardic Jews from Iberia, welcomed by the Sultan after their expulsion following the *Reconquista* (1492 AD). The speaking of Judeo-Spanish Ladino became as common as that of Greek or Turkish, and Salonica (as it was known then) gradually came to be the only city of its size hosting a Jewish majority; for centuries it was known by names such as 'mother of Israel'.

At the beginning of the twentieth century, political reforms, industrial development and population inflows produced new class relations, transformed Thessalonica's social geography, expanded its built environment and 'Europeanised' the urban space (Mazower 2005: ch. 11). These trends affected urban processes and caused dramatic shifts in the population mix of the Ottoman Empire's 'most Europeanised city' (Yerolympos and Colonas 1993: 158). The first Ottoman census (1882–1884) counted 85,000 souls, more than half of whom were Jews; the second one (1902) registered about 126,000 inhabitants, of whom Jews comprised nearly half; by the time of the first Greek census (1913), the share of Jews in a total population of nearly 158,000 had declined to 39 per cent, followed by 29 per cent Muslims, 25.3 per cent Greek-Orthodox, and the rest comprising Bulgarians, Armenians, Western Europeans and various others (Molho 1993: 65).

Towards the end of the nineteenth century, Thessalonica's urban space was still bounded in its medieval walls, with clear residential divisions between religious communities: the areas around the old Hippodrome were home to Christian populations; Westerners concentrated close to the Catholic Church; the Turks lived in the Upper Town; the Jews occupied most of the lower city, particularly around the market and the port; and the Dönmehs (Jewish converts to Islam) were found inbetween the lower and upper districts, marking symbolically their position between two religions (Karadimou-Yerolympos 2008: 105). Historically, socio-spatial 'segregation' and 'inter-communal' relations were to an extent determined by the way in which the Ottoman administration had dealt with 'difference'. In the *Millet* system, the main marker of identity and culture was religion, and 'Non Muslims were divided into religious communities' (Agelopoulos 2000: 142). Each *Millet* had its own organisation and leadership, which were also concerned with secular matters (e.g. taxation, education, legal issues like marriage and inheritance) and enjoyed greater autonomy and self-management in the course of late Ottoman reforms (Agelopoulos 2000; Mazower 2005).

Even so, religious 'communities' were not strictly homogeneous social units. The heterogeneity within religious denominations and their respective spatial units in the city, based on other forms of stratification (origins and language, as mentioned, but also parish, profession, etc.), have led scholars to doubt the term 'communities' as such, since the pattern was rather complex and involved various forms of contact, albeit without much mixture (Mazower 2005; Agelopoulos 2000). Changing social relations with the advent of capitalist industrialisation produced new forms of social differentiation in the urban space based more on class criteria than on ethnic or religious ones. In the early twentieth century, the popular strata lived mostly in the city's overcrowded old historical core, as well as in new settlements in the western part where industry and transport were located. The eastern suburbs, especially the 'European-like' ones by the seafront, were reserved for the elites and the city's growing middle classes.

Tensions occurred occasionally, but the urban authorities did their best to promote communal harmony, within the hierarchies of Ottoman rule and according to the interests of the elites. Soon after the May 1876 consul massacre incident, Sultan Murad V's coronation festivities were celebrated peacefully, with 'Turks, Greeks, Jews, Levantines and Europeans, all mingled together as if their national and religious feelings had not been wounded or irritated by the ... horrid occurrences'.[1] By the early twentieth century, Thessalonica was inevitably found at the epicentre of competing nationalisms in the Balkans, as it was contested by both Greeks and Bulgarians who actively propagated their claims to the city, for instance with the bombings of April 1906.[2] Two years later, however, Thessalonica celebrated the 'Young Turk' constitution, which was welcomed by urban elites across religious lines, as the city was a stronghold of the reformist 'Committee of Union and Progress'.[3] Even the new Greek authority (the Ottoman garrison surrendered on 26 October 1912) was initially positive towards the city's pluralism and proclaimed the safeguarding of 'perfect equality for all peoples living under the roof of the State' (Karadimou-Yerolympos 2008: 113): the Turkish mayor remained in power until 1916 and most Muslim residents stayed in the city, while the new rulers sought the trust of the Jewish community.

The rise of new social antagonisms brings us to a final aspect of Thessalonica's early twentieth century cosmopolitanism, linked to the labour movement (Mazower 2005: ch. 13, 19). The city's first trade union, and the Empire's strongest one, the Workers' Socialist Federation (*Federacion*), was founded in 1909 by Avraam Benaroya. A teacher turned printer, fluent in six languages, Benaroya was born in Salonica or Vidin, raised in Bulgaria and studied in Belgrade. *Federacion* was mostly influenced by Austrian socialism as well as by pre-socialist federative ideas in the Balkans such as those of R. Velestinlis. Although a Jewish-majority organisation, 'it was conceived as a federation of separate sections, each representing an ethnic element of Macedonia – Jewish, Bulgarian, Greek and Muslim' and published its propaganda in the respective languages (Marketos 1999: 39). Nevertheless, its efforts to promote class consciousness proved to be an impossible task, as is bitterly acknowledged in the following extract from its Ladino-printed newspaper *Soridaridad Ovradera* (June 1911; in Mazower 2005: 253): 'Salonica is not one city. It is a juxtaposition of tiny villages. Jews, Turks, Donmehs, Greeks, Bulgarians, Westerners, Gypsies, each of these groups which one today calls "Nations", keeps well away from the others, as if fearing contagion. With conflict in the Balkans and Thessalonica's annexation to Greece, as well as the question of economic exploitation, its agenda also focused on issues of national oppression, antimilitarism and internationalism, calling for neutrality in the war.[4]

Cosmopolitanism no more: making Greece in Thessalonica

Thessalonica's millennia of continuous urban history may be present in its contemporary shape, but never explicitly and always hidden, traceable in scarce and scattered elements that only willing eyes may pick out. Evocatively describing it as a 'city of ghosts', the historian Mazower (2005) found in existing historiography not one, but many cities. The extinction of the city's multiethnic past from both its landscape and living memory owes, of course, much to history itself: cities always change and 'sometimes ... follow one another on the same site and under the same name, born and dying without knowing one another, without communicating among themselves'.[5] If we assume, however, that there generally is a degree of continuity in processes of urban change, Thessalonica's pathway to modernity stands unique in that it was marked by rupture with its past, as a result of combined political events, trends of urban development and deliberate attempts to redraw the city's identity. Making Thessalonica Greek was an ambitious part of the nation-building process, which, as elsewhere, dealt with 'memory' in a forgetful and selective way. Nevertheless, two events occurred that established favourable conditions for such a process to unfold (Hastaoglou-Martinidis 1997).

The first was the August 1917 fire, which destroyed the historical urban core and caused vast populations shuffles, leaving 70,000 homeless, 50,000 of whom were Jews; the pressure to shelter the homeless coincided with an 'opportunity' to uproot this 'integral part of the fabric of the Ottoman city' (Mazower 2005: 327). Restructuring became a vehicle for social, economic and spatial reform and for strengthening Greek political control (Mazower 2005; Karadimou-Yerolympos 2008). An international planning committee was set up, under the direction of the French architect Ernest Hébrard, which came up with a plan providing for modernisation and rational organisation of space. Despite the difficulties imposed by financial shortages and the speculative mobilisation of small capital, restructuring initially proceeded fast, but soon diverted from the plan due to another major development. The 1923 Lausanne Treaty, following the 1919–1922 Greco-Turkish war, envisaged vast population exchanges between the two countries, based on religious criteria. About 20,000 Muslims were forced to leave, while more than 100,000 Christian refugees from Eastern Thrace, the Asia Minor coast, Anatolia and the Black Sea settled in, augmenting Thessalonica's population and dramatically changing its composition. Thessalonica became a 'capital of refugees', who needed to be housed urgently; they were settled in the emptied Muslim properties of the Upper Town, as well as in industrial western areas and undeveloped Eastern suburbs. By 1928, the newcomers represented over half of the city's 245,000 inhabitants: about 48 per cent were refugees, 16 per cent internal migrants and only 36 per cent indigenous Thessalonicans (Karadimou-Yerolympos 2008: 125).

The ongoing restructuring absorbed cheap refugee labour during the 1920s, but the 1930s began with sharp rises in unemployment. The *Rembetika* music sang of the city as the 'mother of the poor', while social tensions took the form of a twofold antagonism involving the newcomers: one between indigenous Greeks and refugees, and one between refugees and the Jews (Karadimou-Yerolympos 2008).[6] Industrialisation and the rise of the labour movement, however, directed popular discontent towards left-wing politics, and the nation-building project constructed a new 'enemy within'. The Greek variety of fascism, however, did not capitalise on anti-Semitism but instead cultivated a spirit of national unity against communism and the northern 'Slavic threat'. The final act in Thessalonica's pluralism ended under German occupation, with about 50,000 Jews, one fifth of the urban population, being deported to concentration camps. As was the case elsewhere, upon liberation, a debate over the fate of Jewish property stimulated anti-Jewish feelings; but even if the authorities were in principle keen on restoring the Jewish property to the Jews, housing shortages became an argument in favour of property takeovers. The civil conflict of 1945–1949 left Thessalonica traumatised, and its legacy strangled everyday life in a city with a large and union-active working class, a significant part of which associated with the cause of the Left.[7] Introverted and closed, planned as a border town against the 'northern enemy' and cut off from its natural hinterland, Thessalonica now emerged as a Cold War city where the interwar social divisions had been replaced by the post-civil war antagonism between nationalists and left-wingers, while its recent cosmopolitanism passed into oblivion (Hastaoglou 2008: 153).

The next decades witnessed Thessalonica's growing dependence from, and intensifying antagonism towards, Athens (Hastaoglou 2008). The Marshall Plan, together with emigrant remittances, contributed to the revival of the urban economy in the 1960s, leading to unprecedented growth and expansion. Large-scale, unauthorised construction and informal settlements that were later integrated into the city-plan conditioned 'spontaneous urbanisation' between 1960 and 1980, often involving clientalist private-public relations.[8] Uncontrolled development and lack of planning led to spreading apartment blocks and shrinking green and public space, which have not only changed Thessalonica's historical physiognomy, but also gradually produced a homogeneous, cement-dominated landscape and car-focused road network, with serious infrastructure and environmental deficiencies (Karadimou-Yerolympos 2008; Hastaoglou 2008). The traditional social map of the city reproduced a division between the working-class north-west and the middle-class south-east, partly through the consolidation of land uses and functions. However, diffused economic activity and mingled spatial uses (Chronaki et al. 1993), alongside the parallel growth of the lower middle classes and the high shares of home-ownership, have resulted in a relatively mixed urban social geography.

Any discussion of the 'nationalisation' of memory and space would be incomplete without taking into account the ideological redefinition of history and place in the city. The construction of Greek national identity involved collective fantasies of continuity and homogeneity. The Greek national myth combined ethnic and religious elements: the former based on the heritage of classic antiquity; the later seeing Byzantine Greece as the successor to ancient Hellenism (see Baldwin-Edwards and Apostolatou 2008). Thus was invented a narrative of continuity, for which Byzantium was primarily Greek and Orthodox and the Ottoman period was perceived as rupture. Building such a myth of national homogeneity also implied an actual process, which employed a 'range of strategies adopted by some state institutions towards any kind of "difference"' (Agelopoulos 2000: 143; Kandylis 2006; Baldwin-Edwards and Apostolatou 2008).

Thessalonica offered a unique example which supposedly confirmed both myths. While Athens reinvented its ancient past, Thessalonica stressed its Orthodox Byzantine one (Mazower 2005). As archaeological excavations in the 1960s and 1970s revealed Byzantine monuments, Ottoman ones were abandoned or left to inappropriate uses (Karadimou-Yerolympos 2008); whatever remained from the past was there to highlight the city's 'Greekness'. Thessalonica's post-war architectural modernity not only prioritised uncontrolled development but also emphasised a distant 'glorious' past, while avoiding any memory of more recent events (Hastaoglou 2008: 166). Thus, in the 1985 celebrations of the city's 2300 years of history, the Ottoman heritage was downplayed and the Jewish presence totally silenced. At the same time, the homogenisation of the population took place in the shadow of broader political conjunctures, such as the forced population exchanges, the tragic departure of the Jews, and the demonisation of the Left in post-war times. New narratives of national unity were adopted, selectively forgetting, excluding or assimilating ethnic, religious or political 'difference'. Soon, however, globalisation – and one of its most visible faces, immigration – was to invert the picture of homogeneity and awaken memories of the city's not-so-distant past.

Cosmopolitanism reinvented: the emergence of a parallel discourse

By the early 2000s, it seemed that Thessalonica's 'cosmopolitan' past had reawakened after half a century of nationalisation of memory and space: 'there appears in hegemonic terms a local discourse which ... offers an imagined community of the city that does not befit the limits of the nation-state' (Agelopoulos 2008: 200). Agelopoulos (2008) has traced the seeds of this discourse in key texts of post-war Thessalonican literature,[9] which observed a distinct identity in the city's Balkan and 'Oriental' character and in the multitude of peoples who had once inhabited it. Even so, the Orthodox Byzantine tradition was highlighted in accordance with the dominant nationalist narrative. It was only in the 1990s that such a new cosmopolitan narrative became possible again, initially as a feature linked to the city's openness 'to the world' with the advent of globalisation and transnational connections. Greece's EU membership since the 1980s and especially the end of the Cold War, not only re-established links with the city's northern hinterland and with Central and Eastern Europe, but also conditioned much the internationalisation of the urban economy and the development of transnational ties. Thessalonica became the base for Greek companies relocating to the Balkans (Labrianidis et al. 2004), and there was an increasing presence of multinational corporations (Hastaoglou 2008). A revived cosmopolitan discourse thus appeared in the mainstream, proclaiming Thessalonica's transnational reach and its new role as 'capital of the Balkans' (Hastaoglou 2008; Kokot 2007).

While the city's conservative elite was prone to such vain rhetoric, at the same time it invested in the revival of nationalism (Hastaoglou 2008). The early 1990s witnessed massive rallies objecting to the name of Macedonia, organised by local authorities and the Church. The frenzy over the 'Macedonian issue' amidst a Greek trade embargo of the former Yugoslav Republic involved the changing of place and business names that pointed to ancient Macedonia (Agnew 2007). In 2000, the city was shaken again by demonstrations orchestrated by the Church against the non-inscription of religion on the new ID cards. This cannot be unrelated to more than twenty years of conservative control in the municipality and the political rise of the far right, represented in Thessalonica with vote shares almost doubling those in national polls (Hatziprokopiou 2006: ch. 5). Even today, on the municipality's website one may read about the city's ancient and medieval heritage, with emphatic references to Alexander the Great and Orthodox Byzantium, while the Ottoman past is limited to '482 difficult years of slavery'; there is no account of the Jewish presence, apart from a vague note on the city's 'cosmopolitan character' over the centuries.[10]

It was in this context that the local discourse on cosmopolitanism gradually gained pace during the 1990s. However, its meaning expanded to include the city's openness to 'difference' in both the past and present. Often conflated with 'multiculturalism', used interchangeably to indicate pluralism and 'diversity', the discourse of Thessalonica's urban cosmopolitanism took a twofold form (Agelopoulos 2000; 2008). One emerged as an alternative narrative of the past, which re-established a sense of continuity and recognised the Ottoman and Sephardic traditions as an integral part of the city's history. Another builds on the challenges of the present, specifically related to the altering of Thessalonica's demographics due to immigration.[11] But the emerging discourse is neither coherent nor homogeneous: it is shaped by a multiplicity of local actors, ranging from council opposition forces to the recently-elected municipal leadership (November 2010), from local media to academic research, from antiracist groups and the Left promoting the rights of immigrants to far-right politicians opposing them. Thus it has developed in contradictory terms, coexisting with 'the parochial nationalist narrative' which until recently remained dominant politically, despite failing 'to pronounce a convincing reading of the city's history, denigrating the presence of populations who did not identify with the Greek nation and whose incorporation was subject to a difficult negotiation' (Agelopoulos 2008: 200).

These contradictions became apparent when Thessalonica hosted the Cultural Capital of Europe in 1997. As the city was officially recognised as a 'meeting place for different nations' throughout its history, the promotion of its 'multicultural character' ('*polypolitismikos charactiras*') was among 'the basic targets' of the programme of festivities, which, however, 'attempted to find a compromise between two distinctively opposite views, the Hellenic and the cosmopolitan one' as proclaimed by the then Minister of Culture, a Thessalonican himself.[12] Although some elements of the city's Ottoman and Sephardic history (restoring Ottoman buildings and modernist villas, opening a Jewish museum, etc.) were brought out, the Orthodox Byzantine past was more extensively stressed and highlighted (Agelopoulos 2000; 2008; Kokot 2007). For example, after three years of preparations and thanks to European funds granted for restoring antiqui-ties, Rotonda – a circular Roman monument that had functioned histori-cally both as Church and Mosque – was turned into a religious site, instead of a public cultural space as groups of citizens had argued for (Mazower 2005: 470). It is indicative that, at the opening ceremony of the 1997 fes-tivities in 'one of the most multi-cultural cities in Europe', politicians 'un-derscored the historical significance of the Orthodox legacy for Europe as a whole' (Mazower 2005: 171), and that the Cultural Capital's major event was an exhibition of treasures from Mount Athos.

Nevertheless, the way in which the city's cosmopolitan past was ap-proached was also problematic, in that Thessalonica's multi-ethnic history was 'multiculturalised' (Agelopoulos 2000). The Cultural Capital 'followed a folkloric approach to cultures', treating them as static and reified, homo-geneous categories, and as commodities to be consumed (Agelopoulos 2000: 149–50).

As the organisation's agenda capitalised on the past, at the same time it silenced the city's 'multicultural' present. References to migrants were marginal, limited to publications such as an anti-racist pamphlet inspired by relevant EU documents (Agelopoulos 2000: 148). Immigrants, until then still undocumented in their majority, 'would create unpleasant percep-tions of who we, the citizens of Salonica, are' (2000: 148–49). In fact, their presence was not only marginalised but also perceived in rather hostile terms. Pavlou (2001: 140–45) analysed the exclusionary local media rheto-ric favouring city marketing strategies in 1997, which saw the presence of migrants in open urban spaces as harmful to the public image of place. Accordingly, the visibility of poverty and 'difference' was judged to be 'an-noying', and the redefinition of spatial uses for tourist promotion required them to be 'cleaned' of migrants and other 'vulnerable' groups through their physical removal.

This raises questions about the relationship between the cosmopoli-tan and the parochial in processes of urban regeneration and branding (Hemelryk-Donald et al. 2009) and indicates a shift in discourses and ac-tual policies promoting specific place identities. If nationalism had been the principal force of homogenisation of peoples, cultures and space in the past, it now finds itself in contradiction with the present forms of ho-mogenisation characterised by urban development and competition in a globalising market economy. Such forms are related to the 'cultural turn' in post-industrial urban economies, whereby 'culture', history and space be-come commodities and lifestyle choices (Zukin 1995; Binnie et al. 2006) and 'ethnic spaces' are transformed 'into places of leisure and consump-tion' (Rath 2007). Thessalonica's parochialism is located exactly in its ongo-ing introversion and the revival of nationalism alongside attempts to adapt to the post-industrial economy and international urban competition. The emerging recognition of its cosmopolitanism as an aspect of urban identity becomes a matter of the city's past, which is now packaged for tourism and consumption, reproducing the uneasy coexistence between modernity and memory in the contemporary city. While the later was devalued and abused, the former (i.e. modernity) has been viewed in a rather distorted way, which produced early forms of post-modernity (Hastaoglou 2008: 194; Leontidou 1996). An example of this process, evident in recent interventions on the space of the city, can be seen in the awakening of architectural memory since the 1980s (Hastaoglou 2008: 178), which drew on the kind of Greek national folklore invented for Thessalonica in earlier decades (Kokot 2007: 14). One may argue that this type of folklore, resulting mostly in picturesque recreations in the historic centre, is deprived of any historical or contemporary life-world, other than that which is promoted through the pursuit of profit.[13]

It is on similarly parochial grounds that the revival of urban cosmopolitanism is currently being based. But there is an additional dimension: Thessalonica's cosmopolitan past is increasingly perceived as a marker of its identity and character, one that crucially differentiates it from Athens (Agelopoulos 2000; 2008). This may also be seen as parochial, because it stems from the relationship of antagonism between the two cities, involving an inherent provincialism in discourses about Thessalonica's dependence on Athens. But it does offer an attractive alternative, as it builds a new narrative of continuity that reintegrates Ottoman times into urban history, revealing the contradictions of the dominant nationalist paradigm (Agelopoulos 2008: 200). Mazower's (2005) historical account of Salonica's multiethnic past was published at this critical point in time, as the echoes of the nationalistic paroxysm of the 1990s were gradually fading out. The warm reception it received locally was expressed not only in high sales but also in fruitful public discussions, indicating how appealing such a narrative was to sections of the Thessalonican public (Agelopoulos 2008: 199). Politically, this attitude also featured in the local elections, where the city's cosmopolitan past was stressed in the agendas of centre and centre-left municipal campaigns (which, however, failed to challenge conservative control in the council until November 2010). It is therefore not by chance that recent scholarly critiques of the 'multiculturalist' discourse begin their analyses with references to Mazower's book (Kokot 2007; Agelopoulos 2008). The historian himself, however, is particularly cautious about the buzzword of 'multiculturalism' and well aware of present-day challenges (Mazower 2005: 472).

Kokot's account (2007: 8–10), in particular, criticises the mono-dimensional perceptions of 'multicultural' or 'cosmopolitan' Thessalonica for overstressing the past 'as a focal point for the city's identity' and neglecting the contemporary reality of immigrants. Nevertheless, some of the political actors shaping the discourse are not only aware of the new reality, but refer deliberately to the past in order to account for the present. During the tenth Antiracist Festival (July 2007), for instance, the keynote speaker – a local Green politician – stressed Thessalonica's Ottoman 'multiculturalism', remarking that with immigration 'Thessalonica becomes multicultural again' (Agelopoulos 2008: 207). Translating politically the past in such a way may be understood as a goodwill response to nationalist, xenophobic and racist stances at the local level. But it remains anachronistic in ignoring the earlier historical context and evasive about the fifty and more years of Hellenising the city.

However, one may acknowledge Thessalonica's urban continuity but at the same time draw a line distinguishing between cosmopolitanism and multiculturalism in the past and present. Hastaoglou (2008: 185) argued that 'migrants represent the multiculturalism inscribed throughout the European space, but have nothing to do with the cosmopolitanism of the late nineteenth century, a time of imperial decline'. Such a distinction accounts for the historical differences in the sociopolitical context framing pluralism and 'diversity' in the city. Thus 'multiculturalism' in the present is seen as a demographic and sociocultural phenomenon[14] shaped by contemporary immigration in the context of European integration and globalisation of the post-1989 and 9/11 geopolitical order. But it also implies a specific political objective for the recognition of difference in the public space and institutions, and it has been subject to critique.[15]

Both this contradiction and its various criticisms are apparent in the diverse rhetoric characterising the multitude of actors who organise the city's annual antiracist festival, which has taken place since 1998. Ranging across a wide spectrum of the Left and involving anti-racist initiatives, NGOs and migrant associations, the discourse in this case focuses mostly on present-day demands for rights and recognition that are not local but rather universal in character.[16] Together with (and as part of) such demands, expressed formally or informally and in multiple ways by those involved, including the migrants themselves, there appears to be a claim of migrants' 'right to the city' (Lefebvre 1996). More than just a matter of defining the cosmopolitan or multicultural city, in the past or present, contemporary challenges impose a political and social rethinking of the possibilities of conviviality and participation on equal terms, which needs to be asserted, claimed and fought for. The right to the city, however, is being contested both politically and in socioeconomic terms. On the one hand, nationalist considerations in immigration policy divide different groups of migrants, accepting some as citizens while excluding the majority as unwanted. On the other, market forces not only commoditise urban space in ways that exclude those deemed 'unwanted', but also reserve for migrants specific physical and social space in the city. Some of these contradictions of the city's contemporary migratory reality are explored next.

Rise of the 'post-cosmopolitan' city: migrant landscapes in Thessalonica

Greece's transition to immigration in the early 1990s involved, on the one hand, large-scale labour migration, especially from neighbouring Balkan states, primarily Albania. On the other, it also involved a wave of ethnic migration, mostly Pontic Greeks from the former Soviet Union. In the latter case, the ethnic Greeks were welcomed by the State, but became subject to differential legal statuses, with citizenship granted to those from the former Soviet Union but not to those from Albania or elsewhere. In the former, the majority of immigrants remained undocumented until the end of the decade, due to an exclusionary legal framework focusing on policing and control; a series of regularisation programmes (1998, 2001, 2005, 2007) partly restored this, though recent developments brought new challenges. The picture becomes ever more complex in the 2000s, with growing numbers of migrants and refugees from Asian and African countries and a migration crisis under way, involving increasing clandestine arrivals, declining asylum approval rates, and EU pressures to 'combat illegal migration' and 'control external borders'.

Thessalonica naturally became the second major destination of migrants in the country; but although its migratory landscape inevitably reflects the situation in Greece as a whole, it also exhibits some rather peculiar characteristics. In 2001, the entire Thessalonica Prefecture concentrated about 9 per cent of foreign nationals in Greece, more than 80 per cent of whom lived in the city itself, making up a share of 7.6 per cent among the urban population.[17] Considering that nearly one third of the 155,139 'repatriates' recorded by 2000 lived in Thessalonica (Katsavounidou and Kourti 2008), the total number of migrants in the city exceeds 100,000 people, among whom the proportion of Soviet-born Greeks reaches 30 per cent (Labrianidis et al. 2008). The respective share of Albanians is over one quarter, that of migrants from former Soviet republics approaches 16 per cent, Western country nationals constitute 12.2 per cent, while Asians and Africans form less than 3 per cent. In general, Thessalonica's migrant population is characterised by relatively low heterogeneity and rather regional features. Its composition seems to reflect historical bonds dating back to Ottoman times and the Greek diaspora communities of the Balkans and the Black Sea (Labrianidis and Hatziprokopiou 2008: 225).

Historical resemblances are also apparent in processes of migrant settle-ment, given the changes in context, size and scale (Kandylis 2006; Has-taoglou 2008). The geographic distribution of immigrants across the city not only reflects, but also reproduces, the traditional social map, i.e. the division between a relatively prosperous south-east and a somehow less privileged north-west (Hatziprokopiou 2006; Labrianidis et al. 2008). Prin-cipally driven by the housing market (home prices and rents), and to a lesser extent as a result of additional factors such as job location or social net-works, immigrants are generally more concentrated in the western parts of the Conurbation (Hatziprokopiou 2006).[18] Moreover, migrant settlement has conditioned much of the growth and spatial trends of Thessalonica's population in the past two decades in at least two respects (Labrianidis et al. 2008). Firstly, it followed existing suburbanisation patterns, which have contributed to rapid population growth and urban expansion in the periph-ery of the city. Secondly, it has to a certain extent intercepted such trends, as immigrants' housing revitalised abandoned properties in the inner city. Thessalonica Municipality has the highest concentration of migrants, who tend to live not just in the cheaper areas but also in older properties and on lower floors, following a vertical pattern of socio-spatial differentia-tion. Moreover, there are relatively strong concentrations of small migrant groups in various districts, statistically insignificant but with a visible and growing presence. The dispersion of the migrant population as a whole adds to Thessalonica's existing social mix and gives way to a 'new social ge-ography' of the city (Hatziprokopiou 2006: ch. 7). The next few paragraphs offer an ethnographic glance at aspects of this emerging geography.

Returning from a trip on a rainy November 2009 morning, I took the bus to Panorama, Thessalonica's posh eastern suburb. Just a few stops before my destination, I realised I was the only male on the bus apart from the driver; women of various ages were chatting in Russian, Tsalkan Turkish, the Pontic Greek dialect and other languages. They were heading to work as domestic helpers, cleaners or carers in Panorama's wealthy houses. Un-like the live-in domestic servants, usually Philippinos working for richer households, I assumed that some might work on a daily schedule, while some others might be hired on an occasional basis. I based that assumption on my doctoral research, when I had interviewed Albanian and Bulgarian women employed in similar jobs (Hatziprokopiou 2006). Female migrant employment activities reflect a gendered division of labour originating in traditional perceptions of women's social roles, and thus counterbalance and further facilitate the exodus of Greek women from the home. Despite high unemployment rates in Greece during the 1990s, immigrant labour has been covering the needs of small companies and private households.[19] By 2001, immigrants officially represented about 10 per cent of the labour force in the Prefecture: about one quarter worked in construction, more than one fifth in manufacturing, 7.4 per cent in agriculture and the rest in services. Their work is mainly manual, often of a servile character and in low-skilled positions, despite the high qualifications of many, and with a clear differentiation between male and female employment patterns.

A few months earlier, driving from the airport towards Thermi, also in eastern Thessalonica, I came to one of my fieldwork sites. Just before entering the district, I noticed young and middle-aged men hanging around at the side of the street. I recalled the so-called job-finding 'piazzas', 'meeting points where immigrants gather and where Greek employers know that they can find labourers to work for them' (Hatziprokopiou 2006: 147). Formerly a village settled by refugees from Asia Minor, Thermi has been transformed into an upmarket, middle-class suburb hosting various economic activities, such as large supermarkets, big commercial houses and small industries. The casual employment of immigrants by such companies, or by private households and small businesses in small construction projects, roof-work, gardening, etc., offers a type of labour which is not only cheap, but crucially very flexible, unprotected and available at any time. Migrant labour has crucially enabled employers to overcome some of the rigidities of the Greek labour market, often within the underground economy, which may have 'traditional' roots but which has been revitalised by restructuring processes. Partly fed by the prolonged illegality of immigrants, the spread of informal economic arrangements is so wide that many remain at the fringes of the formal labour market even if they hold legal status.

The piazza was now outside the district and exclusively used as a job-finding place, while the one I remembered was at Thermi's main square, and also functioned as a social space. Back in the early 2000s, ethnic Greeks (Sarakatsans) from the regions of Plovdiv and Sliven in Bulgaria were concentrated there after early arrivals found employment; they lived in Greece with temporary residence status that led most to employ cyclical migration strategies (Hatziprokopiou 2006). They used to gather in the square, looking for work in the mornings, or socialising and chatting in the evenings. Immigrant gatherings in open public spaces are a feature common to many parts of Thessalonica. An ethnographic study by Vyzoviti et al. (2006) has mapped fourteen such spots – parks, squares and street-corners which migrants appropriate for distinct social uses, either 'strategic' or 'tactical'. The former refer to survival strategies, as in the example of job-finding piazzas; the latter concern leisure practices, where space becomes a place for rest, socialisation and play. Such an appropriation of public space may reflect the migrants' weak financial position, but it also offers a sense of orientation, and inscribes reference points in their cognitive map of the city, making belonging meaningful by establishing a sense of familiarity. As 'increasingly entertainment and socialisation are linked to consumption', social life in the open becomes less common among indigenous residents, while migrants revive spaces which otherwise tended to be deprived of their social use (Labrianidis and Hatziprokopiou 2008: 208).

Distinct spatial uses may generate fear and suspicion, partly relating to the public visibility of difference. In the example above, Sarakatsans spoke of good relations with locals, but complained about problems with the police because of frequent checks. Apart from inadequate and largely exclusionary institutional responses, the authorities play a crucial role in nurturing broader racist sentiments by criminalising the presence of immigrants in various ways, with the police excessively exercising checks and controls that affect immigrants' daily experiences (Hatziprokopiou 2006). There have been several cases of police brutality locally: in the 1990s these were epitomised in a 1998 incident involving off-duty policemen in Thermi torturing an Albanian migrant; in the 2000s they were brought again to the fore with the death of a young Nigerian. On 21 August 2007, a small demonstration in downtown Thessalonica turned nasty when police forces made excessive use of tear-gas chemicals. This would not be news, given the frequency of protests in Greece and the often harsh way in which the authorities respond, had it not involved dozens of angry Nigerian migrants. Three days earlier, Tony Onua had received a mortal wound to his head after slipping from a balcony while trying to escape two undercover policemen in Kalamaria, a wealthy neighbourhood bordering Thessalonica Municipality to the south-east. As his friends and colleagues said, his past experiences at the hands of Greek police, common to those of many of his co-nationals, were marked by verbal and physical abuse, which explains why he ran as soon as he realised they were after him. Originating in the 1980s, the small but visible Nigerian 'community' now numbers about 400 people, mostly of Ibo roots, but also Benin and a few Yoruba, with a male majority, partly due to restrictive family unification procedures. Largely concentrated in two downtown districts, where a small number of Nigerian businesses are also located, the majority are occupied in street-peddling activities across the city, while some women are involved in sex work.[20]

Since 2006, the law grants street-selling licences to Greek nationals only (including ethnic Greeks), thus directly excluding all other migrants from an activity that is commonly used by many as a survival strategy. Partly as a result of labour market disadvantage, partly as an active 'integration strategy', the migrants' diverse pathways to various forms of entrepreneurship are having an growing impact on Thessalonica's economy and urban landscape (Labrianidis and Hatziprokopiou 2008). Their past experience as waged labourers or entrepreneurs, their social networks providing start-up capital, labour and a customer base, as well as opportunities in the local market, have conditioned the emergence of ethnic 'specialisations' and specific market niches. So, Nigerian street-pedlars sell pirate-copied CDs and DVDs, posters, leather bags and African artefacts, while newcomer Bangladeshis offer cheap sunglasses or mobile phone SIM cards. Ethnic Greeks from the former Soviet Union have been involved in flea markets since the early years, trading anything from old Zenit cameras to USSR communist party identity cards. Even when they enjoy a favourable legal status, some do not escape informal economic activity, for instance women selling herbs at the Vlalli market, or smuggled cigarettes at Dikastirion square (Spilok-Malanda 2007). In the later case, however, an interesting shift is under way, with the advent of 'ethnic' shops like travel agencies specialising in various destinations of the former Soviet Union, or food stores offering delicacies from these countries. And if this is a central marketplace for Soviet Greeks, a bigger one exists at the north-western fringes of the city, a huge closed market at Yusurum with a capacity of nearly 170 stalls; here one may buy products from Russia, Georgia, Armenia and elsewhere (Agelopoulos 2008: 208–9).

Back in the inner city, another type of 'ethnic' market has developed, strategically located between the railway station, the western city entrance and the port. Here lies Thessalonica's peculiar 'Chinatown', where shops trading in cheap clothes and shoes attract a wider customer public (Labrianidis and Hatziprokopiou 2008). The four Chinese stores that I counted on the main street in 2000 grew to around twenty-one on a second visit in 2002, with many more now springing up in the surrounding streets. Until recently, the area hosted a Roma camp, which was removed in the early 2000s to build a parking space; many small enterprises (such as carpentry, metal work and car repair workshops) are closing down and the red light district is declining; brothels are gradually pushed out with the spread of Chinese businesses and also with the coming of migrant families. Walking in the narrow streets on a weekday morning can be quite an interesting experience in this grim but diverse place. On Sappho Street one may observe Chinese workers unloading boxes of clothes, while middle-aged women walk around searching for cheap fashion. A group of Greeks are chatting outside the garage next door and the little old house with the pink light on the front entrance seems quiet. Towards the street's eastern edge, smartly dressed lawyers are enjoying a coffee break in the new trendy bar across from the central courthouses. Round the corner, the translation agencies are busy as Albanian migrants queue outside their consulate.

To what extent does this picture really suggest a second path to cosmopolitanism for Thessalonica? The examples above offer a glance only at the multitude of new labour geographies, uneasy relationships, state repression, emerging 'multiethnic' markets and novel spatial uses in Thessalonica. Such an account by no means exhausts the city's contemporary migratory reality, nor the complexities involved in evolving processes of social change. But it is indicative of the modes through which this new reality challenges established perceptions of urban identity and imposes new ways of imagining the city. Some of these imaginaries, as we have seen, feed an emerging discourse of cosmopolitanism; but this discourse is mostly inspired by the city's past. The problem remains that the challenges of the present lie above and beyond any such discourse. Such challenges are to be sought in the city's growing exposure to a transforming world order, in changing class relations that reserve a specific social and physical space for migrants in the city, in still unresolved issues of social and legal equality, in a problematic understanding of 'who we are' that remains uneasy towards strangers of any kind.

Over the last two decades, the presence of migrants has become increasingly noticeable in the city's streets or buses where Albanian, Russian or 'broken Greek' accents now sound familiar, in shops and kiosks where Latin, Cyrillic, Georgian or Chinese scripts are commonplace, in civil society initiatives where immigrant associations are increasingly active (Labrianidis and Hatziprokopiou 2008). Sometimes highly visible, more often less apparent, the presence of migrants inscribes itself in new encounters, transnational connections, everyday practices and new types of relationships. The complex set of processes that are currently under way seem to deprive the emerging cosmopolitan urban imagery of any meaning, apart from mere wishful thinking for the present and restitution in collective memory of a long-forgotten past.

Conclusion: beyond cosmopolitanism

In her seminal work on cosmopolitan urbanism, Sandercock (2003: 127) has posed a key question about how migrants can be integrated into cities 'unused to thinking themselves as multicultural'. The relevance of this in the case of Thessalonica may be contested, although its early twentieth-century cosmopolitanism elapsed with the ascendance of nationalism, and migrant newcomers today encounter a city 'predominantly Greek in culture and Orthodox in religion' (Mazower 2005: 472). Still, the coming of migrants forced it to remember its pluralism of old. But for a city that is now perceived as once-cosmopolitan, history seems to repeat itself only as farce: 'cosmopolitanism' may be too vague a concept to account for present-day challenges and rapid social change. As we have seen, the local discourse uses it interchangeably with multiculturalism, thus limiting both concepts to simple descriptions of actual diversity (i.e. ethnic and cultural heterogeneity) of either the past or the present.

Despite its merits as an alternative to the hegemonic narrative, the emerging cosmopolitan discourse remains parochial, reflecting the city's clumsy search for a distinct identity, and thus anachronistic, in that it seeks answers for the present in a past that has little to do with the experiences of migrants or indigenous Greeks. It is predominantly an elitist discourse, which finds a safe haven in a rather exotic past instead of facing the challenges of an uneasy and difficult present, where the presence of the Other, now, here and among us, is feared, suspected, or unwanted. But it also seems necessary, as 'other futures may require other pasts' (Mazower (2005: 474): retelling the past becomes a discourse of the future, as the present can no longer fit into the narrow space of the nation state. Beyond the historical tensions and present-day contradictions, Thessalonica has in fact much in common with many cities around the globe, in that it faces similar challenges and is being shaped by similar processes of change. The cosmopolitan city may be a 'dreamed' one, 'in which there is an acceptance of, connection with, and respect and space for "the stranger"' (Sandercock 2003: 127). The new municipal leadership (as of January 2011) may signal a new era now that the nationalist rhetoric has been overcome by a more 'cosmopolitan' official discourse. But beyond utopian notions of the 'good city', it is rather the everyday modalities of living together that provide the frame in which to ground 'cosmopolitanism' as urban experience (Binnie et al. 2006; Hemelryk-Donald et al. 2009).

Thessalonica's growing multiethnicity and inevitable opening to global and transnational flows call for a rethinking of the basis of urban symbiosis. It emerges as a 'city of Others', where immigrants are incorporated into a pattern of ethnic hierarchy (Kandylis 2006), by being constructed as a distinct category on the basis of exclusionary mechanisms (Hatziprokopiou 2006): the restrictive immigration policy, the spread of xenophobic attitudes, the particular space migrants occupy in the labour market and urban geography. However, during the last two decades, one may observe a multiplicity of forms and ways of adjustment, belonging and building a life: immigrants have gradually become an organic element of Thessalonica's dynamics, they are here to stay and their incorporation depends on processes similar to those conditioning all citizens of the *polis*.

Thessalonica's ambivalent position between past and present, modernity and memory, multiculturalism and parochialism, at the time of globalisation and international migration, make it inevitably a 'post-cosmopolitan' city. This is not just another of the fashionable 'post-isms', according to which Thessalonica may be described, for instance, as a postmodern or post-industrial metropolis. As the editors suggest in their introduction, 'post-cosmopolitanism' may serve as an alternative concept to the opposition between nationalism and cosmopolitanism. In the case of Thessalonica, 'the heritage and contemporary conditions of multiethnic coexistence', that is, its past and current pluralism, should be understood through the contradictions and dynamics that inevitably structure them and give them shape and meaning in the present.

NOTES

1. Mazower (2005: 174). In May 1876, the abduction by Christians of a village girl converting to Islam led to the massacre of the German and French consuls by Muslim crowds. The unrest that followed threatened the city's 'Frankish' quarter and interfaith relations at large.
2. In April 1903, the 'Boatmen of Thessalonica', an anarchist group of students at the Bulgarian Men's Gymnasium, used several bomb strikes to draw attention to Ottoman oppression in Macedonia.
3. After all, this was the birthplace of Mustafa Kemal Ataturk, allegedly of Dönmeh origin, then a minor Young Turk officer, who later became founder of the Turkish Republic.
4. *Federacion* became the founding core of the Socialist Workers Party of Greece, which allied with the Third International in 1920 and was renamed the Communist Party in 1924.
5. Mazower (2005: 1) quotes from Italo Calvino's *Invisible cities* (30–31).
6. Alongside measures to incorporate refugees in the 1920s, the Jewish community was pressured to Hellenise its school curriculum and to hand over needed areas to the authorities. Anti-Semitist propaganda led to the Campbell riot of June 1931, when nationalist squads set a poor Jewish neighbourhood on fire.
7. Thessalonica became the epicentre in a series of events that gradually led to the colonels' dictatorship (1967–1974), when in May 1963 the left-wing politician Grigoris Lambrakis was murdered by right-wing extremists.
8. See Leontidou (1996), Karadimou-Yerolympos (2008), Hastaoglou (2008).
9. Such examples are the writings of N.G. Pentzikis, G. Vafopoulos and G. Ioannou.
10. Thessalonica municipality website: www.thessaloniki.gr. Considering the coming of centre-left forces in municipal power as from January 2011, however, this may soon change, as the new Mayor, a progressive local businessman, has invested ideologically in stressing elements of the city's cosmopolitan past.
11. In relation to this, recent academic publications on immigrants in Thessalonica have also been shaping the cosmopolitan discourse by seeing in the presence of migrants the emergence of a 'cosmopolitan' or 'multicultural' city (e.g. Hatziprokopiou 2004; 2006; Piperopoulos and Ikonomu 2007; Kokot 2007; Labrianidis and Hatziprokopiou 2008).
12. See Agelopoulos (2000: 148) which comments on official documents of the Cultural Capital Organisation and quotes the 1997 Minister of Culture Mr Evangelos Venizelos.
13. For example, the 1990s redevelopments that turned Ladadika (once full of busy warehouses serving the harbour) and Athonos Square (until then part of the thriving central market) into 'traditional' tavernas and/or bars and nightclubs (Hastaoglou 2008).

14. Labrianidis and Hatziprokopiou (2008: 219); also Hatziprokopiou (2006), Age-
    lopoulos (2000; 2008).
15. Agelopoulos (2000; 2008); see also Žižek (1997).
16. Agelopoulos (2008: 208); see also Glarnetatzis (2001) and Hatziprokopiou
    (2006).
17. The data discussed here and in the following paragraph are, unless otherwise
    stated, from the 2001 census, as analysed by Hatziprokopiou (2006) and La-
    brianidis et al. (2008).
18. In particular, Pontic Greeks from the former Soviet Union tend to live in the
    same parts of the city as the Asia Minor refugees of the 1920s, primarily in
    Thessalonica's north-western districts; their housing has involved similar
    kinds of informal settlement and property speculation by local contractors
    and politicians (Katsavounidou and Kourti 2008). There are of course excep-
    tions to this rule: Western country nationals live mostly in the south-eastern
    areas, while Albanians are relatively dispersed across the city (Hatziprokopiou
    2006; Katsavounidou and Kourti 2008). On the other hand some are marked
    by the clustering of smaller groups, such as the Chinese who live at the west
    end of the centre, the Nigerians at the east end (north-west and south of the
    University Campus), or the Philippinos in Panorama (Labrianidis et al. 2008:
    53, Table D8).
19. On immigrants' labour market integration in Thessalonica, see Labrianidis et
    al. (2004); Hatziprokopiou (2004; 2006: ch. 6).
20. On Nigerians in Thessalonica, see Leven (2007), Labrianidis and Hatziproko-
    piou (2008) and various items of press coverage on the incident, e.g. an arti-
    cle by Agelopoulos and Andrikopoulos in *Macedonia* newspaper (24 August
    2007).

References

Agelopoulos, George. 2000. 'Political Practices and Multiculturalism: The Case of
    Salonica', in J. Cowan (ed.), *Macedonia: the Politics of Identity and Difference*.
    London and New York, pp. 140–55.
———. 2008. 'Multiple Times, Places and Cultures: Aspects of Modernity in Thes-
    salonica', in Gr. Kafkalas, L. Labrianidis and N. Papamichos (eds), *Thessalonica
    on the Verge: The City as a Process of Change*. Athens, pp. 199–216 (in Greek).
Agnew, J. 2007. 'No Borders, No Nations: Making Greece in Macedonia', *Annals of
    the Association of American Geographers* 97(2), 398–422.
Baldwin-Edwards, Martin and Katerina Apostolatou. 2008. 'Ethnicity and Migra-
    tion: A Greek Story' (introduction), in M. Baldwin-Edwards (ed.), *Ethnicity
    and Migration: A Greek Story*, special issue of *Migrance* 30: 5–17.
Binnie, J., J. Holloway, S. Millington and C. Young (eds). 2006. *Cosmopolitan
    Urbanism*. London.
Calvino, Italo. 1974. *Invisible Cities*. London.
Chronaki, Z., C. Hadjimichalis, L. Labrianidis and D. Vaiou 1993. 'Diffused Indu-
    strialisation in Thessalonica: From Expansion to Crisis', *International Journal
    of Urban and Regional Research* 17(2): 178–94.

Driessen, H. 2005. 'Mediterranean Port Cities: Cosmopolitanism Reconsidered', *History and Anthropology* 16(1): 129–41.

Glarnetatzis, Yiannis. 2001. 'A View on the Anti-racist Movement in Greece: The Case of the Anti-racist Initiative of Thessalonica', in A. Mavrakis, D. Parsanoglou and M. Pavlou (eds), *Immigrants in Greece*. Athens, pp. 391–99 (in Greek).

Hastaoglou, Vilma. 2008. 'Modernity and Memory in the Formation of Post-war Thessalonica', in Gr. Kafkals, L. Labrianidis and N. Papamichos (eds), *Thessalonica on the Verge: The City as a Process of Change*. Athens, pp. 151–98 (in Greek).

Hastaoglou-Martinidis, V. 1997. 'A Mediterranean City in Transition: Thessalonica Between the Two World Wars', *Facta Universitatis: Series Architecture and Civil Engineering* 1(4): 493–507.

Hatziprokopiou, P. 2004. 'Balkan Immigrants in the Greek City of Thessalonica: Local Processes of Incorporation in an International Perspective', *European Urban and Regional Studies* 11(4): 321–38.

———. 2006. *Globalisation and Contemporary Immigration to Southern European Cities: Processes of Social Incorporation of Balkan Immigrants in Thessalonica*. Amsterdam.

Hemelryk-Donald, S., E. Kofman and C. Kevin (eds). 2008. *Branding Cities: Cosmopolitanism, Parochialism and Social Change*. New York, pp. 1–13.

Kandylis, G. 2006. 'From Assimilation to National Hierarchy: Changing Dominant Representations in the Formation of the Greek City', *The Greek Review of Social Research* 121 (C'): 157–74.

Karadimou-Yerolympos, Aleka. 2008. 'The Urban Space of Thessalonica: Long Durations and Rapid Transformations, with the Balkan Hinterland at the Background', in Gr. Kafkals, L. Labrianidis and N. Papamichos (eds), *Thessalonica on the Verge: The City as a Process of Change*. Athens, pp. 95–150 (in Greek).

Katsavounidou, G. and P. Kourti, 2008. 'Homogeneis Migrants from the Former Soviet Union in Thessalonica and the Transformation of the Western Quarters of the City', in M. Baldwin-Edwards (ed.), *Ethnicity and Migration: A Greek Story*, special issue of *Migrance* 30: 61–70.

Kokot, W. (ed.). 2007. *Beyond the White Tower: Transformations in Thessalonica*. Munster.

Labrianidis, Lois and Panos Hatziprokopiou. 2008. 'Migration and Social Change in Thessalonica: Immigrants' Integration and the New Multicultural Reality in the City', in Gr. Kafkals, L. Labrianidis and N. Papamichos (eds), *Thessalonica on the Verge: The City as a Process of Change*. Athens, pp. 217–64.

Labrianidis, L., P. Hatziprokopiou, M. Pratsinakis and N. Vogiatzis. ca 2008. 'Thessalonica City Report', report prepared for the GEITONIES Project, European Commission Research DG, 7th Framework programme, Thessalonica.

Labrianidis, L., A. Lyberaki, P. Tinios and P. Hatziprokopiou. 2004. 'Inflow of Immigrants and Outflow of FDI: Aspects of Interdependence Between Greece and the Balkans', *Journal of Ethnic and Migration Studies* 30(6): 1183–1208.

Lefebvre, Henri. 1996. 'The Right to the City', in E. Kofman and E. Lebas (eds), *Writings on Cities*. Cambridge, pp. 61–181.

Leontidou, L. 1996. 'Alternatives to Modernism in (Southern) Urban Theory: Exploring In-between Spaces', *International Journal of Urban and Regional Research* 20(2): 178–95.

Leven, Kathrin. 2007. 'African Migrant Women in Thessalonica', in W. Kokot (ed.), *Beyond the White Tower: Transformations in Thessalonica*. Munster, pp. 59–82.

Marketos, S. 1999. 'Avraam Benaroya and the Impossible Reform', in *Remember Salonica*, special issue of *Justice: Magazine of the International Association of Jewish Lawyers and Jurists* (Spring 1999): 38–43.

Mazower, M. 2005. *Salonica, City of Ghosts: Christians, Muslims and Jews 1430–1950*. London.

Molho, Rena. 1993. 'Le Renouveau..', in G. Veinstein (ed.), *Salonique, 1850–1918: la 'Ville des Juifs' et le Réveil des Balkans*. Paris, pp. 64–78.

Pavlou, Miltos. 2001. 'The "Smugglers of Fear": Racist Discourse and Immigrants in the Press of a Potential Metropolis', in A. Marvakis, D. Parsanoglou and M. Pavlou (eds), *Immigrants in Greece*. Athens, pp. 127–62 (in Greek).

Piperopoulos, P. and Th. Ikonomu. 2007. 'Entrepreneurship in Ethnic Groups: The Case of the Multicultural City of Thessalonica, Greece', *International Journal of Business and Globalisation* 1(2): 272–92.

Rath, J. 2007. 'The Transformation of Ethnic Neighbourhoods into Places of Leisure and Consumption', *Centre for Comparative Immigration Studies Working Paper Series* 144, San Diego, CCIS, University of California.

Sandercock, L. 2003. *Cosmopolis II: Mongrel Cities of the 21st Century*. London.

Spilok-Malanda, Nikola. 2007. 'Vending Herbs on the Agora Vlali: Strategies of Ethnic Greek Migrants from the Former Soviet Union', in W. Kokot (ed.), *Beyond the White Tower: Transformations in Thessalonica*. Munster, pp. 43–58.

Vyzoviti, Sofia, Dina Basiakou and Maria Raskou. 2006. 'Piazzas, Meeting Places and Gardens', in *Architectural and Urban Transformations in Thessalonica Due to the Phenomenon of Immigration*, ed. TEE/TKM, Thessalonica, ch.VI.

Yerolympos, Aleka, and Vassilis Colonas. 1993. 'Un Urbanisme Cosmopolite', in G. Veinstein (ed.), *Salonique, 1850–1918: la 'Ville des Juifs' et le Réveil des Balkans*. Paris, pp. 158–76.

Zizek, S. 1997. 'Multiculturalism or the Cultural Logic of Multinational Capitalism', *New Left Review* 225: 28–51.

Zukin, S. 1995. *The Culture of Cities*. Oxford.

Chapter 8

'For Badakhshan – the Country without Borders!': Village Cosmopolitans, Urban-Rural Networks and the Post-Cosmopolitan City in Tajikistan[1]

MAGNUS MARSDEN

Introduction

'I used not to be this way', commented Shah Firuz having consumed the latest in a long sequence of teacups of *Vodka Tajikistan*. 'No, he didn't', replied the gathering of men sitting in the Dushanbe cafe where we were toasting 'artists' day' on a cold and wet February afternoon. 'The war did this to me', Shah went on, 'before the war I was a strong man, a boxer, you wouldn't have recognised me in the era of the Soviets – no vodka or ciga-rettes ever passed my lips. Now I've lost my strength – look how my stom-ach has become big'. The gathered men nodded again in agreement: 'I lived in Moscow and – do you know – I even fought in a boxing competition in Japan, yes Japan!'

Shah, now in his late forties, is originally from Tajikistan's southern and semi-autonomous Badakhshan province, although he has lived most of his life in Moscow and now Tajikistan's capital city, Dushanbe. During Tajiki-stan's civil war Shah was an influential commander; he fought for the op-position Islamic parties against the government of the Republic. Two years previously, I had met Shah whilst trying to find a seat on a minibus to Ba-dakhshan, the small villages of which are about a twenty-four hour drive from Soviet-built Dushanbe. Shah had invited me to join him in his jeep. During the course of the journey, Shah pointed towards the places where he had spent weeks fighting the government forces during the civil war –

the mountainous Badakhshan region, however, was never captured by the government and remained largely peaceful during the war. During the civil war, Shah had travelled both to Pakistan and Afghanistan, where he sought hospital treatment after being injured during a battle; he had even been sent as a refugee to Canada. Nowadays, Shah lives a relatively comfortable life in Dushanbe: he holds a very good government post, which although not well paid allows him to own a vehicle and a house in Dushanbe where he lives with his family. Shah's next toast was to Badakhshan: 'For Badakhshan,' said Shah raising his teacup, 'the country without borders!' 'Yes,' he replied to his companions, amongst them journalists, school teachers and labourers working in Dushanbe but all from Shah's valley in Badakhshan, 'our country doesn't have borders, we've always welcomed whoever has come: the English came, the Russians came, Magnus has come, and we've welcomed them all: Badakhshan does not have borders.'

This vignette raises two important and interlinked sets of concerns that run throughout this chapter. On the one hand, Shah's discussion of the ways in which his body and its needs, as well as his habits, have undergone significant transformations since Tajikistan's civil war in the 1990s underscores the long lasting effects of the conflict on personal and collective forms of self-understanding in Tajikistan. It would be easy to think that the vacuum created by the collapse of the Soviet Union has been one-dimensionally filled by a class of hyper-masculine warlords and one-time Soviet bureaucrats, men who identify either with assertive forms of political Islam, or the mafia. Yet Shah focuses on the degradation of an active, disciplined and well-trained form of masculinity to something that is a shadow of its former self – undisciplined and, importantly, in relationship to this volume, non-international. At the same time, Shah emphasises the status of his own region of Badakhshan as being a 'world without borders', somehow impervious to the divisive effects of both Russian and Soviet expansion and Tajikistan's civil war: a place where hospitality and encompassment overshadows the forms of social and political divisions that, according to most accounts, have defined the modern historic development of Tajikistan.

In this chapter, I explore what the editors of this volume refer to as 'post-cosmopolitanism'. Ethnographically, I explore these issues in relationship to the ways in which people in Tajikistan talk about the ongoing effects of Tajikistan's civil war on the country's society, something that also shapes the multivalent and complex strategies through which they seek to negotiate city life in the country today. I seek to explore these post-cosmopolitan forms of urban life, however, from a unique perspective, that of the very category of people whom, it is all too easy to assume, are the key agents behind the degeneration of open forms of urban-cosmopolitan subjectivities: rural-urban 'migrants'. A consideration of the ways in which such people reflect upon and play an active role in forging new forms of urban sociality in Tajikistan today reveals the importance, however, of a constellation of very different processes central to the production of a myriad of more hardened forms of identity, notably those emerging from state-derived discourses of national culture.

Ethnographically, this chapter takes as its point of departure the networks that connect Pamiris living in their home region of Badakhshan to others living in Dushanbe, as well as other cities in Tajikistan, notably Khujand. It explores the significance of these networks to people's collective and personal self-understandings of being Pamiri in Tajikistan today. Tajikistan people, I suggest, conceptualise different cities in their country as being characterised by unique forms of sociality and diversity, and as also offering different types of personal and collective possibilities, with both affective and economic dimensions. Critical to note are the ways in which the people with whom I work make choices about where to live in relationship to local understandings of the extent to which different cities in the country are held as being more or less 'cosmopolitan': for many of the Pamiris I know, life in a cosmopolitan city is talked about as nourishing personal and communal forms of moral and cultural life, and as being safer than cities associated with a dominant ethnic or regional identity.

More broadly, this chapter seeks to contribute to the comparative analysis of different types of urban social life important in post-Soviet Central Asia today. Along with Humphrey and Skvirskaja, I have elsewhere considered the ways in which Muslims living in Bukhara, Uzbekistan, negotiate during their everyday lives a shared perception that their city has transformed from being a great urban centre of Islamic learning, thought and knowledge, to a peripheral and even declining urban space, both in Central Asia and the wider Muslim world (Humphrey, Marsden and Skvirskaja 2009). This chapter turns its attention to a very different setting: Dushanbe. As in Bukhara, Pamiris living in Dushanbe talk about the degradation of their city's moral and cultural landscape, often too focusing on a decline in those everyday forms of mixing, openness and interconnection between people from different backgrounds that we might label as 'cosmopolitanism'. There is much talk about the departure of the city's Russians (during the civil war period), as well as the difficulties these people have faced since returning to their 'home' country, and the ways in which new forms of immorality have seeped inside what were once the high cultural nodes of their city: for example, the Soviet-built swimming pools to the north of the city that were once a place of morally proper relaxation for modern families have now become dominated by young men cavorting openly with Tajik prostitutes.

What is different about the significance of these concerns as they are expressed in Dushanbe as compared to Bukhara, however, is that the perceived and ongoing degradation of the city's cultural diversity and moral life is rarely simplified by local people in terms of discourses that posit underlying differences between different ethnic groups, for example, Uzbeks and Tajiks. Rather, the complexity of the types of moral and cultural hierarchies that people in Dushanbe deploy to perceive and understand the wider changes currently affecting life in their city are animated by more finite distinctions between different regional groups of Tajik-speaking people. Whilst there are significant communities of Uzbeks in Tajikistan, and the treatment of these by the government of Tajikistan has received growing levels of international criticism in recent years, the vast majority of conversations about difference and coexistence I heard in Dushanbe concerned the complexity of relationships between people from different regional localities within Tajikistan. This will not surprise readers familiar with Tajikistan's recent political history: whilst the opposition and government forces in Tajikistan's civil war deployed discourses of Islamism, market economy and democracy to distinguish their political claims to authority, the conflict's contours were most clearly defined by the attempts made by regional solidarity groups, commonly referred to as clans in political science works, to secure influence in the Tajik state (e.g. Akiner 2001; Heathershaw 2009; Collins 2006).[2]

It is especially significant to note that distinctions between different regional groups in Tajikistan are not simply made by Dushanbe people in relationship to the levels of political influence, power or authority these groups are perceived to hold, although accusations of corruption by powerful regional networks are often expressed in everyday conversation. Distinctions between Tajiks identified as belonging to different regional sub-sets are also often invested with ethnic-like boundary markers: differences are readily read by local actors in terms of the accent or dialect that people from different regions of the country speak. Moreover, these dialects are also held to signify deeper and more immutable forms of distinctions between Tajikistan people, something often expressed to me in terms of a contrast between the humanity (*insaniyat*) of some and the animality (*haiwan*) of others. On the one hand, all of this is a reflection of the ongoing legacy of the country's civil war on life in Tajikistan. At the same time, it also points towards a theme running throughout this volume: apparently diminishing forms of ethnic and linguistic diversity in once cosmopolitan urban centres have simultaneously led to the creation or at least crystallisation of 'new constellations of ethnic differences and statuses', which emerge alongside new urban practices, and require the active creation of new 'rules of engagement' deployed to negotiate and understand emerging urban social forms. At first glance, these new constellations of differences, as well as the urban practices and discourses with which they are entwined, might appear to point towards the emergence of either a new or even a more developed form of a cosmopolitan cultural sophistication, previously constrained by state socialism and then dissolved during the civil war. A closer consideration, however, reveals the ways in which the cosmopolitan celebration of cultural difference not only conceals but is also central to the objectification and valorisation of new interests and identities, which are, more often than not, conceived of and experienced as being 'specific and exclusive' (Osella and Osella 2007: 2).

Background

The chapter is concerned, thus, with the ways in which Pamiris encounter and perceive Tajikistan's diverse urban spaces as well as how they formulate complex practices and rules of engagement within these. I now want to explore the nature and importance of regional patterns of migration from Badakhshan. Pamiris offer particularly unique insights into both the complexity of the types of overlapping difference that are currently important in Tajikistan and people's ways of navigating these: Badakhshan is distinct in important religious, linguistic and cultural ways from other regions in Tajikistan. Whereas the majority of Tajikistan's 8 million or so Muslim people identify with Sunni forms of Islamic doctrine (themselves of course diversely constituted in relationship to the influence diverse Sufi brotherhoods or *turuq*), almost all Pamiris are Shi'a Ismai'li Muslims, who regard the Aga Khan as their spiritual leader – the 'Imam of the time' (*hozir imam*).[3] At the same time, whilst Pamiris are considered to be ethnically 'Tajik' by the state, most of them speak one of several Iranian-Pamiri languages which are not understandable to Tajik speakers. These differences of religion and language from Tajikistan's majority Sunni and Tajiki-speaking people play themselves out in complex ways. Some Pamiris are from villages that are Tajiki speaking yet they also identify themselves as being Shi'a Ismai'lis. Such people, however, contrast their cultural values and practices, not to mention ways of being Muslim, with those of other Tajik-speaking Sunni Muslims in the country, who they label as being 'Tajik'.

Importantly, Tajikistan's Pamiri-Ismai'lis are not a national religious 'minority' in any simple sense; nor are they newcomers to Tajikistan's largely Tajik-speaking cities. Pamiris, rather, played a central political and cultural role in the Soviet Republic of Tajikistan: many were employed as major state officials in the central government in Dushanbe, while others were influential sporting and cultural figures (Collins 2006: 281).[4] Pamiris, thus, have a long history of experience of life at the geographical extreme of the Soviet Union: a narrow river divided their homes from those of their one-time relatives and also religious authorities in Afghanistan. Yet at the same time, they talk about the depth of their connections to the Republic and to Dushanbe life. The complex status of Pamiris as people both at the geographical peripheries and ideological centre of 'Tajik' national life continues to be reflected upon in their experiences of social and political transformations following the collapse of the Soviet Union. Since the civil war many Pamiris have talked about the decline in their people's political influences in the Republic, claiming to have been purposefully excluded from high government positions in the state because during the civil war they were allied with parties, such as the regionalist La'al-e Badakhshan, against the regional network now held to be most influential in Dushanbe, that of Kulob, a town in south-west Tajikistan. The rise to political power of the Kulobi networks in Tajikistan was far from being a simple product of 'victory' in the civil war, itself the result of a complex intermeshing of factors, including, notably, the president's use of the law and order forces, the mass media at his disposal, and Russian patronage (Collins 2006: 280) partly derived from a fear of the 'Islamisation' or 'Afghanisation' of Tajikistan in Russian political discourse. In the years after the presidential election of 1994, these networks have been further consolidated by distributing political appointments to Kulobis, and by cutting other regional networks – notably the formerly powerful Khujandi 'clan' – out of state resources. Pamiris had firsthand experience of the brutalities of the Tajik civil war: Pamiri men and boys living in Dushanbe were targeted and killed by pro-government forces in the city. Indeed, during my fieldwork in the Chitral region of northern Pakistan I encountered many Pamiri boys and men who had fled Dushanbe, returned to the Pamirs and then walked to Chitral in order to find work as agricultural labourers. Moreover, as I explore below, the perceived and real exclusion of Pamiri networks from contemporary political realities in Tajikistan is also a source of much discussion and reflection by Pamiris today.

The experience of Pamiris in Tajikistan's cities today thus affords important insights into the ways in which overlapping forms of regional, ethnic and religious difference interpolate with one another and are invested with wider political and cultural significance in the country. In particular, their experiences of life in a border region, alongside their changing experiences of urban life in Dushanbe over the past century, challenge the value of models that contrast urban cosmopolitanism with the maligned other of rural homogeneity.[5]

Dilemmas of nationhood

Urban cosmopolitanism and the forms of interethnic and linguistic mixing with which it is entwined has been widely recognised by anthropologists as posing important anxieties to national elites and the forms of cultural nationalism they seek to promote (e.g. Dresch 2005). Tajik national identity discourses today are frequently configured around the loss to the Tajik nation of the great centres of Persian and, thus by extension, Tajik thought and culture: the cities of Bukhara and Samarqand, today in Uzbekistan (in this discourse 'Persianate' has ultimately sought to mark distinctions between Tajiks and Uzbeks, both within Uzbekistan and Tajikistan). This issue was of great importance during the Soviet period too. Yet, given the tense political relations between Tajikistan and Uzbekistan, Tajikistan's divisive civil war, and Tajikistan's expanding relations with the wider Persianate world, notably Afghanistan and Iran, these issues of the content of 'Tajik' self-definition have been invested with even more prominent forms of political significance today.

On the one hand, Tajik national identity is often framed by state discourses in terms of ancient Persianate forms of refined, urban behaviour, spiritual achievement and high cultural learning, as well as, importantly, 'statehood' (Heathershaw 2009: 71). These discourses are vigorously promoted by the state in numerous television programmes about the country's 'national' Persian poets, as well as in the teaching of Tajik literature in the country's universities. Yet Tajikistan is made up largely of villages and small towns, whilst the vast majority of the figures of Tajik culture, whose work is promoted through the state media, were originally from urban centres stretching in an expansive arc through Herat in eastern Afghanistan to Bukhara and Samarqand. The genealogy of the word Tajik is a recurring feature of state discourse on Tajik national identity, for example, its origins being said to go back to the writings of the great Persian mystic Rumi, himself claimed as a 'Tajik' in national cultural discourses (e.g. Chvyr 1993).

In the context of Bukhara, we sought to emphasise the ways in which projects of identification with Persianate forms of high culture and values, notably those emphasising refined sentiment and moderated emotions, served to mark the importance of ethnic distinctions between the city's Tajik speakers, especially the city's Iranis, and Uzbekistan's Uzbek-speaking majority. Bukhara's expansive and inclusive Persianate tradition is also deployed to emphasise the city's historic place in a wider world where ethnic distinctions were of less importance in comparison to those of the universalising dimensions of Islamic civilisation. In contrast, Tajikistan national discourses depict the country's people as being the authentic core and true heirs to the Tajik language – part of a wide and expansive world, yet also distinct from and, in some sense, more authentically 'Persianate', than that wider world.

Yet such discourses are invariably caught up in complexity, historical and social. On the one hand, the effects of Russian and Soviet influences on Tajikistan are ever visible, be these, as I explore below, positive or negative.

In recent years, the state has taken positive steps to emphasise the Tajik-ness of the Tajik nation: in July 2007. For example, the country's president gave a speech in which he argued that Tajikistan's official language should be Tajik only; Russian would no longer have a place in the official business of the state, despite Russian's ongoing importance as a lingua franca in the region, the fact that a very significant proportion of people in Tajikistan rely on labour remittances from their relatives working in Russian cities, and the fact that Tajikistan remains closely politically wedded to Russia to the extent that a large picture of the country's president walking side by side with an albeit comparatively diminutive President Putin could be seen on Dushanbe's central street in my last visit to the city in 2007.

Dushanbe: languages of region and religion

In what ways are these complex constellations of difference and similarity enacted, instantiated and managed in everyday urban social life? Impor-tantly, unlike Bukhara and many other cities in Central Asia, notably Tash-kent (Sahadeo 2007) and Osh (Liu 2007), Dushanbe is not divided into old and new sectors. Dushanbe, rather, is a predominantly Soviet city made up of central wide boulevards, lined by Russian-style offices and state build-ings, whilst its residential areas are comprised mostly of apartment blocks. As I am often told by friends and informants in the city, what is now Du-shanbe was until the creation of the Tajik SSR in 1929 nothing more than a weekly village market, or bazaar. Morgan Liu has explored the ways in which the urban form of the Kyrgyz city of Osh 'integrates both a so-called colonial city and a traditional city of the mahallas' mediated by a bazaar sit-ting at the interface of these distinctive spaces.[6] These distinctions in space, Liu suggests, 'mark distinction in livelihood, lifestyle and aspiration', even if from the perspective on the ground there is considerable hybridity and blurring between them. Liu explores these spaces as raising questions and providing useful indicators about the ways in which Central Asia should orientate itself today. On the one hand, more 'traditional' parts of the city point towards the possibility of the region's people choosing to identify with Islamic and moral order. On the other hand, the new urban spaces suggest the possibility of life being defined above all by commitment to liberalism and democracy. At the same time, of course, the hybridism of everyday life points towards a more real and 'on the ground' accommodation between these different forms and representations of future possibilities.

Dushanbe's spatial organisation, in contrast, provides no such helpful hints or simplifying clarifications for understanding the varying orientations that the city, country or region should take in the future. In Dushanbe there are no fast distinctions between Soviet sectors and traditional mahallas. Whilst there are some neighbourhoods with old houses, much of the city is a predominantly Soviet-inspired space with the elegant main street – Rudaki Prospect – running through the centre, surrounded on either side by government buildings, shopping centres and apartment blocks that extend to the city's limits in both directions.[7] Certainly, Dushanbe people do not talk of their city as being comprised of 'old' and 'new' parts, as is the case not only in many other Central Asian cities, but also in neighbouring Afghanistan. The division of space here is not so much between different sectors of Dushanbe, but between Dushanbe and the world beyond: only a few miles outside of the city's limits the wide and well paved boulevards of Dushanbe are gone, replaced instead by broken roads destroyed during the civil war and now only just being rebuilt. Dushanbe, in short, is something akin to a modern, urban enclave in a country of villages, mountains and dispersed small towns. That this is the case is quickly felt by people when they enter the city from the village: their cars must be washed before arrival, if not they will be fined by the police, as too will those foolish enough to drive old jeeps within the city limits.

As I have already noted, whilst the majority of people living in Dushanbe are Tajik speaking, people living in the city talk about the different linguistic registers that distinguish the city's people from one another. At one level, people claim to be able to distinguish between people from different regions of Tajikistan by the dialect of Tajik that they speak. This reflects the ways in which different dialects use different Tajiki words, as well as grammar; it is also often a reflection of the different accents (*lahja*) spoken. One change that people in the city talked about was the ways in which many of the city's people choose not to speak either 'literary Tajiki' or the form of Tajiki spoken in their own region, but instead speak with distinctively Kulobi accents, using Kulobi linguistic forms and vocabulary. All the Pamiri people I spoke to emphasised the differences between high Tajiki and low Tajiki. They also asserted that Kulobi Tajiki was even less refined than other everyday forms of Tajiki, and that everyone in the country could identify Pamiri forms of Tajiki, even though Tajiki was not 'their' language. One evening, for example, I was watching a Tajik discussion programme on state television with a Pamiri friend, although from a largely Tajiki-speaking village. He exclaimed during the programme how he was shocked to see people speaking in the Kulobi dialect on television: 'What can become of our country where there are even Professors on television who are unable to speak proper Tajik?', he commented. At one level, thus, Kulobi linguistic styles are said by Pamiris to mark almost ethnic-like distinctions between Kulobis and other regional groups in Tajikistan; they are also held to point towards the inability of such people to grasp literate forms of Tajiki, and, thus, point towards their cultural crudeness.

At the same time, many Pamiris I spoke to also claimed that other influences lay behind what they described as the expansion of the Kulobi dialect in Dushanbe. In particular I was told that many of the city's policemen had started to speak in a Kulobi-style dialect despite the fact that many of these men were not from Kulob at all. Aka Islam, for example, is a Major in Dushanbe's traffic police; his main job is bringing the city to a complete halt when the country's president drives from his downtown residence to his newly built palace in the nearby mountain resort of Varzob. Islam is from a largely rural region to the north of Dushanbe called Ayni, today about a five-hour drive from Dushanbe, but he has been living in Dushanbe for the past twenty years. His circle of friends in the city is made up mainly of networks of kin from his home region. When I stayed with him in Ramadan 2005 we spent each evening visiting his Dushanbe-based relatives from Ayni in their homes in Dushanbe's apartment blocks.[8] Yet Aka Islam's friendships are not wholly defined by his region of origin. He also has a close Pamiri friend, although he has never visited the Pamirs; the two met whilst they were course mates (*hamcors*) at Dushanbe University.

Aka Islam often expresses resentment about the influence of Kulobis in the city and the country more widely today. As with many others, he claimed that Kulobis tended to be unrefined in their way of speaking and that not only had they taken over all government jobs in the city, but they had also used their connections to buy profitable businesses elsewhere. Near his home in Ayni, for example, some Kulobi men had bought a chaikhana (tea house) that was a profitable business because the road which it served was frequently blocked by landslides. Kulobi, thus, is widely seen as a language of power, something that represents and marks out Kulobi influence not only in Dushanbe but in the country more widely.

One day, I was stopped by a policeman in Dushanbe and aggressively asked to show my passport immediately. Later in the day, in the company of our mutual Pamiri friend, I mentioned to Islam what had happened: 'Kulobis, they both sighed, 'our once beautiful Dushanbe is now a village'. A few minutes later, however, our Pamiri companion commented to Islam that he had heard him 'speaking like a Kulobi' when he was on duty during the day. Islam rather apologetically asked us what he could do; 'all the people around me are Kulobis', he commented, 'unless you speak like one of them they give you no respect'. It is also important to note the degree to which the unrefined Kulobi accent is itself something consciously cultivated by Kulobis. On a trip to Afghanistan in March 2008, for example, I travelled to the Tajik-Afghan border at Sher Khan Bandar to meet some of my Afghan friends.Shortly after their arrival they told me that Kulobis were 'bullish' (*boqa*) fighters, a positive collective attribute that made them more similar to their Afghan friends than their non-Kulobi Tajik compatriots.

What emerges from a consideration of these ways of speaking about different dialects of Tajiki is the emergence of important forces behind the homogenisation of ways of using language in the post-cosmopolitan setting of Dushanbe. It would be easy to assume, given the Tajik state's emphasis on the importance of 'high' Tajiki for national cultural identity, that the key force behind such processes were state attempts to sanitise local language usage in line with state-led national identity building projects. In contrast, however, the reflections of Dushanbe's inhabitants on these matters point more to the emergence of the Kulobi dialect as being the language of state power and to the ways in which people experience this dialect in relationship to the theme of domination, whilst also cultivating strategies to benefit from the power of Kulobi, by using it in their own professional lives, in public spaces and as a way of ironically mocking the Kulobis amongst themselves, for example.

Making distinctions of the ways in which different people speak Tajiki and how some people switch between different dialects of the language during their daily life is not only understood by the Pamiris I have met in terms of the impact of the politics of region on Dushanbe life. Tajiki is a form of Persian and similar in important ways both to Iranian Persian and Afghan Dari. Some Dushanbe people also seek to speak forms of Tajiki that do not reflect their regional identity but offer other, more transitional, transnational and even transcendent possibilities for Tajik self-understanding. What could be seen as active attempts to transcend being identified according to region by speaking forms of Tajiki – associated with neighbouring states as it is – appear to be especially important for Dushanbe dwellers seeking to enact publicly expressed forms of self-consciously Muslim forms of thought and identity. Importantly, given that the Soviet border regime on the Tajikistan-Afghan border was strict, and that the Soviet Tajikistan Republic exerted considerable efforts towards the formulation of a 'national' Tajiki language which was devoid of Arabic loan words with clearly religious connotations and meanings, such hybridised forms of Tajiki-Dari are a predominantly post-Soviet phenomenon.[9] Interestingly, these complex interactions between linguistic styles and personal forms of religious transformation are often talked about in relationship to local discourses concerning the body and its needs.

Public forms of religion are a visible dimension of life in Dushanbe, and something that is often mapped onto the bodies of Tajik men and women, yet here, as elsewhere in Central Asia, the state has also played a major role in shaping what it considers an acceptable form of public Islam (e.g. Stephan 2006). This is partly a reflection of the important role played by Tajikistan's Islamic parties in the negotiation of the end to the civil war in 1995. More recently, the Tajikistan state has taken more active steps to police the boundaries of public Islam and extend its surveillance of personal forms of religiosity as well. During my research in Tajikistan in February and July 2007, for example, a number of Pamiri students taking courses in philology and Tajik literature at Dushanbe University told me how some of their class mates had refused to take off their veils when told to do so by the Tajik authorities. Some of these women had compromised with the state and kept their places; others had refused to remove their veils and had been sent 'outside'. In contrast to Collette Harris (2006) who has argued that such reform-minded forms of public Islam are important only to small sections of Tajik society, people in Dushanbe have told me that they are surprised by the growing religiosity of the city's people. Significant numbers of women in the city can be seen wearing the Hijab (*ruhmol*), while some men do not merely wear 'national' Tajik clothes – notably the robe, or chapan – but also wear loose shirts and trousersassociated by many men in the country with Afghanistan's mujahidin.

Scholarly works on post-Soviet forms of Central Asian Islam have debated the degree to which new styles of veiling in the region are either voluntary and personal assertions of individual adherence to Islamic norms, or more a reflection of forms of social control, which themselves point towards resurgent local patriarchal values, or particular kinship forms. Yet these debates animate a great deal of discussion amongst Muslims in Tajikistan themselves and it was quite normal for the men with whom I walked around Dushanbe to click their tongues as they passed veiled women in the street and claim that such forms of veiling were a threat to Tajikistan's status as a 'democracy'. At the same time, these men's wives themselves led predominantly home-based lives in deference to what they and their husbands referred to as 'Tajik cultural values', or their sisters, happy to wear skirts and jeans during the day, would studiously wear 'traditional' dress in the presence of their elder brothers.

Equally prominent are stalls throughout the city where translations of the Qur'an in Tajik, books about good Muslim practice, prayer instruction manuals and cassette recordings as well as DVDs Islamic preachers are sold. These materials mostly address questions pertaining to personal Muslim life – how to pray, which verses of the Qur'an need to be memorised, and how relations should be constructed and enacted across the boundary of sexual difference. At the same time, other works also address more overtly political and legal concerns, such as how far a democratic state such as Tajikistan may also be considered to be governed by Shari 'a law. These works also outline the ways in which Muslims should change their behaviour to conform to Islamic doctrinal standards, by no longer selling alcohol in their shops, for example. The men and women who work at these stalls frequently claim that people in Tajikistan are not Muslims by practice but, rather, *musulmanzada*, the descendents of Muslims, or Muslims by name alone. Importantly, whilst such stalls are particularly evident in the enormous yet largely empty outdoor trading zones on Dushanbe's peripheries, they are also found along Dushanbe's main street, Rudaki Prospect, signalling the lack of any simple association of particular urban spaces with particular modes of public religiosity.

At one level, and as is the case elsewhere in Central Asia (notably Liu 2007), such public modes of being Muslim in Dushanbe represent the performance of political power by those associated with the Islamic parties during the civil war and, perhaps too, the growing influence of global ways and modes of being Muslim (e.g. Roy 2007), yet they also point towards more complex processes. In particular, Pamiris took very careful note of the dialect in which Tajikistan's media Muslims voiced their calls to commitment for the country's Muslims to follow more strictly Islamic doctrinal requirements. Having bought a DVD of an especially well-known religious leader in Tajikistan, Eshon Nuruddin, who, I was told by several men in the city, was especially religious and spiritual but also closely watched by the country's president, Imam Ali Raman, I watched it in the home of some Pamiri friends. The Eshon is shown in the video presiding over a large 'gathering' (*majlis*) of men, who are sitting, eating and listening to the Eshon's sermon. The Eshon introduces the gathering by quickly saying that this is no normal gathering where people come to eat – he instructs those who have just come to the meeting for food to leave immediately as now they have filled their stomachs the real spiritual work must be done. The world is divided, thus, between those whose ultimate aim is to fill their stomachs and the believers who have higher ethical and moral goals. One of the Pamiri men with me said that the version of Tajik spoken by the Eshon in the video sounded more like Afghan Dari or Afghan Persian than Tajiki. Some people in the city distinguish not only between different regional versions of Tajiki, but also associate other ways of speaking Tajiki with attempts to emulate other national forms of Persian, suggesting that some opinion-making figures in the city have sought to transcend regional forms of difference by identifying themselves with linguistic forms widely associated with Afghanistan.[10]

Finally, the relationship between such avowedly 'Islamic' modes of self and collective identification projects and those embarked on by Kulobis in the city, particularly those associated with or employed by the Tajikistan state's interlocutors, are complex. At one level this shows that the types of political divisions fostered and sharpened during the civil war are of central importance: distinctions between pro-government and opposition 'Islamic' movements in Dushanbe may be said now to be taking the form of distinct and even conflictual models of self-identification, with one emphasising regional power, bullish forms of authority, and political influence, and the other the authoritative claims of more universal and Islamising forms of religious piety.

Yet there are also important similarities in the ways in which Tajiki people talk about these apparently conflictual modes of self-identification, and recognise how they are deployed, managed, manipulated and sometimes also subverted by Dushanbe people. Here too it is frequently with reference to the ability or otherwise of different categories of Dushanbe dwellers to control their bodily urges that these differences are vocalised. Thus, policemen consciously adopt Kulobi linguistic styles, yet also deride Kulobi ways of speaking as being both uncontrolled and unrefined – in short, animal-like. Likewise, other men I spoke to in Dushanbe told me that the Eshon and his way of speaking was 'too emotional' (*ehsosi*): mullahs like him, they told me, brought dangerous influences to Tajikistan – such mullahs were 'terrorists' bent on destroying Tajikistan's modernity. 'If it were not for the Soviets,' Aka Islam told me, 'then today we would be the same as the Afghans and if the country is left in the hands of men like the Eshon then we will once again take the colour of the animal-like Afghans.'[11] Moreover, the fact that the Eshon and other mullahs claim to be focused on spiritual perfection is also a constant source of derision, and it is in the bodily comportment of such men that their inability to control their insatiable appetites is most clearly held to be visible: 'It's easy to be a mullah,' I was often told, 'all you need is a cloak, an insatiable appetite for more wives, and a big stomach.'

Alternative configurations of language and religion

At one level, then, different everyday usages of language and modes of bodily display signal stark differences in the ways in which categories of people in Dushanbe identify themselves. Yet the distinctions thus created reflect more complex tensions than a simple conflict model between some Dushanbe people who emphasise identifying with distinctly post-Soviet and secular ways of being Muslim, and others with more abstract and reform-minded ways of being Muslim.

Many Pamiris, for example, were affiliated to the opposition Islamist parties during the civil war. At the same time, they identify themselves as being Shi'a Ismai'lis – an Islamic doctrinal tradition, the ritual practices and attitudes towards supposedly core Islamic ideas of which is the source of much contentious debate amongst Sunni religious authorities, both in South and Central Asia. Importantly, most Pamiris claim that Tajikistan has no history of the type of sectarian conflict that has become important in other regions of the Muslim world; whilst Ismai'lis were treated 'with cruelty' in the Emirate of Bukhara in the pre-Soviet period, they say, when Tajikistan was a part of the Soviet Union matters of doctrinal difference were something the country's people neither thought or, more pertinently, talked about: 'In Soviet times', I was often told, 'nobody interfered with another' (*kasba kas kor nadosht*). This recognition by Pamiri Ismai'lis today that Soviet religious 'tolerance' was rooted more in a veil of silence concerning matters of religious difference than it was in the actual views that Muslims adhering to different Islamic doctrinal clusters held of one another, should problematise any simple attempt to characterise the Soviet past as either any more or less 'cosmopolitan' than today's realities. In Dushanbe today questions of religious difference do seem to be growing in importance. Yet the extent to which these will develop, or the ways in which people will seek to negotiate them, remain unknown.[12]

The emerging importance of distinctions and differences between Tajikistan Muslims was raised in conversations with Pamiris in Dushanbe during the course of my visits in 2007. In July 2007 the worldwide Ismai'li community was celebrating the jubilee of the current Aga Khan's accession to the Imamate, or spiritual leadership of 'the community'. The Aga Khan was to deliver a televised address to the world's Ismai'lis, which would be beamed across the world on Sky Television. On arriving in Dushanbe, however, I was told by some Pamiri friends that 'the state' had refused permission for there to be a gathering of Dushanbe-based Ismai'lis at the city's football stadium to watch the address on specially arranged television sets – such a gathering would, according to state officials, contravene the laws of the Republic which forbade the use of loudspeakers to deliver religious sermons or messages. In contrast, I was told, Ismai'lis living in Badakshan Province were to be allowed to watch the event in the region's rayon and provincialheadquarters. Some people I spoke to did talk about the government's refusal to allow the gathering in Dushanbe as proof that the country's Ismai'lis were being unfairly treated. The majority, however, merely commented that the meeting was not to go ahead. Others said they had not even been aware of the possibility of such a gathering taking place. On the day of the Imam's jubilee, instead, I went with a family of Pamiris and one of their Tajik Sunni friends to a restaurant in the centre of the city, where toasts were said and much vodka consumed. Yet towards the end of the meal, the Sunni man and his Ismai'li friend agreed that it was important for Tajikistan not to become like Pakistan or Afghanistan, where Sunnis and Shi'as declared each other as being non-Muslims and killed one another. What is evident in such conversations is a clear awareness of the limits and possible weak points of the values of religious co-existence said by Dushanbe dwellers to shape their relations with one another. Evident too are attempts to negotiate and manage these new crystallisations of religious difference, and this willingness of Tajik people to discuss these matters 'openly', as a way of reaffirming friendships between Muslims from different doctrinal traditions is an important manifestation of these processes.

Yet such differences cannot be simply wished away or successfully negotiated. Pamiri Ismai'lis living in Dushanbe told me that they had heard that Sunni Tajiks in the city were spreading rumours that the Aga Khan was not merely providing assistance to people from Badakhshan, but that he had bought the entire region lock, stock and barrel. Young women I spoke to, moreover, told me that if Pamiris were not opposed to their daughters marrying Westerners, they would never give their daughters to Sunni families. Of course, such discourses betray more complex social realities – many Pamiri men in Dushanbe have married Sunni Tajik girls. One couple I met had married shortly before the civil war. During the civil war, when Pamiris were targeted by opposition forces, the couple fled the city to the comparably safe northern city of Khujand. Yet these mixed marriages between Pamiri Ismai'lis and Sunni Tajiks – which were a relatively frequent, and, probably, officially valorised feature of life during the Soviet period (cf. Humphrey 1983) – appear to be subject to more social and moral control today.[1] Moreover, whereas men and women who have participated in such unions emphasise the fact that they are both Muslims and highlight more the differences in language and tradition (*urf-adat*) that distinguish them from one another, with the growing importance of shared forms of commitment to an exclusive Ismai'li community, complex questions are likely to emerge in the future regarding not merely the ways in which such mixed unions are judged morally by communities and kin, but also the religious identities of mixed Sunni-Ismai'li marriages.

Importantly, Pamiri people appear to be taking the religious demographics of Tajikistan's urban centres into consideration when making important family and personal decisions about where to live. As I noted in the introduction, many Pamiri families are now moving from their houses in the Pamiris and relocating in Tajikistan cities. At the same time, other Pamiris left Dushanbe during and after the civil war in order to either return to the Pamirs or live in cities they considered to be safer. Alongside a rapid increase in the cost of rent and housing over the past five years in Dushanbe, these factors have contributed to quite significant changes in the demographic distribution of Pamiris in the country.

One city that Pamiris talk about as being attractive to live in is the northern city of Khujand. Khujand, once the powerbase of Tajikistan's Soviet-era elite, a regional network now in political decline, is widely talked about both by Pamiri and other Tajikistan people as being a city inhabited by polite and sophisticated people (*mardom-e bahurmat*). This stands, increasingly, in contrast to Dushanbe's growing reputation as a city dominated by

Kulobis, those said to pride themselves on their bullish (*boqa*) ways. A consideration of the types of choices that Tajik people make concerning where to buy and rent houses is critical to the theme of this volume for two reasons. Firstly, as shall become clear below, these decision-making processes do appear to be leading to a significant clustering of regional communities within particular neighbourhoods in Tajikistan's cities. Secondly, however, this clustering, is not, perhaps, leading to the straightforward ethnicisation of the Tajik urban landscape that we might expect. One of the central reasons that Pamiris gave for Khujand's sophistication was that it was said to be ethnically and linguistically diverse in a way that Dushanbe was not. Pre-existing ethnic and linguistic diversity, in other words, is sometimes a positive force behind the clustering of Pamiris themselves in particular urban locales.

I travelled to Khujand with a family from the Pamirs who were seeking to move from their region and establish themselves in a city in the country. The family had about US$15,000 at their disposal and after spending several days trying to find a three-room flat to buy in Dushanbe for this price, they decided to travel to Khujand in order to see the possibilities of buying there. At first, the family looked at flats located about a fifteen-minute bus ride from Khujand's city centre. The dormitory wardens of apartment blocks were asked if any of the people living in the blocks had rooms available for rent, which they inevitably did. We were led around the flats, noting which ones had been recently repaired and which needed extensive work. Of about thirty flats we saw, around ten were being sold by Russians, mainly elderly women, who were leaving the city to live in Russia. Many of the Pamiri people who showed us round the city claimed that this was one of the greatest benefits of life in Khujand: if Dushanbe had become overrun by villagers and townspeople from southern Tajikistan then Khujand continued to be home not only to Uzbeks, but – of more significance to the Pamiris I spoke to – to significant populations of Russians, Tatars and Jews.

All of the Pamiris I met in Khujand were fluent Russian speakers. Firuz, for example, told me that he was better at speaking Russian than he was at Tajik. He was especially keen to emphasise that some of the Russians we spoke to were unable to distinguish him from a Russian. Tajiks distinguish the different ways in which their people speak Russian: some are said to speak a 'strange' or *ajoib* Russian – as soon as they open their mouths, I am told, everybody can tell that they are Tajik. Others say they can speak proper (*asil*) Russian – they tell stories of having so impressed Russians they met whilst working in Russia that they were invited to work as Russian teachers in schools. Nevertheless, many also speak of the incomprehensible language that 'new Russians' speak, which they claim to be barely intelligible. Tajiks not only distinguish different categories of Tajik persons on the basis of the way in which they speak Tajik, but distinctions are also made in relation to the types of Russian they speak, and speaking proper Russia is one way in which Pamiri men emphasise their capacity to move, profit from and be respected within a wider international realm.

Firuz, for example, had recently returned from Russia where he had been working as a builder in the city of Yekaterinburg. He told me how he felt bored in Khujand and longed to return to Russia: he was not 'happy' with living in the Tajik city, but did not have enough money to travel to work in Russia. His father, moreover, had told him that after seven years of working in Russia it was time for him to return. Firuz's stay in Russia had also been eventful, although he emphasised that he felt content in Russia in a way that he did not in Khujand. One of the reasons his father had asked him to stay at home was because of the increasingly anti-Tajik violence Firuz had experienced in Yekaterinburg. He had lived with a Russian girl in the city, and one night had been accused by a group of twenty Russian men of beating her while he was drunk. He told them that he was prepared to fight them one by one but they refused to accept and instead set upon him as a group: he spent the next six weeks in hospital with a broken jaw and a very visible scar where the gang of young men had smashed a bottle on his face. Yet Firuz told me that he had become adept at 'looking after' himself in Yekaterinburg: his fluent Russian and dark skin meant that he was skilled in persuading people that he was not a Tajik or Central Asian at all, but in fact a gypsy. Another Pamiri told me that when faced by young, drunken men who rode in his taxi, he concealed his Tajik identity and told them that he was Greek. There is thus a profound awareness of a perceived rise in racist attacks on Tajik labourers in Russia, yet some Pamiri people continue to talk about and valorise their status as persons able to move with skill through this international world.

The costs of flats in central Khujand were high too, however, with most being sold for between US$15,000 and 18,000. The relatives of the family with whom I was travelling were told that many Pamiris were now living in a small town, Choye Rukh, about twenty minutes drive from Khujand. The road to Choye Rukh was served by a large bus that ran in the mornings and the evenings so travel to and from work was not difficult. Choye Rukh, moreover, was known across the Soviet Union for its steel factory, operated, I was told, directly out of Moscow rather than Dushanbe. Today, the steel factory continues to function – one of the reasons that the small industrial settlement, with houses built for its once strong workforce, a school teaching Russian and a worker's club, makes Choye Rukh an attractive place to live for Pamiris. The family with whom I had travelled to Choye Rukh, indeed, decided that the peripheral steel town would be a good place to live. Not only were the houses with large gardens cheap and good Russian-language education available, but they were also impressed by the behaviour of the Uzbek bar owners – they had played Pamiri music when they recognised their clients in the bar were from Badakhshan. Other Pamiris living in the city advised the family to move there, moreover, because Armenians, Tatars and Russians had continued to live there after Tajikistan's independence. Choye Rukh's ongoing internationalism in a world of increasing ethnic and regional bleaching, coupled with the emergence of more conflictual intra-'Tajik' regional and religious identities, was an important signal to Pamiri people that it was both a secure and safe place to live. If Dushanbe and, to a lesser extent, Khujand are associated in the minds of many Pamiris with unrefined forms of ethnic or regional difference, then there are other, less expected urban spaces where what Humphrey refers to as Soviet forms of internationalism appear to be valued and re-invested with a type of culturally and morally nurturing significance.

Conclusion

New constellations of difference are thus an increasingly important dimension of Dushanbe city life. I have highlighted the complex and shifting forms these take, ranging from increasingly ethnic-like distinctions associated with the regional origins of people, to modes of religious identification that seek through the deployment of linguistic registers and practices to transcend questions of region, and to the gradual sharpening of distinctions between the city's Sunni and Shi'a Ismai'li Muslims, itself a category that does not go uncontested. I have explored the paradoxical processes of what the editors of this volume refer to as post-cosmopolitanism, which include the 'bleaching out' and displacement of public expressions of difference in terms of the emergence of shared standards of Kulobi speech in the city of Dushanbe. On the one hand, my emphasis has been on the multilayered ways in which differences are expressed and come to be invested with wider meaning, which highlight the problems with associating such forms of linguistic difference with either ethnic or religious 'identity', and the presence, rather, of more complex urban modes of both interaction and pulling apart. At the same time, however, I have also pointed to the ways in which another more totalising and perhaps potentially chilling way of thinking, talking about and categorising Tajikistan's urban diversity also occasionally comes to the surface. This discourse, hardly unique to Tajikistan in the post-9/11 world, is one that posits a basic difference between Republican civilisation and the public expression of barbarity, whether it is associated with irrational and over-emotional mullahs, or the immoral, uncontrollable and animalistic bodily cravings of those perceived as being the country's dominant urban group. The potential of this argument to sideline what appear to be the decidedly vicarious attempts by the state to promote an encompassing classical Tajik culture and everyday strategies of urban coexistence remains to be seen. Yet with civil war memories of the random shooting of young men in Dushanbe and talk of the horrific forms of torture meted out to political enemies during what is referred to as the era of 'human slaughter' (*odam kushi*), it is hardly surprising that a small, declining steel-producing town in northern Tajikistan is considered to be as good a place as, if not better than, Dushanbe's elegant avenues to watch new practices of urban coexistence unfold.

Notes

1. The research on which this chapter is based was conducted during three research trips made to Tajikistan between 2005 and 2007, and the chapter itself was completed in 2007. Whilst I have tried to incorporate into the chapter important changes I have seen on visiting Tajikistan since 2007, the chapter largely reflects the outcome of my first fieldwork in Central Asia. I would like to thank Caroline Humphrey and Vera Skvirskaja as well as Diana Ibañez-Tirado for their helpful comments, criticisms and suggestions, and the Nuffield Foundation, the British Academy, the Leverhulme Trust and Trinity College, Cambridge for supporting the research on which it collectively draws.
2. On Shi'a Ismai'lism generally see Daftary 1990.
3. During the Soviet invasion of Afghanistan, moreover, many Pamiris travelled to Afghanistan and worked as interpreters for the Soviet Army. Today, however, they also claim that even looking across the border was forbidden in the Soviet era.
4. My ethnographic work on Pamiris living within and beyond Badakshan is part of a broader and ongoing interdisciplinary project on the capillary networks that connect Muslim life in an expansive region including northern Pakistan, Afghanistan and Tajikistan. The research for the project is concerned with the ways in which Muslims in the region perceive and understand the interconnected transformations that they have experienced and actively participated in over the past thirty years and negotiate life in a world in which minute distinctions in space often mark radical differences in everyday modes of being Muslim. My interest in these issues crystallised during long-term ethnographic fieldwork in villages and small towns of the Chitral region in northern Pakistan. In some places, Chitral is only separated from Tajikistan by about twenty miles of Afghan territory: my main fieldwork village, for example, lies about a five-day walk from villages in Tajikistan's Badakhshan Province. During the war years Badakhshan was cut off from the rest of Tajikistan by a blokkade by pro-government forces. This was because several men of influence in Badakhshan had joined the opposition Islamic movement, although many of these 'commanders' organised themselves around ideas of Pamiri cultural

identity and autonomy rather than supporting the creation of an Islamic state. As a result of the association between the opposition movement and Pamiris, many Pamiris living and working in Dushanbe were selected for targeted killings, leading to thousands fleeing their homes in the city and returning to their villages in the Pamirs, villages which some of them had only visited during their summer vacations. Given the government blockade of the region, however, Pamiri people also faced a severe shortage of basic food items. This was further compounded by the presence of thousands of refugees from other regions of Tajikistan who fled to the region because it remained outside government control and largely free of violent conflict. In these circumstances, men, young boys and some women from Tajikistan walked to northern Pakistan and beyond.

5. There is an expanding body of anthropological work seeking to challenge the dichotomy between rural homogeneity and urban cosmopolitanism. See Gidvani and Sivaramakrishnan 2003 for a particularly sophisticated theoretical treatment of these issues. See Marsden 2008 for an ethnographic treatment of cultural and religious diversity in the Chitral region of northern Pakistan.

6. There is an extensive body of literature on the importance of the mahalla to both collective identity and governance in Central Asia. See Rasanayagam 2009 for a particularly sophisticated theoretical discussion of the mahalla as a moral frame.

7. Dushanbe's urban landscape is, of course, also undergoing rapid transformations. Striking, for example, are the mushrooming of coloured glass buildings, which can be found in cities elsewhere in the region such as Kabul and Peshawar in Pakistan, and appear to derive as much from a Dubai-inspired, post-9/11 construction boom as they do from any simple distinction between traditional and modern.

8. As in most former Soviet cities, the '*zemliachestva*' – mutual help associations formed in the city of people from a particular region – are also an important feature of life in Dushanbe. Elsewhere these are widely held to represent ways in which particular groups gain ascendancy, partly because original city dwellers do not have such organisations. For case studies, see Alexander et al. 2007.

9. On the differences between Tajiki, Dari and Farsi, see Spooner 1993.

10. On a later visit to Tajikistan I was told that the Eshon had been asked to leave the country by its political authorities, and was, as a result, now based in Kazakhstan. I was also told that a year after the 2007 research visit on which this chapter is based the Eshon's CDs were so popular that men would drive all the way from Khujand to Dushanbe when they heard of the release of a new one. On the celebrity-like dimensions of other religious figures of authority important in the region, see also Devji 2009.

11. As Madeline Reeves (2007) has put it, Afghans are the archetypal violent 'other' for many Soviet Muslims. In Tajikistan today, however, such stereotypes of Afghans are also changing rapidly: Afghans are also known as merchants par excellence, and are sought out as good, wealthy and honourable husbands by some Tajiki women. See Marsden (forthcoming).

12. The growing importance of distinctions between Sunni and Shi'a Ismai'lis in Dushanbe is likely to be most affected by the growing role played by the Aga Khan Development Network in Tajikistan and the expanding role of the worldwide offices of the Aga Khan Religious Board in instructing the country's Ismai'lis (Pamiris) in Ismai'li thought. These concerns are a topic of much debate amongst Pamiris in the country today, especially in the wake of the opening of a specially constructed Ismai'li prayer house (jamaat khana) in Dushanbe in 2009. Both of these bodies are already influential in the country (especially in the Pamirs) and the books for the teaching of Ismai'li courses are distributed to Ismai'li children being educated in the region's schools. Yet it is likely that the growing importance of a shared sense of global Ismai'li identity that these seek to foster will have their most significant implications for Pamiri Ismai'lism living in cities such as Dushanbe, the population of which is predominantly Sunni. For a comparative study of the emergence of doctrinal distinctions between Sunnis and Ismai'lis in northern Pakistan, see Marsden 2005. On the complexities of the Ismai'li tradition in the Pamiris, see Iloliev 2008; and on the shifting identity and political dynamics of Central Asia's Ismai'lis, see Devji 2009.

REFERENCES

Akiner, S. 2001. *Tajikistan: Disintegration or Reconciliation*. London: Royal Institute of International Affairs.

Alexander, C., V. Buchli and C. Humphrey (eds). 2007. *Urban Life in Post-Soviet Asia*. London: Routledge.

Chvyr, L. 1993. 'Central Asia's Tajiks: Self-identification and Ethnic Identity', in V. Naumkin (ed.), *State, Religion and Society in Central Asia*. Reading: Ithaca Press, pp. 245–61.

Collins, K. 2006. *Clan Politics and Regime Transition in Central Asia*. Cambridge: Cambridge University Press.

Daftary, F. 1990. *The Ismailis: Their History and Doctrines*. Cambridge: Cambridge University Press.

Devji, F. 2009. 'Preface', in M. van Grondelle, *The Ismailis in the Colonial: Modernity, Empire and Islam*. London: Hurst.

Dresch, P. 2005. 'Debates on Marriage and Nationality in the United Arab Emirates', in P. Dresch and J. Piscatori, *Monarchies and Nations: Globalization and Identity in the Arab States of the Gulf*. London: I.B. Tauris.

Gidvani, V. and K. Sivaramakrishnan. 2003. 'Circular Migration and Rural Cosmopolitanism', *Contributions to Indian Sociology* 37(1-2): 339–67.

Harris, C. 2006. *Muslim Youth: Tensions in Transition*. Oxford: Westview Press.

Heathershaw, J. 2009. *Post-Conflict Tajikistan: The Politics of Peacebuilding and the Emergence of Legitimate Order*. New York and London: Routledge.

Humphrey, C. 1983. *Karl Marx Collective: Economy, Society and Religion in a Siberian Collective Farm*. Cambridge: Cambridge University Press.Humphrey, C., Skvirskaja, V., and Marsden, M. 2008. 'Cosmopolitanism and the City: Interaction and Coexistence in Bukhara', in S. Maryam (ed.), *The Other Global City*. Routledge: New York.

Iloliev, A. 2008. *The Ismai'li-Sufi Sage of Pamir: Mubarak-e Wakhani and the Esoteric Tradition of the Pamiri Ismai'lis*. New York: Cambria Press.

Liu, M. 2007. 'A Central Asian Tale of Two Cities', in J. Sahadeo and R. Zanca (eds), *Everyday Life in Central Asia: Past and Present*. Bloomington: Indiana University Press.

Marsden, M. 2005. *Living Islam: Muslim Religious Experience in Pakistan's North-West Frontier*. Cambridge: Cambridge University Press.

—————. 2008. 'Muslim Cosmopolitans? Transnational Life in Northern Pakistan', *Journal of Asian Studies* 1 (February): 213–47.

—————. forthcoming. 'Fatal Embrace: Trading in Hospitality on the Frontiers of South and Central Asia', *Journal of the Royal Anthropological Institute*, Special Issue, *Anthropology and Hospitality*.

Osella, C. and F. Osella. 2007. 'I am Gulf": The Production of Cosmopolitanism in Kozhikikhode, Kerala, India', in E. Simpson and K. Kresse (eds), *Struggling with History: Islam and Cosmopolitanism in the Western Indian Ocean*. London: Hurst.

Rasanayagam, J. 2009. 'Morality, Self and Power: the Idea of the *Mahalla* in Uzbekistan', in M. Heintz (ed.), *The Anthropology of Moralities*. New York and Oxford: Berghahn Books, pp. 102–17.

Reeves, M. 2007. 'Unstable Objects: Corpses, Checkpoints and "Chessboard Borders" in the Ferghana Valley', *Anthropology of East Europe Review* 25(1): 72–84.

Roy, O. 2007. *The New Central Asia: Geopolitics and the Birth of Nations*. New York: New York University Press.

Sahadeo, J. 2007. *Russian Colonial Society in Tashkent, 1865-1923*. Bloomington: Indiana University Press.

Spooner, B. 1993. 'Are We Teaching Persian? or Farsi? or Dari? or Tojiki?', in M. Marashi (ed.), *Persian Studies in America*. Salt Lake City: University of Utah Press, pp. 175–90.

Stephan, M. 2006."*You Come to Us Like a Black Cloud*': Universal Versus Local Islam in Tajikistan', in, C. Hann & the 'Civil Religion' Group, *The Postsocialist Religious Question: Faith and Power in Central Asia and East – Central Europe*. Münster: LIT Publishers.

⊰ NOTES ON CONTRIBUTORS ⊱

Martin Demant Frederiksen received his PhD from the Department of Anthropology and Ethnography, Aarhus University. He carried out several periods of fieldwork in Tbilisi and Batumi, the Republic of Georgia, from 2005 to 2012, focusing on subjects such as masculinity and criminal networks, post-conflict, youth and imagined futures. He is currently External Lecturer at the Institute of Culture of Society, Aarhus University, working with questions of urban planning, time and morality.

Panos Hatziprokopiou studied in Greece and Britain and earned a DPhil from the University of Sussex. He teaches Human Geography at the Department of Spatial Planning and Development, Aristotle University of Thessaloniki. His research interests focus on aspects of migration and immigrants' incorporation in Greece, and on the relationship between multiethnic coexistence, social change and the space of the city in urban contexts.

Caroline Humphrey has worked in the USSR/Russia, Mongolia, Inner Mongolia, Nepal and India. Her research interests include socialist and post-socialist society, religion, ritual, economy, history, and the contemporary transformations of cities. Until 2010 she was Rausing Professor of Collaborative Anthropology and she is now attached to the Department of Social Anthropology at the University of Cambridge as a Research Director.

Joanna Kostylo specialises in Venetian history and has worked extensively in Venice. She obtained her doctorate in Italian history from the University of Cambridge. Her research interests include religion, medicine, inter-cultural relations in early modern Venice and Poland, and the history of copyright and authorship. She is currently an Assistant Director at the British School at Rome, Italy.

Magnus Marsden has conducted fieldwork in connected regions of northern Pakistan, Afghanistan and Tajikistan. His research interests include the anthropology of Islam and Muslim societies, borderlands, mobility and the trade diasporas. He is Senior Lecturer in Social Anthropology with Special Reference to South and Central Asia at the School of Oriental and African Studies, University of London.

Michał Murawski grew up in Warsaw and Norwich. He studied Social Anthropology and Politics at the School of Oriental and African Studies and University College London. He is currently completing his PhD at the Department of Social Anthropology, University of Cambridge, which focuses on the relationship between ideology, materiality and the city's legacy of Stalin-era architecture.

Marina Sapritsky received her PhD from the Department of Social Anthropology at the London School of Economics. She has worked in Israel, Russia and the Ukraine. Her current research deals with post-Soviet Jewish identity, migration and projects of religious and ethnic revivals in Odessa, Ukraine.

Vera Skvirskaja is currently a Postdoctoral Researcher at the Department of Anthropology, Copenhagen University, Denmark. She has worked on kinship, new economic forms and religious change among the reindeer herding communities in arctic Siberia. She has conducted fieldwork in Russia, Uzbekistan, Ukraine and Denmark. Her recent research interests include cosmopolitanism, post-Soviet migration, economy and urban market places.

⊰ INDEX ⊱